UFOs

OVER ROMANIA

Dan D. Farcaş Ph.D.

UFOs OVER ROMANIA

By Dan D. Farcaş Ph.D.

Edited by Philip Mantle

First edition published in 2016 by FLYING DISK PRESS

FLYING DISK PRESS
4 St Michaels Avenue
Pontefract
West Yorkshire
England
WF8 4QX

Published by
FLYING DISK PRESS

Designed and typeset by: Bob Tibbitts (iSET)

Cover artwork by Daniel Del Toro

ISBN 978-0-9934928-8-4

CONTENTS

ACKNOWLEDGEMENTS

T HIS book would not have been possible without the contribution of many remarkable people. I'd like to express my gratitude to all of them:

To the memory of the late Ion Hobana for his friendship, for his pioneering work in investigating and promoting UFO data, as well as for his leadership of the main Romanian UFO organisations. To Florin Gheorghiță for his enthusiastic work of almost half century in understanding mysteries of UFO and of many related areas and to the late Călin Turcu, the most hardworking investigator of UFO cases in Romania.

To Adrian Pătruț, Alexandru Mironov, György Mandics, Emil Străinu, the late Dan Apostol and others, for sharing in their various books knowledge of UFOs, extraterrestrials and related strange phenomena and also to all those who are no longer active in the field of UFO research and to whom I owe so much.

To the late aviator Doru Davidovici, to the astronaut Dumitru Prunariu and to the many military pilots who had the courage to report their encounters with unidentified aerospace phenomena.

To my fellow researchers at ASFAN, to all witnesses who have shared their experience with me and colleagues. To my family and my friends who helped me in this endeavour.

Also, we all owe a debt of gratitude to the thousands of ufologists worldwide, who by examining hundreds of thousands of cases, have shown that UFOs exist, -outlined their main characteristics and have developed the appropriate tools of investigation.

Special thanks to Daniel Del Toro for his wonderful UFO artwork and cover design and also Robert Snow and John Hanson for their proof reading of my text. Last but not least, I express my gratitude to veteran UK UFO researcher and publisher Philip Mantle, for his initiative to publish a book about UFO cases in Romania, for his editorial effort, including the hard work required to transform my raw text in readable English.

FOREWORD

"THERE are more things in heaven and earth than are dreamt of in your philosophy", said William Shakespeare in a scene from Hamlet. The UFO phenomenon is among them; it exists, even if no one knows with certainty exactly what it is. To many researchers it still remains "unidentified".

We know that only 5-10% of observations are completely unexplainable, but these are too many sightings that are too similar and their behaviour is too intelligent to be natural phenomena, which suggests that we may be dealing with technologies that are too advanced to be human creations.

The UFO phenomenon has apparently accompanied mankind throughout its existence. It has left traces in legends, in folk tales, in shamanic traditions, in religion, as well as in many ancient texts. We can find these traces everywhere in the world and obviously also in Romania.

My grandmother told me that more than one hundred years ago, in her home village, sometime in the evening, floating along the roof tops was "the man with the lantern". It was real, though somewhat puzzling, but an encounter with this mysterious character could happen randomly and be seen by any of the villagers. On one occasion a number of horses, frightened by this occurrence, overturned a wagon into a ditch. My grandmother was not an academic. She and her fellow villagers were convinced that such encounters are uncommon, but somehow they are still part of the order of things.

On the evening of September 6th, 1978, I travelled home, driving a car on the A1 motorway. I was about 20 kilometres from Bucharest, when I saw above me, at about 45 degrees, a very bright light. It was like a car headlight pointing toward us. Next to me was a friend and we discussed the apparition without slowing the car down. We could hear no noise and we did not see any red, green, or intermittent aircraft signal lights, so it seemed that this light was not an airplane or a helicopter. It was no astronomical object either.

The light crossed the road, dimmed its brightness, then reappeared in an unexpected, location to our right, at an angle of 50-60 degrees, then faded again. The observation lasted less than thirty seconds.

The fact that during the thirty seconds of the sighting we had covered quite a long distance, having the light still in front of us, suggests that it was either at a very great height, or it was going in the same direction as us. A curious but significant fact is though we were not in hurry, neither of us had the idea to stop, to get out of the car in order to get a better view. Nor did we think to report the event to anyone.

In time, I found that many people went through similar experiences. Most have provided an explanation for why they reacted in such a manner and afterwards they had simply forgotten everything. But there are also dramatic UIFO encounters which the witness can not ever forget.

In the following pages I included a limited selection of representative UFO cases from Romania, most of them investigated either by people that I know and trust or by me personally. Only a small part of these cases are known abroad, simply because of the language barrier. Some cases are even unpublished in my home country of Romania.

The selection contains encounters with "nuts and bolts" UFOs, but also cases with strange connections with other realms of the unknown. The cases confirm, on the one hand, the main features of the UFO phenomenon as they are known worldwide and on the other hand, bring some new features, specific to local customs and traditions of various regions of Romania: Transylvania, Moldavia, Walachia, Maramureş, Banat etc. By this, they add new details to the complexity of the UFO phenomenon and perhaps deepen the Great Mystery.

THE BEGINNINGS

Early sightings

AS far I know the oldest UFO cases from Romania are two 16th century UFO reports. The first is in the year 1517. On November the 8th a great sign was seen in the sky. "It was glowing in the northern sky and looked like a human face. It remained in one place for a long time before slowly fading from view."

The text is from the "*Letopisețul țării Moldovei*" (Yearbook of the country of Moldavia) and written by Grigore Ureche (1590-1647), a landlord with important connections at the court of the ruler of Moldova. This case was mentioned by Dalila-Lucia Aramă, senior palaeographer at the manuscripts office of the Library of the Romanian Academy in the paper „*Să fi fost oare farfurii zburătoare?*" (Could they be Flying Saucers?) in „*Magazin Istoric*" (Historic Magazine) 12/1968. This was the only paper dedicated to UFOs in this publication.

In the same article a mention is made about a second sighting. On the 15th of October 1595, when Michael the Brave, prince of Walachia, besieged the city of Târgoviște, the capital of Walachia, temporarily occupied by Turks, above the military camp "a large comet appeared". After three days, the Turks were defeated and expelled.

Many contemporary sources describe this event. Once such is a newspaper from Transylvania which stated that "the comet... lasted an hour or a little more". In a report in Italian, in Prague on November the 14th, 1595, is it mentioned again that the "comet" was seen for two hours. There is also an old German engraving, printed in 1665, about the 1595 Târgoviște case [Fig.1].

As no astronomical record mentions a comet for this date and no comet is observed in only one place and on one day, the sighting should be accepted as unidentified.

In his book „*Extratereștrii in România*", Călin Turcu featured more than 60 strange celestial observations before 1800. Most of them are probably bolides, meteor showers, northern lights (?) and some could be rare meteorological pheno-

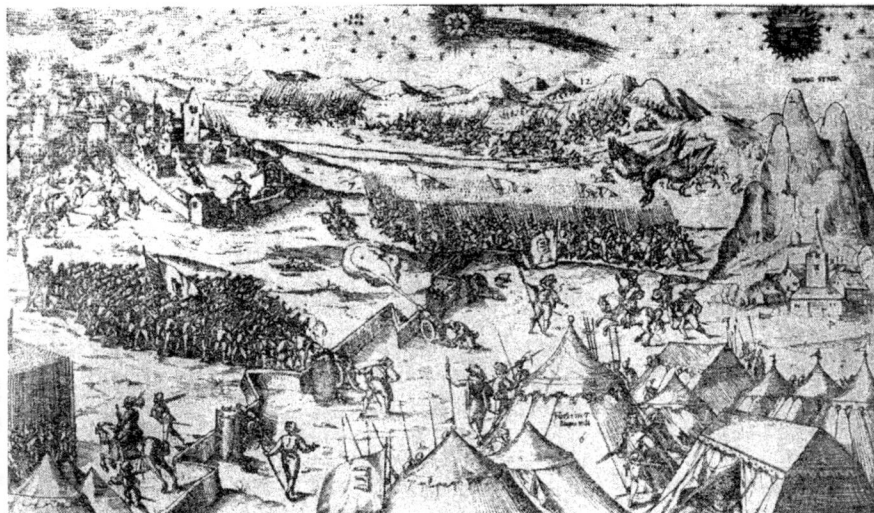

Fig.1 Old German engraving, printed in 1665, about the 1595 Târgovişte battle.

mena. They were commonly interpreted by witnesses as heavenly "signs" or a sign of events yet to come. In the following I will show only a few examples, noting that some old Romanian expressions are difficult to translate and even harder to understand.

In 1657, February 2nd, in Transylvania. "On February 2nd, three fiery stars in a black cloud, fighting with each other, were seen in the sky. Then it came near them a fourth star, which was also full of fire and much larger than the others. This lasted about two hours and is a portent that there would be in future many princes and many territories" (Kraus, Transylvanian Chronicle, p. 197).

In 1737, December 5/6 (16/17) at 20:00-02:00, in Banat: "When it was the year of 1737, after dinner, in the eve of the day of Saint Nicholas, they showed a sign in the sky from the north, red as blood and wide. After two hours, it broke in two and then were joined back together and moved westward". (This note, made in Braşov, appears on a Romanian manuscript now in the Romanian Academy Library, No.2342).

In 1768, October 5th, in Romania. "The gentleman captain Potlog Dumitrescu told me that when he was at his home in Tarnauca (North Moldavia; now in the Ukraine), Sunday night to Monday at 4 hours of the night, they saw a sign in the sky, namely, they saw a fiery horizon on the sunset sky and much it have played, as half an hour, climbing and descending – and a black cloud above calmed down the flaming fire and underneath were made white horizon. Saying all that [to the people], the people have said that when they were at Godineşti, to the mill, they saw it too, but as a chair of fire and a crown above and the same cloud was its ruin".

In 1793 November 27th, "Sunday, at two hours and a half in the night, the earth trembled three times. I was at the table at Floreşti [north of Bucharest], with the gentleman sardar Constantin Poenaru. The following evening, at the same time, the Moon did wonder, that in half an hour it has travelled through the sky from lunch time right through until the sunset and then it stopped".

The first report of a UFO type phenomenon in the media has appeared in the newspaper from Iaşi, "*Albina Românească*", No.71 of September 9th, 1837. It states that: "In the night of 29 to 30 August, were seen, in particular places of the country, from the Highlands to Moldova, a meteor, or physical apparition, whereof we share the following: the day was serene, heat – 24 degrees Reaumur [30 degrees C] when, at eleven hours at night, was seen, just above Neamţ Monastery, one bright spheroid, longish globe, large as twelve hands. This meteor descended into the atmosphere obliquely, toward sunset, flying slowly over the monastery courtyard, illuminating all meadows with a very vivid and glittering colour and spreading sparks as shooting stars. From the closer neighbouring parts, as Târgu Neamt Monastery, it seemed like the monastery would be burning. This meteor was observed at Dorohoi at the same clock". It was probably a bolide.

A lot more interesting is the sighting made in city of Sibiu, on December 20th, 1853, at 21:00. "On the 20th of the current month at 9 pm, over Sibiu an aerial phenomenon was observed. Above the city a conical cloud was seen, moving around its axis. It has shifted to Sfânta Elisabeta [St. Elizabeth, name of a neighbouring village]. This movement was accompanied by a noise similar to a locomotive which starts moving; the noise intensity alternated, when stronger when weaker. Finally, the phenomenon disappeared through a small lightning".

Of course, in winter, the occurrence of a "cloud cone" that produces functional noises is not easy to explain. The very disappearance raises questions too. This seems not to be a meteorological phenomenon.

The great Romanian poet and philosopher Lucian Blaga (1895-1961), includes in his autobiographical book „*Hronicul şi cântecul vârstelor*" (The Chronicle and the Song of Ages) a case which occurred in the summer of 1904, in the Apuseni Mountains (Transylvanian Western Carpathians). "One night, late after the high hour, an old man sat with his cart out in the fields. He was awake at the time. Suddenly he sees a wheel of fire coming down from the horizon across the Apuseni Mountains. The wheel is spinning and quickly approaching. The man looked mad. When it was nearby, the wheel of fire pretended to be a man; and man with man looked at each other; long and without saying a word. This vision was interpreted by the local villagers as some sort of 'sign'".

The story is indeed very close to the experience through which the prophet Ezekiel passed, as is detailed in the Old Testament of the Bible.

UFO representations on the walls of churches in Romania?

As everywhere in the world, ancient testimonies of UFO sightings are not only in the written documents, but also in paintings, mostly in churches perhaps because ordinary people interpreted these phenomena as divine signs.

The city of Târgoviște was the capital of Walachia for several centuries. The construction of the Princely Church in the city was completed in 1583. The frescoes inside have not been repainted but only retouched with all of the original figures and objects remaining the same. As journalist and ufologist Gabriel Tudor noted, on the west wall of the nave, the fresco depicting the moment of receiving tablets of the Law by Moses on Mount Sinai, we see a character not mentioned in the Bible: depicted as an angel and placed between two concentric circles, looking as if it had just come out to watch the proceedings. What are those two circles? In any case, surely not clouds which are clearly represented in the nearby paintings in a completely different manner. Also they can not be stars or the moon, because on the same fresco the sun is seen, whose rays are prominently depicted, to draw attention that the scene takes place in broad daylight. Could it be that the two circles are a graphic representation, in a primitive manner, of a disc-shaped UFO with a domed top, which the anonymous painter, having not a very good capacity to represent things in a three-dimensional perspective, drew as a circle inside another circle?

The writer and researcher of mythology Victor Kernbach (1923-1995), in his book "*Enigmele miturilor astrale*" (Riddles of astral myths), detailed that similar frescoes have been in churches from Bucharest as the (old) "Saint Spiridon" and "Bucur". Unfortunately, the first was demolished under the communist regime, but the second exists today and the pictorial representations are of the same type as those at the Princely Church of Târgoviște.

As the ufologist Călin Turcu (1942-2006) noted in his book "*Extratereștrii în România*" (Aliens in Romania), "On the walls of the chapel Lainici (Gorj County) can be distinguished a picture quite different from the others. The drawing, done in the early seventeenth century and representing the "Annunciation", depicts, above the Archangel Gabriel and the Virgin Mary, a heavenly "vehicle" with the shape of a double balloon which again can not be a cloud. The flying object ends with a narrow open tube, where red streaks appear to burst and absorbed behind by a red cloud.

Fig.2 Mural fresco in the Monastery Church, in the city of Sighişoara.

On the walls of Tutana monastery (Argeş county), built in 1577, is depicted an "astronaut", equipped for space flight. It is by no means an earthly character. Images such as those presented above are reported not only in Romania but also in other countries of the Orthodox faith, as in the Decani monastery in Kosovo and on a number of Russian religious icons.

Gili Schechter and Hannan Sabbath, from the *Israeli Extraterrestrials and UFOs Research Association*, commented in an article of a photo of a mural fresco in the Monastery Church, not far from the Clock Tower in the city of Sighişoara (Transylvania) [Fig. 2]. The photo reproduced in the article was made by Cătălina Borta. Under the image is written in German, a passage from Psalm 130, 7: "Israel trust the Lord!" In the image is a large building, possibly a church, above which floats, slightly oblique, a large disc-shaped object, divided in to about 10 large sections. From the centre of the disc pointing down is a sort of spike. Above the bright object is a short column on which you see other objects that are hard to identify.

The authors could not find who did the painting, nor when. However the text can not date before Luther had translated and published, in 1534, the Bible in German. The authors also noted that the same disc hovering, diagonally divided into sectors and with the stick underneath, appears on a number of medals from the seventeenth century, probably chips used in gambling. It issued its opinion that these objects represent the cartwheel described in Ezekiel's vision.

A similar picture exists in Liber Prodigiorum, a book, written by Julius Obsequens, a fourth-century Roman historian. But the book, which describes the unusual heavenly appearances over Rome, was printed, with engravings added, only in 1552. The authors noted some differences between Sighişoara painting and the objects on the medals; for example, these have almost all a circle of stars on the circumference, while they are not on the object depicted in Sighişoara.

Ghost aircraft over Romania – January 1913

By searching the old Romanian media at the library of the Romanian Academy, Ion Hobana discovered that in January 1913, in Romanian air space a number of weird flying objects were observed all of which were brightly illuminated. Eyewitnesses said that the objects performed sharp turns in the air above their villages, showing a predilection for the military barracks in Focşani, Iaşi, Brăila and Târgovişte. These intruders were observed with "optical devices" and traced over considerable distances. By executive orders of the minister of war, soldiers even fired volleys of bullets at them but all to no avail.

Given the involvement of these military units, Ion Hobana asked the archives of the Ministry of National Defence for documents of this event. Nine reports were made available. They were those submitted to the General Inspector of the Rural Gendarmerie – General Alexandru Averescu – also Chief of General Staff of the Army. If we add the 14 articles in newspapers, it means there were 23 reports of these observations in less than a month.

It was argued then that the sightings were of Russian reconnaissance airplanes; but the overall state of aviation in January 1913 excludes this interpretation. In those times, aerial observations of fortifications and of troop movements were carried out exclusively in daylight and the existing civil and military airplanes lacked any reflectors or other strong light sources. It seems also impossible to describe all of the luminous phenomena to be celestial bodies (planet Venus), because of the hours and the directions indicated and the movements of the unidentified lights are inconsistent with those of a celestial body.

The first half of the twentieth century

In the first part of the twentieth century, the observations continued. I mention just a few Romanian cases that were known outside of Romania thanks to the book *UFOs From Behind the Iron Curtain*, by Ion Hobana and Julien Weverbergh.

A school director, born in 1901, recalled in 1969, an event that occurred in Bujoreanca village (30 km north of Bucharest, in Dâmboviţa county), when he was aged 13 or 14. In the autumn of 1914 or 1915 around nightfall, he was with his family at the table in the garden, when their attention was drawn to a reddish object that appeared in the sky. It had the apparent size of a football or a human head and had a sort of protuberance that resembled an "exhaust pipe". It moved eastward, about 20-25 m above the gardens. The object gave off a whistle-like noise and produced a stream of air that twisted the tops of the oak and acacias trees and left behind a shower of bright sparks some 8-10 m long. The witness went on to say that it was as if the object had materialised over a house which was located at 800 m away from them and then would have dematerialised over another. This flying object reappeared for five or six days in a row.

Another witness, the farmer Ion Bunescu told Ion Hobana in his own words of the odd event he went through when he was aged 38. "One night in June 1926 I went with our cattle to Leurda [a plateau 400 m high, near Colun, some 25 kilometres east of Sibiu]. I had found there some rich grass pastures for the cattle. It was just after midnight. Suddenly, from village Cârţa, a light appeared looking as if the moon was about to rise. Shortly thereafter arose an illuminated globe travelling quickly towards Leurda. For a few moments it disappeared behind a hill and then it reappeared and was right over me; at least so it seemed to me. The light was so strong that even illuminated the river Olt some 4 km away.

Fig.3a & 3b A UFO-like object near the church tower of the Transylvanian city of Sebeş, in 1923, and the object magnified.

Terrified, I threw myself into the grass. Behind the light I saw something dark. It looked like a boat, about three meters long and two wide, darker in the middle. It made no noise. What seemed strange was the kind of wind that did not blow neither from one side nor from the other, but against me from top to bottom. The object remained motionless for I don't know how long before it started to move, with the light ahead, upstream of the river Olt, circled a patch of forest, then simply "died" disappeared. Back then people were somewhat backward and superstitious. I told others of the sighting on the following day in the village. Some old women arrived at the conclusion that I saw Lazăr Teca, a man from our village, suspected of being "*strigoi*" ... [kind of living undead, believed to be in connection with the devil and dealing with spells and charms]. In fact, Lazăr Teca was not "*strigoi*", but he used to walk at night and to steal some cow milk. (...) I don't know what to say. But I'm sure that it was not any kind of mirage".

It is also worth a mention that Ion Hobana received, many years ago, an interesting old photo, made in the Transylvanian city of Sebeş in 1923 [Fig.3 a & b], showing an unexplained UFC-like object near the church tower.

After 1950

Around the years 1970-1980, Romanian ufologists Ion Hobana, Călin Turcu and others unearthed a series of older UFO events. I will summarise below some of these cases from the 1950's and early 1960's.

Dumitru Coca, a retired teacher told Călin Turcu the following story: "I lived for a while in Hârşeni, in one of the valleys of the Făgăraş Mountains, Braşov County. On one particular summer night in 1955, between midnight and 01:00, I was on the road with my wife, looking at our house. On the right, between Făgăraş and Hârşeni, flows a small stream and to the left are the plains. At about 500m from the village, I noticed, at about 1,000 meters height, an object strange enough for me to fear its approach. It was an ark, which emitted a ring of white sparks. The object flew at high speed towards the left side of the mountains. It was blue, with stripes of bright white. I could hear no sound. This sighting lasted three minutes or a little more. The night was calm and clear and I must say that the observation was made in excellent viewing conditions, which excludes the possibility to confuse what I saw there with any of the atmospheric phenomena that are observed day or night in mountains."

One day, in 1957, the cadastral engineer Pantelimon Mizof had a strange encounter in the Bucegi Mountains, Prahova County. In his own words he stated: "While doing work for the cadastre and with our team which was composed of four people, a flying machine approached and over flew us at about 200 meters.

When it passed over our heads we noticed that there was no noise", so surely it could not be a helicopter. The object landed a little further in front of us and those from the team that were curious went to take a look at it. "When we approached and were within 40-50 meters of it, it took off suddenly, but quietly, doing some kind of dance over us, was very agile and then disappeared".

A female doctor aged 50 back in 1971, recounted to Ion Hobana an observation she made in a morning of June 1958. She demanded not to make public her identity "because people will laugh at me". She was at Sinaia, a resort in the Bucegi Mountains, and at four o'clock in the morning was at the hotel window, located on the second floor, watching the first rays of the dawn. The sky was clear and cloudless, when, as she declared:

"An object appeared from behind the mountains, coming from the east at about 500 m height. It had the apparent size of a car, with a dome on top, like a soft hat. Underneath it was a triangular protruding portion, smaller than the rest of the unit, with rounded points distributed all around. The device had a silvery glow and the raised portions were blue; but at the top were two small domes both of the same colour as the rest of the unit. The strong luminosity it gave off made me think that it reflected the sunlight. I could not hear any noise, so there was no question of a jet or helicopter which would have easily heard. On the other hand, there was no trace of smoke or vapour. Although the device came straight to the hotel, there was no discernible psychological effect. It was moving slowly and was not animated by any other visible movement. I think it came closer, up to three hundred meters or less and then flew over the settlements and down the valley. My husband, who died in 1962, was also witness. We didn't think to try and photograph it."

Mihail Sadoveanu (1880 – 1961) was a political figure and one of the greatest Romanian novelists and also president of the Writers Union of Romania. His son in law, Emanoil Manoliu, recounted to Ion Hobana the following story: "In the fall of 1961, I was at the Neamț Monastery. It was a very nice evening and I walked towards a summer house located at the bottom of the park. Then suddenly I was blinded by a vivid multi-coloured light which faded just as quickly as it had appeared. Half blinded, I just barely made out a kind of boat, upside down, over a small hill, beyond the lake. After a few seconds, the object suddenly rose vertically, like a helicopter, but certainly much faster. It was like a disc with a concave base, which could be 6-7 meters long and about 3 meters wide. It disappeared like a whirlwind in the air. I noticed even the air movement caused by its take-off at a fantastic speed. But I didn't hear any noise. After staying up all night without any sleep the following morning I went to see the place where the object was and I was accompanied by a priest, who was very sceptical of what I told had him. To our great surprise, we found there scorched patches of grass and a small footprint on the ground, as though it was made by a solid object".

This seems to be one of the first records of a UFO landing in Romania. Unfortunately, the witness of the event has not thought then, in this autumn 1961, to take photographs or drawings of the place in question.

In 1996, Florin Gorănescu, then 51, had reported to Călin Turcu that in 1961, "when I was 15, I was at the resort *Lacul Roşu* [Red Lake, Harghita County], in the [state owned] villa "Mura". One evening, I can not remember if it was July or August, just after sunset, I was in front of the building with two colleagues. It was dark, the sky was clear and the stars were out. We watched the landscape towards the high cliff named "*Altar*" [Shrine], talking with two colleagues, when I noticed a red light which drew our attention because it was located on "Altar". Now we started joking that it was "electrified" the red star, made of painted tin plate, placed in the top of the hill "Altar" by the then communist authorities. The light was red and sparking. The difference in altitude between the villas and the top of "Altar" is about 300 meters. For a while, the light apparently remained motionless then began to move slowly towards the north-east. It was only then that we realised that this was something unusual. During the observation, I did not hear any noise. The apparent size of the object was about a big coin [of 2.5-3 cm diameter] held at arms length. It was round in shape and very intense red colour. The height of the object was about 60 degrees above the horizon."

From the 16th century right through to the 20th century a curious collection of oddities, UFO sightings and landings were documented throughout Romania. At the time no one was able to predict the coming wave of UFO sightings that would dominate UFO research in Romania in the 1960's and beyond.

THE UFO WAVE OF 1968

The observations are multiplying

THE book "*Extratereştr i în România*" (vol.I, 2004; vol.II, 2005), by Călin Turcu, is so far the most complete overview of the UFO observations in Romania since the sixteenth century until about 2005. The cases mentioned in the book reveal a "wave" of UFO reports in 1968. If between 1957 and 1965 there are 0 to 3 cases per year (total of 11), the next years there are as follows: 1966: 4, 1967: 10, 1968: 94; 1969: 26, 1969: 26, 1970: 17, 1971: 14, 1972: 9, 1973: 4, 1974: 28, 1975: 3, 1977: 20.

One of the causes of the increase in sightings was certainly the rising awareness of the UFO phenomenon across the country as well as the activity of a number of ufologists, among them: Ion Hobana, Călin Turcu and Florin Gheorghiță. A number of eyewitness testimonies from this period were collected later but many were recorded at the time.

David V. Marin, from the village of Poienarii Burchii, Prahova County, recounted to Ion Hobana that in the afternoon of 21st of November 1967, at around 16:30-16:35, he walked into his yard to chop some firewood. Suddenly, he saw in a north-westerly direction, at about 30 m at an angle of about 30 degrees above the horizon, a luminous body that looked like an upside down candlelight. The witness estimated that the apparition had a length of 1.70-1.80 meters. He commented: "I watched all the time. It stood still for about ten minutes. I don't know when it first appeared there. Then it made a curve upwards, during which its tail was greatly elongated (5-6 meters). After that it took a position parallel to the ground, the tail lengthening again to about 10-11 meters. Its colour was at first pale white and then looked like a flame. It then started to move slowly, towards north-west, reaching the speed of a cargo airplane. Now, its front seemed to look a dark colour. I watched until it disappeared over the horizon. I shouted at the doctor at the dispensary as well some neighbours to try and draw their attention to the event. But they were too far away and nobody heard me. I didn't want to leave and didn't want lose the sight of the object in question.".

The phenomenon could not be seen from the village, since the object was quite low and the house of David Marin is at the edge of the settlement. From here it's flat field, while other houses are lower than the witness's house, in a kind of valley.

Asked how he got the idea to inform the press, the witness said: "I have not notified the press. The next day, on November 22nd, 1967, I read in the newspaper that in Bulgaria there was a report of an unknown flying body, the same day I had seen it myself. I was surprised that nothing was written in the Romanian media about what I saw, since I was convinced that it must have been seen by everyone. Then I sent a letter to the Meteorological Institute in Bucharest. It was only some time ago they told me that what I reported had apparently appeared in the newspaper".

Ion Hobana also investigated the next case. Ladislau Schmidt, an official in the mining industry in Petrila, Hunedoara County, told the following story: "On November 22nd, 1967 at around 12:30, I was sitting at home in the kitchen with the door opened. All of a sudden I found that the hens are running toward me without being called or attracted by the offer of grain. I drove them back out but they came back in the kitchen, more scared than ever and trying to hide. Then I drove them again out into the yard and following them to see if a hawk had been attacking them. In their panicked fright the poultry seemed to be looking up. I looked up and in the sky I noticed, very distinctly, a disk-shaped shining object, a silver or aluminium colour, having at the bottom a smaller rising and at the top a higher one, with more extra-rods like antennas. I called my wife to come in to the yard to see this strange object. Both of us ran into the street and watched the object. At about 5,000 meters, it looked like size of a cowboy hat. I mention that the first time I saw it, in the yard, it was motionless in the air, but when I went out into the street it rotated and moved away at a high speed towards the northwest, spiralling into the sky until it was out of sight. At the same time, I drew the attention of several people who were on the street. I must say that at the time the weather was beautiful and the sky was completely cloudless."

In September or October 1967, at an antiaircraft artillery unit in Floreşti, located only 6 km from the city of Cluj-Napoca (called until 1974 Cluj, name kept, colloquially), another strange incident occurred. A witness reported it to Călin Turcu, asking him not to make public his identity nor the names of other people involved. He recounted: "We stared at the artillery gunners who positioned their weapons to point in all directions. Suddenly, a corporal who was leading the group and was looking up with the telescope sight of his rifle warned us: "Hey! Do you see that thing up there, what the hell is it?" All of us who were there, which amounted to 40 soldiers and NCOs, were all looking up. We all observed a fascinating aluminium-coloured object, hanging motionless in the sky at about 800 m above us.

It was briefly obscured by some thin cloud for a short time but once the clouds had passed it was still there in exactly the same place. It was afternoon, about a quarter to five. I know this, because all the officers in the barracks were gathered at the gate to get on their bus [at 17:00] to go to Cluj.

The corporal from the second battery ran to the gate to ask our captain to come and to see this suspicious and peculiar object that was at low altitude 'spying' on the weapons platform. All of the officers that were there gathering at the gate, from small to large ran toward the end of the barracks where there was gunnery platform and they all stood in amazement and stood there just staring at the sky. The object was still there hanging motionless in the sky. The unit commander fled to the Telex area and reported the event to the General Command in Bucharest. From there he received the order to load cannon with ammunition and take aim. He was ordered to shoot only if the object performed any hostile manoeuvres. The officers went to the warehouse where they obtained several pairs of binoculars in order to get a better look at the object. I grabbed the binoculars and I have studied very carefully the aerial intruder. I remember well that nobody uttered the word UFO, but rather "American spy device". After more than two hours the device was still there. The officers were very nervous. After a while, a cloud passed below it and when the cloud was gone the device wasn't there anymore".

The sightings of Banat

At the end of March 1968, at least one unidentified object was seen wandering around in south-west Romania, mostly above the highlands of the historic region of Banat.

Associate professor of geodesy Dan N. Mihăilescu, from Bucharest, founding member of ASFAN, compiled a wide variety of observations in an article entitled "The Case from Banat", published in Romanian, in the *Quasar* journal No.3 (September), 1992. In summary the following occurred:

On March 29th 1968, at 16:00, meteorologist Ştefan Bălaşa of the weather station on Semenic Mountain (1447 m), along with a group of skiers, saw in the sky "a shiny object that stood still in an easterly direction and was about 75-80 degrees above the horizon". Through binoculars (6x30), the object appeared to look like a cone with a bright sun-lit side. The meteorologist continued to observe it until after sunset (18:40 local time) when "the objects brightness gradually disappeared without changing its position". Many other skiers said they also observed, between 17:30-18:00, "a truncated silvery cone shining brightly in the sun". Half an hour later, the UFO left the point at which it stood, moving very slowly towards Ţarcu Peak (2196 m, located about 40 km east-northeast) where there was also a weather station. The object eventually faded from view in the twilight sky."

Nicu Tomoniu, M. Ungureanu, Boris Lemac (medical assistant) and Vasile Mihalcea (technician), were at a football match in Tismana town (45 km southeast of Țarcu Peak). They reported that between 18:50-19:00 "at a very high altitude we saw an extremely bright blue-green object which seemed to perfectly stationary", It was a conical-shaped object and it was slowly changing its colour, becoming more red, until it was completely gone by about 19:30. In the city of Târgu-Jiu (65 km southeast of Țarcu), at 19:00, two pupils and two teachers saw in the sky at 60-65° to the southeast, a white isosceles triangle shining very brightly. Then it changed colour and departed to south-west, disappearing into the night.

In the mining village of Ciudanovița, in southern Banat, at 22:00, the engineer Gheorghe Tănase, together with a number of others, saw in the sky a "bright object" which remained visible until the next day at 16:00. On March 30, 1968, from 06:30 to 07:00, the same engineer and employees here tracked the object with a theodolite. But even to the naked eye it looked like a "geometric body shaped like a truncated cone, upside down, slightly inclined and having the size of half of the New Moon". It zigzagged around the sky for about five hours.

Another sighting was reported 20 km south-west of Ciudanovița, in the town Oravița (35 km southwest of Semenic weather station) at 02:30 in the morning, the UFO was seen by a group of people, "like a rugby ball, or a 40W light bulb". In the same place, at 06:10, a yellowish-white object positioned at about 35-40 degrees above the horizon, to the northeast. These observations were made by Teofil Iorga, who was working on a construction site in the area. He photographed the object at 08:00 and then watched it at 08:15 by theodolite, stating that it had the shape of a truncated cone, with a shiny side exposed to the sun and that it was stationary. He tried unsuccessfully to photograph it through the theodolite telescope. At 9:00, the UFO started to rise in altitude, heading south. It was observed by about 120 people at the site.

At the weather station on Semenic Mountain, at 07:50, meteorologist Ștefan Bălașa observed once again the same object; it deviated slightly southward and was also very brightly lit on its sunny side. At 09:00, it moved imperceptibly towards the southwest. At 10:00, Bălașa informed his colleagues of the sighting at the neighbouring weather stations: Caransebeș, Țarcu Peak and Cuntu Saddle. Ten minutes later, those other weather stations confirmed seeing the object, which continued moving slowly southwest. At 12:00, it was out of sight.

In the industrial city of Reșița (the county capital, 20 km northwest of Semenic Mountain) at 10:00, a group of technicians and officials from the steelworks saw a bright opaque spot over the hill of "Gol" (southwest). Through binoculars it appeared as an isosceles trapezoid with the small part pointing down, brightly lit on the sunny side and showing the colours of rainbow on the opposite side. Witnesses signed a joint declaration to confirm this observation.

I can add here that I personally have other reports from people I know in Reșița (e.g. Petru Ursuță), who watched the object, which "made triangles in the sky and moved at sharp angles". The next day, in the newspapers, a calculation was published on how much money the local industry lost through disruption of work.

At the meteorological station on the Țarcu Peak, meteorologist Vasile Coțoi and his colleague, Mrs. Ingeborg Vityi observed the object. They declared that "at a first glance it appeared to be an ordinary upper-air sounding balloon. The shape was of a cone, with a number of rounded edges, resembling an egg, matt white, with the side facing the sun very bright. However due to the strong sunlight reflection and the chaotic vertical movement of the object and other movements against the wind (movements not typical for a survey balloon), we found ourselves watching it very carefully. I looked at it for two and a half hours until it disappeared because of the position of the Sun (nearly in the same direction). Its movement was slow then it would speed up and then it would suddenly stop dead".

At 13:00, the UFO was observed at the meteorological station near the Berzasca village, on the Danube, about 85 km southwest of Țarcu Mountains. Locals said they saw it earlier, possibly even at 11:00. The object was observed for about one hour at about 3 km inland from the river Danube. Meanwhile, the object was seen also at Marila some 12 km from Oravița, at an altitude of 700 meters.

At 16:00, from the Semenic Mountain, the object appeared pretty much in the same point where it was seen the day before. It was tracked until sunset during which time the witness kept in touch with the meteorological station at Țarcu. From there, Vasile Coțoi was of the opinion that when observed on previous day, the object was "much closer and bigger, with well defined contours, the shape of an isosceles triangle, advancing with the larger side. The speed was constant and the object was at an altitude of approx. 30,000 m. This altitude was determined by observing two airliners that passed the over (in this position the object was photographed) ... This time, its movement was almost linear with very large curves and heading in almost the same direction. The size of the object (which despite being at a height of 5-6 times larger than that of airplanes) was approximately the same (like airplanes). When the sun set, it began to lose its glow, becoming a pale white. Later, after the emergence of the first stars in the night sky; the object became a bright red, with the contours of triangle barely visible. When it became very dark, it took on a round shape, emanating a bright light (through binoculars it looked like a planet like Jupiter or Venus, but much larger and much brighter)".

In the town of Anina (19 km southeast of Semenic station) at 17:00, Michael

Bachici went out in to the yard accompanied by his neighbour Ion Arnăutu. They saw to the east, an object which they estimated to be about 5-8 meters in size hanging stationary in the air and continuously changing shape and colours. Bachici reported that: "At sunset its brightness had not changed; in my opinion, it had its own internal light source. After sunset it became bright and had the appearance of that of a bright star". Mircea Matei, from Semenic Mountain, also observed the object at 17:30 and described it has being "a tronconic shape with a small base. We believe that it had its own source of light, because Sun was had set and the object was an intense silvery colour".

The object was seen also from the weather station situated in the city of Caransebeş (located in the valley, at about 30 km from both the stations Semenic and Ţarcu and lay between them), towards south-east at 70-75 degrees above the horizon. It looked like a truncated cone and was very bright. It remained still for about an hour, after which it moved slowly to the east-northeast (on the route from the Semenic Mountain to Ţarcu Peak).

On the night of 30th /31st March, the UFO was followed and photographed from the Ţarcu weather station. It was present all night and shone brighter than any star.

On March 31st, 1968, in the early morning, the object was seen above the Ţarcu Peak. Vasile Coţoi stated: "In the morning it had the same episodes as before when it changed brightness, but its movement this time was in the opposite direction", namely towards Semenic Mountains. Here, as wrote Ştefan Balaşa: "At 06:00, it was again over Semenic, but the developing weather accompanied by misty cloud cover prevented me from observing it further".

In conclusion, Dan C. Mihăilescu was of the opinion that the object could not be a stratospheric balloon. Perhaps the most vigorous support for this conclusion are the observations made through the theodolite (which magnify at least 25 to 30 times), as well as the quality of the observers – meteorologists accustomed with stratospheric balloons. We shall add to this was a nocturnal light and manoeuvred in a zigzag path unlike any weather balloon or astronomical body.

In addition, during the same period, a similar phenomenon was reported in Yugoslavia and – throughout 1968 – "flying triangles" were reported to be repeatedly seen over Transylvania, the "apparitions" showing the same features as the object observed at Banat. One example, as Ion Hobana wrote, was on April 4, 1968, between 19:30 and 20:00. George Roth, a university student in industrial chemistry, along with several colleagues, observed in the sky, over the city of Timişoara (about 100 km northwest of the places mentioned above), an object described as conical in shape, then frustoconical, then like a dot. This object also would vary its brightness as well.

A Romanian airliner meets a UFO in 1968

Arguably the most important sightings of this year were in August and September. On August 17th, 1968, an IL-18 airliner, of the Romanian *Tarom* Company, flying from Constanța (Mihail Kogălniceanu Airport) to Düsseldorf, Germany, at an altitude of 7600 meters, was near Oradea, north-west Romania, very close to the Hungarian border, when the crew saw an unidentified flying object.

Captain Benjamin Gabrian stated: "We noticed suddenly an oval object to our right, at a distance of about one kilometre and about 300 meters above. It travelled at high speed and issued a dazzling, extremely strong, greenish light. I checked the clock. It was 20 hours and 21 minutes. We watched this bright object for a few seconds and then it accelerated and disappeared to the west. We observed the object for 10-15 seconds but it was enough to appreciate – for my colleagues: Alexandru Niculescu, Marian Constantinescu and me – its dimensions. As far as I could see, it had a diameter of about 2.5 to 3 meters".

By contacting the control tower of the airport in Vienna, the Captain learned that in an area 400 kilometres around him there were no other aircraft.

A few minutes later, the Budapest, Hungary, airport called to report that the crew of an airliner of the Hungarian company *Malev* saw, in Austrian airspace, a similar UFO, moving rapidly westward, about two and a half minutes after the Gabrian observation. If it was the same object, its speed should be 14,000 kilometres per hour. No plane could achieve this speed, at an altitude of 6000 m. In an interview, given by Gabrian to the August 18, 1968, edition of the *Dobrogea Nouă* newspaper from Constanța, he said: "I think, what we have seen is routinely described, in international media, under the term UFO. The chance that we could watch it for 10 to 15 seconds is due to the fact that the object had apparently reduced its speed [...] Perhaps because the alien crew was interested in our machine and in what was inside it ?."

Humanoids in the Hoia-Baciu Forest

Hoia-Baciu Forest, west of Cluj-Napoca, a recreation place for the locals, became famous through by a variety of accounts of paranormal phenomena. Since the 1960s, biology teacher Alexandru Sift studied here luminous, magnetic and radiological phenomena that were very hard to explain, gathering about all these a rich archive of photos that were lost mysteriously a few days after his death in 1993. Apparently they were stolen by unknown individuals which just added to the mystery of this location. The few remaining photographs that survived were published in 1995 in the book named "*Fenomenele de la Pădurea Hoia-Baciu*" (The phenomena from Hoia-Baciu Forest), by Adrian Pătruț PhD [Fig. 4], professor of chemistry at Babes-Bolyai University of Cluj-Napoca and friend of Sift. Pătruț continued the scientific research of the strange phenomena in this area.

Adrian Pătruț writes that on Saturday, July 20, 1968, around 11:00, in a hot summer day, Alexandru Sift and his wife Viorica Sift were on one of their regular trips to a preferred area known as "Valea Bongarului" in the Hoia-Baciu Forest. Sift, who observed the surrounding areas with his Zeiss 8x30 binoculars, noticed that up on the ridge, at the edge of the "Pădurea Popilor" forest, at a distance of about 250-300 meters, were

Fig.4 Adrian Pătruț PhD, university professor in Cluj-Napoca.

four humanoid beings with a very unusual appearance. Two humanoids stood motionless with their back to the observers, near the edge of the forest, peering

occasionally in to the perfect blue sky. Another humanoid was lying on the ground, on his back, as if 'sunbathing'. The humanoid closest to the observers was moving swiftly and with his hands behind his back, to and fro, on a route parallel to the edge of the forest [Fig. 5]. After about five minutes on object appeared in the sky that was described as looking somewhat like a pear shaped grey balloon with a diameter estimated at 20-25 meters. It was moving at a speed of approx. 50-60 km/h, at an altitude of about 100 m above the forest, from west to east.

When it was over the four humanoids, the "balloon" ejected, one after another, in rapid succession, three large spheres in a vertical downward path and nine smaller spheres on a parabolic trajectory, also downward. The bigger spheres had a diameter estimated at 5-6 m and the smaller ones 2-3 m.

The four humanoids, now all standing up, raised their arms above their head. Within seconds, a kind of white parachute-bell covered all four of them, from their head to their mid body. After

Fig.5 Humanoid spotted, in July 20, 1968 by Alexandru Sift and his wife, in Hoia-Baciu Forest.

a few tens seconds, the four parachute-humanoids ascended slowly, becoming increasingly diffuse, until, a few meters above the ground, they were completely gone.

As the witnesses estimated, the humanoids were small in stature, approx. 1.30-1.40 m, robust looking, with short legs and with the muscles on their buttocks and legs that looked highly developed. Their skin was dark red to brown. The distinctive feature was a relatively large head with a canine type muzzle. Their hair, of about the same colour as the skin, was short.

After humanoids were covered by the white parachute-bells, Alexandru Sift took a picture of the scene. Unfortunately due to the large distance and the absence of any telephoto lens, the picture was not considered as conclusive evidence for the reality of the observation.

I can also notice that, as the distance to the humanoids from the witnesses was greater than 170 meters, this case can not be considered, strictly speaking, a close encounter of the third kind. It is however a very peculiar and fascinating case which also typifies the difference between the types of humanoids reported in Romania compared to those in the USA.

Emil Barnea photographs a UFO

On Sunday 18th of August 1968, technician Emil Barnea (then 45 years), went, along with three friends to spend the day in the Hoia-Baciu forest. The weather was hot, 36 centigrade, without any cloud or wind. At around 13:00, Barnea stood in *Poiana Rotundă* (The Round Glade) to collect wood to make a small camp fire. His girlfriend called out to him, shouting that she can see "something in the sky". When he joined her, he saw a large, round, flattened, shining silvery metallic object, at low height, above the treetops. It was moving slowly towards the South-West [Fig. 6 a & b].

After the first moments of surprise, Barnea rushed to get the camera that he had on the blanket on the grass and took in a hurry the first photograph. Since the object was not moving quickly, he took some time looking at it and then exposed the second photograph which was well centred in the viewfinder. Meanwhile, the strange aerial device begun to glow intensely and to tip over, as if its flight position would not matter. Obviously, it looked like a reversed "plate", but back then Emil Barnea knew very little about UFOs.

Suddenly, the object accelerated upwards. Following it through the viewfinder, Emil Barnea managed to shoot three more photos. In the last two images, the object appears, but only as a point that is lost in the immensity of the sky.

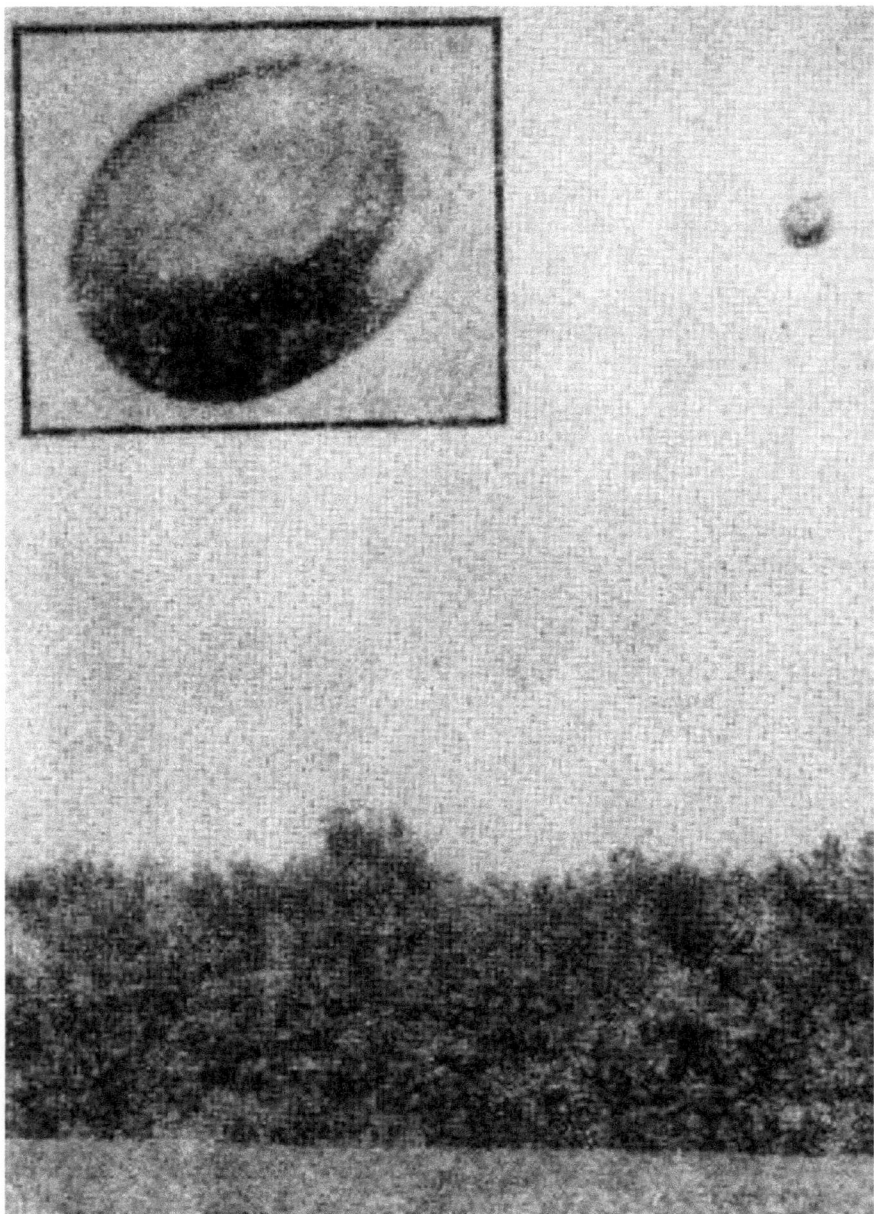

Fig.6a & 6b UFO photos made in August 18, 1968, by Emil Barnea, in Hoia-Baciu Forest.

Returning home, Emil Barnea, apparently uninterested about the sighting, had not rushed to take out the film from the camera. It was a while after before he exposed the remaining frames, had the film developed and made copies of the strange images.

Reporters from Bucharest came to interview the witnesses. The pictures obtained by Emil Barnea were taken by the Romanian news agency "*Agerpres*" and, after checking the film and then the witnesses' statements, they were shown on the national television and in newspapers across the country. Then the case became known abroad and it was featured in many magazines and books from different countries.

The series of UFO pictures made in Cluj has been recognised as one of the most important ones, because of the outstanding scientific issues raised by a number of very relevant details. The image analysis offered several unusual issues for which nobody has found explanation to this very day.

In the first image, the "flying saucer" appears as an object with a metallic enclosure whose contours are defined by natural sunlight; in the second image some changes have appeared: the shadow on the brim is illogical, reported to the direct sunlight (it is at the top), not being the shadow of the dome, while the centre became blurry. A careful checking of a model by specialists from the Faculty of Architecture in Cluj, led to the following conclusion: the luminosity of the shining object itself became brighter than sunlight and the illogical shadow on the brim had an unknown physical cause, being produced by the position of the object relative to the sun. The conclusions correspond with the details given by Emil Barnea.

The magnification of the third image confirms the findings above, raising some other, difficult, scientific problems. This reveals another inexplicable detail: while the dome is dark, the brim continues to shine. Obviously, the glow is not produced by an electrostatic process, but how is it possible to achieve, technically, the brilliance of only a part of the body of the unidentified flying object?

The photos taken on August 18th, 1968, by Emil Barnea, in Baciu forest, near Cluj, aroused a lot of interest, not only because of the quality of the images and by the details obtained, but also by the series of images that possibly showed us clues on how UFOs fly. As a result, these photos were subject to various types of analyses carried out in several countries. For example, the French UFO magazine "*Lumières dans la nuit*", before publishing the photos, submitted them for some very demanding examinations conducted by the Belgian LAET laboratories (Brussels). In the bulletin dated on March 12th, 1970, the specialist G. Delcorps stated: "The absence of detectable evidence of a possible fake and the conclusions of previous experts, make me conclude that the two photos I'm studying show the major elements of authenticity".

Then, F. Lagarde, a well known French ufologist, sent the photos and the bulletin, to another scientific expert. On October 28th, 1970, he confirmed the following: "Regarding the photos from Romania, I came to the same conclusion as Mr. Delcorps. I must agree with him and the shadows (on the object) have absolutely nothing to do with the sunlight".

Colman S. VonKeviczky, then director of ICUFON, revealed that the photos from Cluj-Napoca, significantly enlarged and displayed in the lobby meeting room, have impressed the participants at the First International UFO Congress held in Acapulco, in April 1977.

September 1968

In September 1968 other observations followed, not as spectacular, but still worth mentioning.

Miron Oprea, a professor of mathematics at the University of Oil and Gas in Ploiești and president of the Mathematical Society for Prahova County, related to Ion Hobana the experience he underwent on the evening of September 15th, 1968:

"It was 22:00. I travelled by car from Vălenii de Munte to Ploiești, with my wife and our two grandchildren aged 14 and 12. Just before the barrier from Blejoi, my wife saw to the southeast of us a glowing object heading slowly westward in the direction of the *Vega* oil refinery. It seemed to hover at a height of some hundred meters and when we got closer; its contours became increasingly clear. It was cylindrical in shape with a shiny ring underneath. It was around 2-3 m tall and about 3 m in diameter. It emitted a very strong bluish light. For about 40 seconds I had the impression that the object stood motionless in front of us at 100-800 m height, but it seems to me that it was descending slowly. When we arrived at the refinery it disappeared behind some buildings. It may have landed near the facilities. I wanted to stop, but my wife and grandchildren were so frightened that they did not allow me to. That night, at the same time and same place, another witness saw an identical phenomenon".

On September 19, 1968, a strange apparition was noticed over several towns in Transylvania. Engineer Florin Gheorghiță made a summary of them in his books and articles. At 15:30, above the centre of Cluj, a big pyramidal balloon had stopped, motionless in the sky. It was of an unusual shape and was shining brightly in the sunlight. Further calculations showed that the base of the "balloon" had a diameter of about 70 m.

The pilots of a *Tarom* aircraft that arrived at that time from Bucharest estimated that it was a stationary object at a height of 8000-9000 m. A similar estimation of the objects altitude was made separately, using theodolite, by both the topographer engineer Ştefan Mureşan of Cluj and the technician Gheorghe Norodot of Apahida (10 km east of Cluj).

The shining "balloon" was observed by thousands of the local inhabitants. The sightings began at 15:15. These witnesses submitted several written accounts describing how the object was moving very rapidly westward, although it was flying against a strong wind. Weatherman D. Peligrad from Cluj stated that: "At the height of 8000-9000 m, where the object was assumed to be observed, the wind strength reached 72-86 km/hour and the predominant direction was from west-southwest".

Then the "balloon" stopped and remained stationary for nearly four hours in a fixed spot in the sky. Those who were watching it with binoculars, with a hand-held telescope, or by an optical instrument made available to the public by the local astronomical observatory, all stated that the object did not react to the wind at all.

The bystanders who stopped to watch the apparition noticed that at on the opposite side to sunshine, the object emitted a continuous variation of lights in different colours. The radiances from the object had a yellow-orange tone which seemed to come from its inside.

For most observers, the "balloon" disappeared at 19:15, when it was covered by a thick cloud front; but some residents of the eastern part of the city did provide some additional details. In his written account, economist Gheorghe Poruţiu said that "at first, the object was stationary, but when the clouds came it departed at high speed travelling against the wind which was blowing from west to east".

By coincidence, a team of reporters from the Romanian state television were in Cluj, to make a programme about the UFO photographs taken a month before by Emil Barnea. They watched and filmed the new "unidentified" object. The film, made on this occasion by A. Croitoru was shown later in Bucharest, in front of a small group of competent people but it failed to clarifying the mystery.

The event that afternoon, as observed by the residents of Cluj, was not an isolated incident. As published in several newspapers and magazines of that time, many towns and villages in Transylvania were also "visited" by an unidentified flying object, at the same time as the strange "balloon" was observed over Cluj. Numerous reports were received from various witnesses from the cities of Deva, Mediaş, Dumbrăveni, Sighişoara, Braşov, Bistriţa and from several villages.

Issue 6033 of the nationwide German language newspaper "Neuer Weg" reported a UFO overflying the town of Bistriţa along with other locations nearby. A bright, iridescent body, which disrupted the TVs. Of the Sighişoara City residents were able to watch a spectacular stationary air show, somewhat similar to that which occurred in Cluj. Schoolmistress Taisia Maftei, who witnessed the event, wrote: "At about 18:00, I was informed by neighbours that in the sky there was a bright object stationed above the downtown area (the citadel). Looking at it, I saw it was a bright blue colour. There was no trail of smoke, nor was any engine noise heard. I watched this object for about an hour. This object was seen by many other inhabitants of the city".

Things proved more complicated than first imagined when trying to account for these sightings. Not only was it impossible to explain how the object remained stationary despite the strong wind, but the astronomer Gheorghe Chişu, from the Astronomical Observatory of Cluj, observed through a telescope at the object and stated that the object seemed to have its own light. As he said, "Balloon's shine by reflecting sunlight. In its middle the object had an area which shone more than the rest of the object", suggesting that the object had its own light source. A local radar station found that within the "balloon" there was a large metal core. Press photographer Rudolf Wagner from Cluj managed, using a telephoto lens, to take a photo which revealed that inside the soft "plastic" cover, there were two bright objects, each with an obvious form of a "flying saucer". They were located inside the main object at a short distance from each other in a position and appearance that is difficult to explain in conventional terms. Scrutinising the images of the two objects has revealed that their brightness was at least as intense as the sunlight reflecting from the other side of the object.

This was undoubtedly the first contemporary UFO wave in Romania. As a consequence it provided a lot of information for UFO researchers and scientists alike to ponder. In 1968 Romania had this huge wave of UFO sightings most of which remained unknown to the rest of the world.

THE 1970's

Ion Hobana, the ufologist

IN the period after 1968, ufology in Romania was strongly influenced by researcher Ion Hobana. He was born on January 25, 1931 at Sânnicolaul Mare, Timiş county, western Romania. His real name was Aurelian Mantaroşie. Ion Hobana grew up in the city of Bârlad (Romanian Moldavia), where his father was a magistrate. Here, in 1949, he graduated at the "Gheorghe Roşca Codreanu" high school. Then, in 1954, he graduated at the Faculty of Philology of the Bucharest University, with a diploma thesis in science fiction literature, the first of this kind in Romania.

Writer, journalist, editor, literary critic, essayist, translator, theorist of science fiction literature, Ion Hobana was a member of the *Société Européenne de Culture, HG Wells Society, Centre International Jules Verne, Associazione Internazionale per gli Studi sulle Utopie.* He has been for a long time the secretary of the Romanian Writers' Union. In recent years, he led the department of literature for children and youth of the Bucharest Writers Association, being also a member of the Board of the Writers Union of Romania. For his work in Science Fiction, he was awarded several international prizes.

With his knowledge and his skills, as well as by the positions he held in Romanian mass-media, Ion Hobana established good relations with science fiction writers and critics in the West, at a period in time when such relations were rare and difficult. As he declared, a Belgian friend – Jacques Van Herp – gave him, in 1967, two well documented books, about UFOs, of a known American author, former Major in the US Navy aviation (Donald E. Keyhoe). These books helped him to understand that the UFO issue is much more serious than it seems at a superficial view and that the "ostrich policy" towards it is not a wise one.

In an interview in 2010, Ion Hobana said that there are two types of arguments for which he takes seriously the study of unidentified aerospace phenomena. "First, there is the testimony of highly skilled people in their fields – military and civilian pilots, astronauts, engineers, scientists – who have made extensive comments. The opinions of these people cannot be removed with an ironic smile. Secondly, we must relate to physical testimonies that we have: radar recordings that cannot be disputed, recordings made with other instruments, traces on the ground and others. The amount of information is huge, especially now, after a number of official files were declassified", mainly military ones, in countries like the UK, France, Brazil, Australia, New Zealand etc. "For example, I believe that the accounts of astronauts, both Russians and Americans, have convinced many people that the phenomenon is real, even if we still have no certainty as to the origin and nature... There are many theories, but unfortunately, all rely, for now, on suppositions only. We do not have evidence to clearly show that these unidentified objects are extraterrestrials ... This is the easiest explanation, but..."

The UFO Circle from the Student House

Ion Hobana immediately understood the importance of the cases in 1968 and, as a result, actively participated in their popularisation. The context was favourable because the subject was quite taboo in other countries of the "socialist camp", but in 1968 the Ceausescu regime wanted to prove that the Romanian authorities' attitude was different.

The UFO "wave" of 1968 had good media coverage in Romania and had sparked the general interest for UFOs. In 1969, it was translated and published in Romanian the first book about UFOs: "*Farfuriile zburătoare – o chestiune serioasă*" (Flying Saucers – Serious Business, 1966) by Frank Edwards, which became a bestseller. In these circumstances, Ion Hobana took in 1971 the initiative of organising, at the Culture House of University Students, in Bucharest, a "Scientific UFO Circle", which attracted, for several years, a great number of young people as well as specialists interested in study of the phenomenon, including many academics. They conducted field research on reported cases and organised briefings and meetings with the public.

In an interview in 2010, Hobana said the success of this circle "is hard to believe today. The public meetings, held in the great hall on the ground floor, were attended by hundreds of students and other people. We travelled to other cities, being warmly welcomed everywhere [Fig. 7]. Interest in the UFO phenomenon then reached its peak. It is true that there were not so many books and dedicated TV shows as there were after 1990; those interested today prefer these ways of satisfying their curiosity rather than active involvement. The activity of the Circle was not subject to interference or obstruction by the authorities; they considered probably that it did not harm the ideological imperatives of the time. On the other

Fig.7 "Scientific UFO Circle" members in Brasov 1973. From left: Călin Turcu and Adrian Pătruț. In centre Ion Hobana.

hand, it was preferable that the students and the general public focus their attention on such harmless themes. As for me, I published dozens of articles and participated in radio and television debates without any hindrance".

Also in 1971, Ion Hobana and the Belgian author Julien Weverbergh published, in Romania, the book: "*OZN: o sfidare pentru rațiunea umană*" (UFO: a defiance for human reason). It was the first book, by a Romanian writer, about UFOs. The second was published by the engineer Florin Gheorghiță (*OZN – o problemă modernă*, Editura Junimea, Iași, 1973). Both authors were involved in the investigation of the 1968 cases. Ion Hobana with Julien Weverbergh also published UFO books abroad, among them *UFOs from Behind the Iron Curtain* (1974), translated later into French and Spanish.

The impact of this latter book was special, because it brought to the English and international readers one of the earliest indications that UFOs are not just an urban legend of the western technological society, but a phenomenon that resounds even in environments so severely controlled as the countries with communist regimes. Because of the opening offered, the volume is appreciated worldwide even today. For instance, Russian ufologist Boris Șurinov, bemoaning the lies that proliferate in the 1990s on the UFO phenomenon in Russia, wrote in 2000 that: "There are only two books in English with chapters where the Russian ufology is presented correctly enough. The first one is the English translation of the book written by my friend Ion Hobana and Julien Weverbergh. Ion Hobana is honest, he respects the ufological community and readers in general and knows Russian well enough to avoid traps and fantastic stories proliferated by many journalists and so called ufologists."

Julien Weverbergh himself had a UFO sighting in Romania. He writes that on the night of December 13 to 14, 1970, when he was in Bucharest, he was awakened at 01:30, by his wife and by a strong red light in the sky. His wife rushed anxiously to the next room, which overlooked the street, where her mother slept, while Julien rushed to open the window blinds of their room.

The light source was somewhere to the right, hidden by the walls of a building. There was a pulsating noise – like a buzz in the ear of the witness – and the red light was becoming increasingly white. When he was called by his wife and her mother and opened the door of the next room, he found that everything was bathed in a bright white light.

But, this light was suddenly extinguished before he reached the window. They were on the first floor and outside, to their left, in the centre of a small square, a bus was parked. A policeman was running towards it, but a few meters from the car, he suddenly stopped. The two women told that they saw then, just above the bus, a sphere, pulsating blue and white colours, which, at some point, suddenly disappeared.

It was quite warm for this time of year; the sky was covered in cloud. The total duration of observation was eight to ten seconds. The distance between the phenomenon and witnesses was about 80 m.

Valea Plopului – September 1972

A typical case, implying the "Scientific UFO Circle", was that of "Valea Plopului". On one of the nights between September 2 and 6, 1972, just after midnight, in the village of Valea Plopului, Prahova county, South Romania, Vasile Cărăbuș, a night watchman at the agricultural cooperative of Posești village, saw from the hill of "Tabacioi" a shiny object – a yellow "star with tail", crossing the sky, hovering and landing smoothly in an orchard located about 2 kilometres from him, on the hill of "La Odaia". After this, the object disappeared. The witness did not hear any noise.

After two days, the guard, along with several villagers had investigated the place in question; a cornfield dotted with fruit trees. Here they found a circular area with a diameter of 4.5 meters in which all the stems were broken at about one meter above the ground. In the centre of the circle there was a small heap of earth with the diameter of 60 cm and 40 cm in height, having in the middle a round, cylindrical hole, with a diameter of 12-14 centimetres and at least 2 meters deep. Around this hole, there were three identical, mechanical footprints, at the same distance of 1.5 meters, spaced perfectly at 120 degrees and well imprinted into the soil. It has been estimated that the weight of the object could have been of several tens of tonnes.

Later, hundreds of curious people visited the area, including the students brought in for "farm work", as it was customary to do so then. To verify the rumours that had spread in the area, Călin Turcu, a teacher in a school in Vălenii de Munte (about 17 kilometres from Valea Plopului) went to the location on November 29. The traces were pretty much still visible. Călin Turcu went back there, taking numerous photos and talking with the witnesses. He sent his findings to the "Scientific UFO Circle" in Bucharest. As a result, in the coming days the specialists who came from that organisation, among them, engineer and inventor Justin Capră (1933-2015) found, with the help of a Geiger–Müller counter, "a substantial increase of gamma radioactivity in the centre of the alleged landing area".

Maybe it is worth mentioning that Justin Capră claimed that he had invented the jet pack. According to an interview he gave later, he proposed this device to the Romanian Academy in 1956 and completed it in 1958. When the Academy declined to show interest, he said he offered it to the American Embassy, which was also uninterested. He was then put into jail for a short while by the communist regime for having approached the embassy. He claimed to have flown the device and received a patent in 1958. Despite the questionable assertions of Capră, it is widely accepted in Romania that at least one of his jet packs was flown two years before any other similar device in the world.

At Valea Plopului, on December 10th, 1972, a group of 11 people made measurements, photographs, sampling of soil and vegetation, tape recording of witnesses accounts and collected written statements. On this occasion, a widely circulated documentary film was made. Judging by the depth of the traces, it was estimated that the object could weight tens of tons. The soil appeared to have been exposed to a high temperature, but not to a flame. The unknown flying object avoided two high voltage lines (at a distance of 135 meters from each other), as well as three apple trees around, landing at an equal distance to them, without harm.

Călin Turcu found that the vegetation on the heap of earth was completely absent for the next four years and frail afterwards. He continued to monitor other aspects of the case, despite the fact that in the summer of 1973, as he wrote, two unidentified persons visited him and "advised" to never go there again.

Observations at Vălenii de Munte

Despite this warning Călin Turcu was passionately involved in the investigation of more unexplained occurrences, mainly around the town of Vălenii de Munte (in Prahova County, 100 km north of Bucharest), where he was a high school teacher.

One such case, which I summarise below, occurred on February 8, 1974, at 07:25. Ten girls from the orphanage school in Vălenii de Munte, aged between 11 and 18 years, had seen, above Bughii hill, on west-southwest direction (about two kilometres around the village Bughea de Jos) at a very low height (5-6 meters) above the trees on the hill, two spheres (or discs) at a short distance from each other. They were easily visible and were a yellow-orange colour and around them was a kind of semi-transparent whitish coating ("like a raw egg white", as stated by witnesses). Between them was a kind of faded orange light, as if their own light would be reflected from one to another.

After staying motionless for about 15 seconds, the two spheres slowly approached each other, merging into one object and taking the form of an elongated oval. On its top, a round shape was seen which was also orange in colour. The shell surrounding the object which was observed in the first phase of the sighting, had suffered no change in shape or colour. Immediately after the two objects merged together the object began to move very slowly towards the west-southwest. Then the object suddenly accelerated, moving away at high speed, in the same direction and disappeared behind the tree line giving the impression that it is moving horizontally. The total time of observation of the phenomena was about 40 seconds.

The witnesses insisted that, at the moment of the first observation, the sky was very overcast in that direction, but after that, it suddenly brightened up, a fact that apparently has strongly impressed them. Initially, Călin Turcu did not rule out an optical illusion. At east, where the sun was rising just above the hills, the sky was clear. The phenomenon could have been some iridescence of light, some effect of the barely risen sun.

After Turcu determined, with each of the witnesses, separately, with the highest probability, the area where the phenomenon was observed, he went to the location the very same day. On the top of the hill, beyond a wooded area, he found a kind of plateau, a relatively flat field that was ploughed by tractors in the autumn. Exactly where the lights had been seen, on the ground, there were two traces – fresh and deep, which, at first glance, seemed to have been left by the rear wheels of a tractor that would have wobbled slightly.

Călin Turcu made measurements and collected samples of water, soil, traces of oil, two screws etc. At first glance, it seemed that a tractor wanted to turn at the end of the field and it slipped heavily with the rear wheels, which sank into the soft earth; the driver repaired the engine which had leaked oil, but he forgot or lost two of the screws.

But – wondered Turcu – if the ground had been ploughed in the autumn and nowhere around were any new traces, then how come these marks appeared exclusively in that spot? There were no other traces, neither of the coming, nor of departure, no traces of the front wheels, or those that would have shown how the two big wheels came out of the mud. In one place, on the edge of one of the recesses there were three ribs, which would have disappeared if the tractor wheels would have been spun around.

The distance between the two traces was 1.85 m. No known tractor in the area had this wheel spacing. The soil at the bottom of the two traces was strongly compacted. Turcu managed only with great effort to thrust the knife into the soil, to take samples from the site. On the bottom of one of the recesses was "a green water", while in all other puddles around the water was grey; why?

On the next evening, on Saturday, Turcu was travelling by train to Timişoara, with members of the "Scientific UFO Circle" from Bucharest, intending to speak in public about the events of Vălenii de Munte. On the train, he told, to colleagues from Bucharest, everything that had happened the day before and gave, in their care, the whole set of collected samples, to be examined upon return to Bucharest. But, due to negligence and the lack of interest of M.D. who led this circle at that time, the samples were "lost" in Timişoara.

On the first day of the following week, immediately after returning from Timişoara, Turcu went again to the Bughii hill and collected another set of eight soil samples. But the "green water" was not there anymore. The new samples were analysed in the laboratories of two separate institutions: *Institutul de Carotaj* (core drilling) in Ploieşti (February 15th, 1974) and the Institute of Nuclear Physics from Bucharest (February 22=). Both gave the same verdict: "The samples do not differ between them and do not contain abnormal radioactive traces".

In the days that followed, Turcu went several times to the Bughii hill, trying to find other clues, other potential witnesses, talking with tractor drivers, machine operators or locals, making new measurements. One day, in the same place where the traces were found, a concrete pillar appeared, with a metal plate, written on it: "Warning! Danger of tipping over. Forbidden to work with tractors". Călin Turcu wrote that only now he begun to not understand anything. In that particular area a tractor could not overturn even if the driver wanted it to at all costs. After all, the whole area was an arable land, worked with tractors for years.

Călin Turcu was to witness for himself a UFO type phenomenon. As he wrote, on a winter's night, on Wednesday, December 11th, 1974, he was working longer than usual at his desk writing an article. At one point, he heard the dog barking insistently in the backyard. He went out to see what was happening. When he returned, he saw his shadow violently projected on the white wall. He turned around and saw, under the edge of the wooded hills, beyond the Teleajen river, a white dazzling light, looking as that given by welding machine and stronger than that of the full moon on clear nights, pulsating with the rate of 1-2 seconds. He ran into the house and took out the camera, an easy-going German "Beirette", suitable for night shooting. It was 01:22. When he returned to the courtyard, the light was in the same place. It had no precise contours. The actual distance could not be more than 800-1,000 m. It made a slow vertical movement, ascending and descending at a range of about 10-12 seconds, at an angle between 32 and 35 degrees. During a pulse, when the light intensity was at its maximum, the forests were brightly illuminated for miles around. At low intensity the light seemed like car headlights somewhere on a distant hillside.

In the next 3-4 minutes, Turcu took between 7 and 10 photographs, changing several times the place where he stood in order to try and obtain the best possible angles and positions. He also changed several times the aperture and shutter speed, hoping that, from all the attempts, at least two or three photographs would be successful. Later, he will regret not shooting the entire film. The total observation time was 12 minutes, until 01:34. After a final ascent, the light faded slowly and disappeared.

At the beginning of 1975, the photographic film was investigated carefully at the Photogrammetry and Remote Sensing Laboratory of the Institute of Civil Engineering of Bucharest. Upon returning the film; a report of several pages, signed by university assistant lecturer Dan Mihăilescu, was attached, certifying that the film is genuine.

The event has been made public – wrote Călin Turcu – in at least two publications abroad: "*The MUFON UFO Journal*" (USA), no. 114 / May 1977 (showing on the front cover two of the photos then) and "*UFO Quebec*" (Canada), no. 13/1978.

The RUFOR movement

Unfortunately after 1974, the activity of the "Scientific UFO Circle" began to diminish. Călin Turcu took the initiative of organising another structure dedicated to studying UFOs. On Sunday, July 17, 1977, he invited to his home, in Vălenii de Munte, three UFO enthusiasts: Valeriu Niculescu from Bucharest, Adrian Pătruț from Cluj-Napoca and Augustin Moraru from Ploiești. Here they decided to establish an informal group called RUFOR ("Romanian UFO Researchers") as a mean of information exchange. At that time, the legal establishment of organisations, even apolitical and non-governmental, was permitted in Romania only by initiative of the appropriate authorities.

However, this group, which, in the next few years, took on many new enthusiasts and published for eight years, between 1979 and 1986, 27 issues of a "samizdat" magazine (also something not officially permitted) with the same name: RUFOR. The hard work of compiling the magazine fell mainly on the shoulders of two passionate researchers: Mihai Harry Danciu from Braşov and Augustin Moraru, the latter being the one who took care of the artistic design of the magazine. As Călin Turcu writes, I'm almost sure the authorities knew and "tolerated" the existence of the magazine and did not intervene as long as it has not represented any political "danger".

On August 8 and 9, 1987, also at Vălenii de Munte, a "10 years of RUFOR" meeting took place, which involved eight people: Lt. col. pilot Doru Davidovici from Bucharest, author of many books, among them a famous one about UFOs and extraterrestrials, Adrian Pătruţ PhD from Cluj-Napoca, Mihai Harry Danciu from Braşov, Augustin Moraru from Ploieşti, writer György Mandics from Timişoara; eng. Justin Capră from Bucharest; eng. Octavian Mişorin from Bucharest and Prof. Călin Turcu, as host. Unfortunately, after this anniversary, the magazine has not been published anymore.

After several years, in 1994-1996, in a completely changed political environment, members of the same group will publish the only widely marketed Romanian UFO magazine, also with the title "RUFOR". It had 21 monthly issues. After that, there was no printed UFO periodical in Romania.

I could mention that in the seventies and eighties a dozen of UFO books, translated or original, were published in Romania. Among the Romanian authors were: Ion Hobana, Florin Gheorghiţă, Dan D. Farcaş, Doru Davidovici (fighter pilot 1945-1989), Dan Apostol and György Mandics. An important book, published in Romanian, in 1978, was "Experienţa OZN" (The UFO Experience, 1972), by the astronomer J. Allen Hynek, university professor, one of the greatest ufologists, for 21 years scientific adviser to UFO studies undertaken by the U.S. Air Force. The number of UFO books in Romanian increased dramatically after 1990, written mainly by Călin Turcu, Adrian Pătruţ, Emil Străinu and some of those above. But most of the titles, in this period, were translations.

Other sightings

Titus Zăgrean, a noted journalist from Bistriţa (Transylvania), also passionate about UFOs, wrote in a letter to Călin Turcu, of an incident which happened to him in 1973. On the evening of August 28, at 22:00, he was driving a car, coming from a job for the newspaper he was working for, in Bistriţa-Năsăud County. It was a clear sky, full of stars and no breeze. Beside him was his friend and colleague, Ion Moise, a staunch opponent of the UFO phenomenon, who often used to say that "those who believe in such things have no culture". At one point – while passing near an area with vineyards, in the area of the Codrişor forest, Budacul de Jos commune – the friend said he saw a big light in the sky, very low, clearly looming over the background hills. Believing that his friend was making a joke, Zăgrean did not react. But after his friend insisted, increasingly troubled, saying that the light was coming to intersect their road, Zăgrean looked through the right window of the car and saw "the most beautiful UFO possible, in all its splendour, in an atmosphere of a phantasm that gives you tingles up your spine". It was round, big, milky white and revolving.

The colleague stuttered, squirmed and asked him to stop the car, "otherwise the engine will stop" and they "will abduct us". The driver was rather curious and even wanted to stop and to try and communicate with it. The moment the object was above the road, he has illuminated like the full beam of car headlamps. "The mass of neon light with a diameter of about one meter" made a sharp vertical jump of several meters and continued on an east-west trajectory. The two journalists sped off in pursuit of the UFO. Once on top of a hill, they saw it as "chandelier hanging in the sky". It moved along the valley, veered sharply to the north and accelerated, changing colour to a yellow-orange, then red, becoming a star and departing with a fantastic speed in the direction of the city of Baia Mare.

The witnesses did not notice any propulsion system, any noise and did not feel any heat or other sensations, except for a state of strangeness. Zăgrean had a camera in the car, but he completely forgot about it.

The next day, news agencies published a statement that a UFO was seen over the airport of Baia Mare and that, the same or another object was seen over the cities of Budapest and Vienna.

Another interesting sighting, made in the same geographical area, was that of Răstoliţa, a commune in the north-eastern Transylvania located on the Mureş River Valley, 63 km upstream from the city of Târgu Mureş, in an area of wooded hills, with 90% of the population involved in wood processing.

The main witness was Dr. Andrei Antalffy, back then associate professor at the Medical-Pharmaceutical Institute (University) of Târgu Mureş, a very serious and trustworthy person, who has followed the phenomenon with his mother, wife and daughter.

On the evening of September 9th, 1974, around 20:30, they were in their cottage, inhabited only in summer and not connected to the mains. The cottage was located 500m from the village, on an isolated plateau surrounded on all sides by trees. The wife of Antalffy noticed a strange light, silvery-white, behind the house. The sky was clear and moonless. Calling her husband, they went outside the cottage. Here they noticed that the source of the strange glow was a "wall of opaque light", perfectly defined, as a rectangle, at a height of about 1.70 m and length of about 25 m, located about 160-170 m from the cottage. In front of the "wall", the witnesses observed four spheres of intense orange colour, with the apparent diameter of 40-50 cm. The spheres were grouped two by two, "with exactly equal distances between them". In the opinion of Dr. Antalffy the objects were definitely on the ground.

The witnesses did not hear any noise during observation and did not feel any other secondary phenomena. After a few moments of fear, they went back into the cottage and continued to watch the phenomenon from inside, until around 24:00. During this time, they had not noticed any change in colour or light intensity and no change in the position of the orange balls. After midnight, the witnesses went to bed and in the morning the phenomenon was no where to be seen.

The case was investigated onsite by a team from Târgu Mureș. They established, among other things, that the phenomenon was on a terrace of the plateau and the actual distance to the witnesses was 134 m.

An intelligent orb and a false Moon

Among the many cases investigated by Călin Turcu, an interesting one is that of Margareta Ivanciov from Timişoara. In 1975 she was 45 years of age and teacher of history in the Teremia Mare commune, at a distance of 70 kilometres from Timişoara. She was commuting by train, having also a room rented in the commune.

In her correspondence with Turcu, she wrote that one night in July 1975 (she no longer remembered the exact date), at around 02:00, she arrived in the village, coming from Timişoara. Descending from the train, she started to walk from the railway station, on the main street. The night was warm, the sky was clear, no wind was blowing. At one point, she observed a bright globe, approximately 50 to 60 cm in diameter. The globe advanced, floating, on the same route, by 10-12 meters in front of her and 2.20-2.50 m above the pavement, without deviating to the right or left. When she tried to approach it, hastening her steps, the globe increased its speed, so the distance between them had not changed.

The globe was composed of thousands of individual bright dots, but which together gave the impression of a homogeneous whole. The colour was intense, something between yellow and orange. All points composing the globe were emanating light of the same colour. Towards the edges, the light was softer, like a fog, like a halo. The witness said that she had no fear and, on the contrary, she was very curious and trying to observe everything consciously and correctly.

The floating orb disappeared around a corner, to the left, on a secondary street, exactly where she had to turn. "When I reached that corner, I turned left and I saw with astonishment that the light globe floated, as before, in front of me, at the same distance between it and me and between it and the ground", she wrote. When she reached the house where she lived in, the orb "remained suspended in the air a few seconds, motionless, as if it was waiting for me and then went over the fence into the yard". Here it stood until she entered, then went over the fence into the neighbour's garden, which unfortunately she could not follow or track.

From the moment she noticed the globe and until it has passed into the neighbour's garden was around 10 minutes in total. The teacher's opinion was that the phenomenon was not a natural one. Its movement was self aware or directed. The thing that intrigued her most was that the globe "knew" where she lived. She ended her story by writing "It's hard to express in ordinary words that special state of good feeling and quietness that I experienced. Words don't have the force required to accurately express what I felt then".

Another case examined by Călin Turcu was that of the UFO sighting at the motel "*Paralela 45*", located north of Ploieşti, on a main highway. The witness, Marian R., 47 years old in 1996, reported that almost two decades before, in the second half of September 1977 he was working as a receptionist at the motel. One night, around 01:00, two usual clients, a delegate and a driver, arrived, requesting accommodation. They transported a trailer with boxes of grapes. The customers said to Marian that, if he wishes, he may choose a couple of bunches for himself from the trailer.

When he went out to the trailer he saw a bright disc and even exclaimed "Look what a big Moon!" The night watchman, "Uncle Babone", replied: "No, Mr. Marian, it is not the Moon! Watch! The Moon is over there!"

Only then he realised that what he mistook as the Moon was actually a giant bright disc about three to four times larger than the Moon. The disc "had an incandescent, orange-red core, like hot embers and its surrounding halo of light was red with shades of yellow". At the beginning, perhaps for 3-4 minutes, it stood motionless; then it fell sharply a few hundred meters, stopped a moment and then continued to fall slowly towards Floreşti village, less than 2 km away.

The witness could not tell if the object hit the ground or not, although he climbed on some garden tables to try and get a better view. After about 20 minutes of observation, he went back inside to put a coat on. When he got outside again, the night watchman, whom he had asked "to keep an eye on the objective", said, "it shot off at an unimaginable speed".

Hoaxes and disinformation

As everywhere, in Romania also were some hot-headed people who spread invented or much embellished UFO stories. Below I highlight two examples which have been publicised abroad as well as in Romania. It is not impossible that behind these cases was a mechanism of purposeful disinformation, meant to ridicule UFO stories, or to spread upon them a curtain of confusion and distrust.

One example is the "contactee" Izsáky G. László, from Satu Mare. Born in 1943, he remained fascinated by the UMMO phenomenon, the well-known disinformation (hoax) that originated in Spain. Izsáky told, on several occasions, that in 1974, he decided to call a UFO. He said that along with a group of friends, they drew on the ground, in a clearing near the Ocna Şugatag village (Maramureş County) a huge sign "Ж" (specific for the UMMO hoax). They organised a group of observers and allegedly on June 7, at 13:00, the UFO landed next to that sign. They said that the event was attended by about 60 people from the area (forestry workers, nearby residents curious individuals etc.). Two ordinary people came out from the landed ship, both with long blond hair. They spoke Greek at first. Then they tried to communicate in four different languages. The visitors wore no helmet and on the back of their coveralls there was the exact same sign "Ж". Finally, they put a box on the ground as a gift to the earthlings. When the organisers wanted to open this box, two trucks and a car suddenly appeared and, out of them, about 100 soldiers from the Army, Militia and Security appeared. They asked to be given the box. After a brief struggle, a friend of Izsáky fled with the box, the pursuers being "paralysed" by a "wave" sent by visitors.

Allegedly, in the box were 84 gold plates of 100 grams each, marked with an unknown writing, containing a message to earthlings. A group member, Zoltán Molnár, hastily made photocopies and spread them among friends.

According to the story, in the days and months ahead a hunt was on for those directly involved in this case, during which time some of them were arrested and isolated in prisons and psychiatric hospitals, some even being killed. The organisers were accused of fighting against the communist regime and of espionage. Molnár, tortured, disclosed the whereabouts of the box, which was confiscated. Then he was liquidated... and so on...

László G. Izsáky said he decrypted the text, finding a number of great secrets, including that under the pyramid of Cheops there is a time capsule left by aliens. He tried, in 1988, to publish a book in this regard, addressing even the Romanian Academy, to intervene with a publisher in the country, to accept his text (back then, you needed many official approvals to publish a book at one of the few publishers). He was advised to seek treatment for mental illness. He published some texts in Hungary and, even now, has a blog in Hungarian, promoting his ideas.

Călin Turcu said that the story was accepted, with some alterations, by a number of foreign authors without checking – even summarily – the information. He cites in this regard William P. Sanders. Turcu tried himself, in the second half of July 1995, to check what can be proven in this story. In this regard, he went to Maramureş County and wandered through the localities: Sighet, Ocna Şugatag, Cavnic, Baia Sprie, Baia Mare etc., all specified in the story of Izsáky. Finally, Turcu found no trace of the alleged events of 1974. What – he says – it does not necessarily mean there was nothing.

It is worth to mention briefly, another similar case (presented, for example, in number 18/1995 of the RUFOR magazine). At one time, among ufologists, the news had spread that in the summer of 1977 in an andesite quarry, next to Bixad (Covasna County), a shiny UFO had landed. People were horrified; they refused to work there from that moment on and then were moved to other careers. Peter Leb investigated the case and concluded that nothing happened, the story being a possible disinformation story. In 1977 in Jiu Valley, there was a huge coal miners' strike and maybe the UFO story was invented to deflect any interest in the strike?

Like the rest of the world Romania has not escaped from those who would try and pull the wool over our eyes with hoaxes and fanciful stories. However, despite their best attempts the real and factual UFO accounts always rise to the top and continue to baffle and excite in equal measures.

THE 1980's

The Løvendal-Papae case

LYDIA B. Løvendal-Papae, a school teacher, was the daughter of the famous Romanian painter George baron Løvendal and descendent of the old aristocratic families from Northern Europe, including astronomer Tycho Brache. She married Radu Mihai Papae, a noted architect, professor at the University of Architecture and Urbanism in Bucharest. In 1987 she wrote a report concerning a UFO sighting she and her husband had in Bucharest. In the following, I have summarised this report, which was signed in person by both of the witnesses.

September 11th, 1987, at 20:15, after a short walk, they left the Herăstrău Park towards Aviators Square. The first stars of the night had appeared. The sky was serene except for a small brown-black layer of cloud, slightly to the left, toward the east. "Our attention was drawn to a 'star', unusually large, of reddish-orange colour, like Mars, but much more intense and bigger (relatively 5 times!)". It was like a ball of coloured glass, illuminated by its own light. It stood motionless over the region Arch of Triumph and gave off a strong pulsating light. After a minute or two, 'the star', with the speed of a plane, appeared right above the witnesses and stopped suddenly. It stayed there for a couple of minutes, without blinking and then began to sway slightly in several directions, like a balloon held by a thread, returning always to the same place. Suddenly, after several flashes of light, it started to make large zigzags movements towards the television building and then, suddenly headed straight to the left, towards the north-east, disappearing behind the brown-black layer of cloud.

They waited for about five minutes for it to reappear. After this, she lowered her head for two to three seconds to rest her neck and to put her spectacles in her purse, when her husband yelled: "Did you see?! It released a white beam, like a puff of smoke!" But the beam disappeared immediately much to her annoyance. Her husband said that "the ray was white, pretty defuse much like a spray-effect.

It had an angle of about 5 degrees and its length was shorter than the Big Dipper constellation".

In the report she added that the object was at an approximate height of 1000 meters. There were no other witnesses. They left the location at 20:30 so the whole sighting took a quarter of an hour.

Arriving home, they considered to whom to inform about the observation. They had many friends, noted specialists, but "the specialists in any field are sceptics and we did not want to be ridiculed". Finally they found a friend, "a multilateral scientist, a PhD, who also had observed similar phenomena, but never had the courage to go public with his sighting. He asked me to write down immediately everything I saw, because he knows someone who gathers such data and said that only in Bucharest, this year, were another 14 reports very similar to ours (all flying in a zigzag, all pulsating with abrupt movements exactly as I described earlier)".

She discovered, unexpectedly, that a next-door neighbour, Mrs. Mioara Iliescu and her nephew also saw, during the same evening, a very large, reddish star, "like a glass globe on the Christmas tree" and that it stood still for a long time, before 20:15.

She added "I know that such reports are mocked worldwide, yet I felt compelled to write down exactly what we both saw, without dreaming, without being hypnotised and we hope that we are still of sound mind without individual or collective psychosis!. Without getting carried away and speculating what this object may have been, it was, for us at least, a truly unidentified flying object!"

She remembered, in the same report, another sighting, several years before, at around 22:00, in the same area. It was a very bright star, moving in the same direction with them. Then the "star" stopped for a moment, blinked and, swaying slightly, began to jump in very strange zigzags, turned sharply eastward, flew again in very agitated zigzags and disappeared at a high speed over the horizon!

A UFO over flies a lake in Bucharest

Gabriel Tudor, a young journalist and ufologist, was in 1998 one of the founding members of the Romanian UFO association ASFAN. He discovered, investigated and published many UFO and paranormal cases. Some of them were included in his book "*Tărâmul Enigmelor*" (The Realm of Enigmas, 2000). Among these is the case of Cristian Tuţă, in 1999 a successful businessman in Bucharest and aged 31 at the time.

In 1988 he was in mandatory military service in a unit located in the Roşu village, adjacent to Bucharest, on the shores of *Lacul Morii* (Mill Lake), between that village and the neighbourhood of Crângaşi. On January 5 (or 15?), he was assigned as a guard for the night shift, from 02:00 to 06:00. It was bitter cold and he desperately wanted to leave his guard duty in order to get warm back in the barracks.

At around 05:00, his thoughts were interrupted by him sensing the presence of a light, in his right, just above the bridge to the only island on the lake. The guard post was on the shore of the lake; but in those days, in the winter, the lake was completely drained of water. Also, because of electricity shortages, the entire city was plunged into darkness. The only sources of light were several windows in the military command unit, which had its own power generator and some red lights on a distant antenna. In these circumstances, the light instantly intrigued the young soldier.

The bridge referred by the witness was about 500 meters away from the guard post. Tuţă said: "The light that appeared was, in my view, at 10-12 meters above the bridge. It had an oval shape and stationed there vertically, perpendicular to the ground. I do not know what size it was; in any case, it was very large, appeared to be 10 to 15 meters high and about 5 meters wide. The visibility was very good. I could see it perfectly! The light was strong, like the one produced by a neon lamp, and the bridge was seen clearly below it. What amazed me even more was that inside the apparition I glimpsed four lights, in the shape of a cross, glowing in the same colour range, but with tenfold intensity, like reflectors. For a couple of seconds, the object or whatever it was the source of that light, stood motionless, at the mid point of the bridge. Then, it began a strange dance over it. The object really danced; it moved amazingly fast, up and down, not sideways, as if it was trembling. At one point, it began to move toward the edge of the bridge, but all in the same style, by repeated climbing movements, comparable with the graph of sinus and cosinus from trigonometry. Arriving at the end of the bridge, it resumed the race to the opposite side. This 'dance' had lasted, according to the clock, 30 minutes and I watched it without blinking. I was fascinated, already aware that I see something that not many people have been able to see. This back and forth movement ended as suddenly as it started and the object remained suspended over the bridge and in the same place where I had seen it originally. It began to move slowly toward the Roşu village, at a constant height, which I estimated as not exceeding 20 meters. It had travelled amazingly slowly compared to how it had moved earlier. It was like it scanned the area. I think it crossed in just one minute a distance of just 50 meters".

At no time did the object make any noise and when the object came near a clump of trees more than 70 meters away from the bridge, it seemed to stand out by showing itself in all its glory. Tuţă said: "I actually gaped at it, watching it, among the branches of leafless trees. The oval object had turned 90 degrees and looked like two plates put together, resembling those 'flying saucers' you see in the movies. I did not know what to say, I can never forget the emotion I experienced. I told myself: 'Here's a UFO, an authentic UFO!' and it was kind of like I could not believe it. The object maintained the initial neon-white brightness, but the four lights were gone. Instead, in the middle, in the region where we imagine that the two 'saucers' were combined, I saw a row of colours: there were small lights, like small light bulbs, going on and off, but not completely. There were only warm colours, with different shades: white, yellow, pink, orange. The harshest colour was a dark orange. The object continued to move smoothly, stationed, for a few moments over a tree, then in a split second, it rushed towards Chiajna [village] at an incredible speed and it was not to be seen again! I had the impression that the sky swallowed it! For years afterward, watching the Star Trek TV series, I have seen such a mode of travel, of disappearing almost instantaneously, with a speed that defies the speed of light!"

"I was shocked by this event, but I was afraid to report it to my superiors. The political times were as they were; you know very well what I mean". The witness mentioned it to one colleague but his reaction was one of fear. Only after a few months, when he was assigned to another unit, did he have the courage to tell the story to an NCO and he learned with amazement that such encounters had been reported by many of his colleagues, from units in Bucharest and countrywide.

After more than a decade after the event, Cristian Tuță declared that: "I am absolutely convinced that what I saw then was an alien ship. Nobody can make me change my mind. What else could it be? Nothing of the kind like a weather balloon or any weather phenomenon could account for what I saw. The object, I saw clearly, had material consistency and was clearly a flying ship. No assumption of a military spying device – American, Russian or of another state – can account for what I saw. Who is capable of building such craft with such amazing manoeuvrability, as seen only in movies or manufactured on computer?"

Unusual phenomenon observed on radar in Romania

Ion Lazeanu is retired senior meteorologist and founding member, in 1998, of the ASFAN association. He made, repeatedly, around 1986, astonishing radar observations of a huge UFO. Below, I present his report about these incidents, a report which was also previously published in the March 2000 issue of EJUFOAS, "The European Journal of UFO and Abduction Studies".

"I was working as a senior meteorologist at the radar laboratory (physics of the atmosphere) at the National Institute for Meteorology and Hydrology in Bucharest (Romania), since 1967. In the same year a British Plessey radar was installed in our

Institute, the training of operators being made by English and American specialists. In 1971 the Plessey device was replaced by a new installation: MRL-2, made in the former Soviet Union, the training being performed by an engineer from the manufacturer company. The radar had a range of 300 kilometres and a narrow angular opening, typical for meteorological radar devices [Fig. 8].

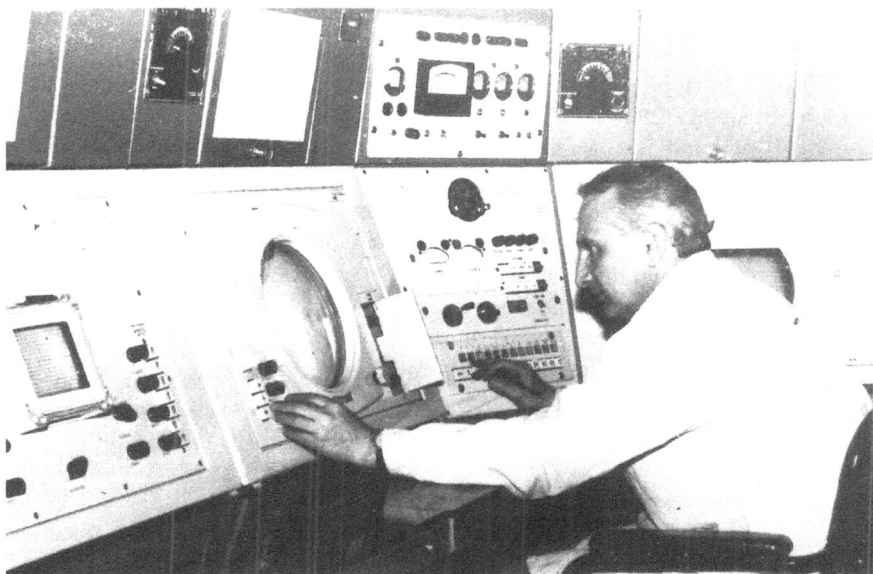

Fig.8 Meteorologist Ion Lazeanu in front of the radar with which he observed repeatedly UFOs.

The meteorological observations were performed each hour, 24 hours per day, working in shifts. During one of the routine observations with this radar, on one night of August 1986, at 02:00, on the screen appeared a sharp horizontal line one centimetre long. The position of the target remained stationary. By specific radar techniques, I determined that the distance to the object was 275-280 km south-west from our station, that is, above the city of Sofia (Bulgaria), at an altitude of 30,000 meters. Through manual operations, I stopped, for about 4-5 minutes, the radar beam on the 'object', which had remained motionless. Afterwards, almost instantly, it disappeared. I found it immediately, on the same vertical, some 5000 meters lower down. I fixed the radar on the new position, continuing the observation, but after a short while it disappeared once again, this time rising back to its initial position. I have a good experience in observing flying objects and I have also two licenses as airplane pilot, but this object and its movements resembled nothing I had seen before.

During this time period I was on duty at night every four days. During three-four weeks, I had the opportunity to observe this strange 'object' almost every time and it was always in the same place. The length of the observations varied between 3 and 20 minutes. I discovered also the same object (or another, identical), above the city of Cluj-Napoca (Romania), located at some 300 kilometres northwest of Bucharest. Afterwards, the object disappeared and it was impossible for me to find it, despite my extensive efforts.

The object reappeared in February 1988, again in the area of Sofia and again at night, between 02:00 and 04:00. My observations were made several times, in conditions of good weather and a cloudless sky. Once again, the 'object' made its vertical movements. After one month, a change occurred; during one of my observations, the object disappeared suddenly, but this time horizontally; I found it more than 200 km eastward in the area of the city of Varna (Bulgaria). In the next observations, I found it in this new location. When I fixed the radar beam on it, the object performed the same quick movements upward or downward. On one night, after repeating this operation several times, when I fixed once again the radar beam on it, all of our radar installation was disconnected spontaneously. I started it again only for the next planned hourly observation. After the usual routine operations everything was functioning once again without any problems. However the 'object' was no longer visible on the radar screen. After this incident, I stopped to study the strange object. I saw it several times for a short while, but I avoided stopping the radar device on it. I must mention that the morning after the incident I called the electronic technician. After checking all the components of the equipment he told me that he did not found any explanation for the spontaneous malfunction of the radar systems. As a matter of fact, the radar worked perfectly afterwards without any further problems.

The dimensions of the object could be estimated by analogy. A big ship (e.g. 200 meters long), at a distance of 35-40 kilometres offshore, appears on the screen of a similar radar, installed on the coast of the Black Sea, as a horizontal one centimetre line. Taking into consideration the distance of 275-280 kilometres, the 'object' could have had a length of at least 1500 meters. We must also remember its tremendous speed, both horizontally and vertically, as well as the property to reflect the radar beam".

Following a number of sceptical comments which contested the possibility to stop the radar device on the target, Ion Lazeanu stated that there are several types of radars and there are differences between military and meteorological radars, as follows: The military radars transmit radio waves, with a great angular opening, to detect small targets. There are often two antennas moving horizontally and vertically. Only when they are moving they can "see" the target. The meteorological radars, as the MRL-2, have a small angular opening. Their purpose is to detect targets of a large size and low speed (such as a cloud systems). They operate by emitting two microsecond pulses of radio waves. When they "catch" a target, the echo of the pulses is received by the same antenna, in the same position. Unlike military radars, the meteorological ones can observe a target being stopped on it.

Sightings on the sea

By 1990, the (state owned) maritime fleet of Romania – commercial vessels and marine fisheries – had over 350 ships, many of them big ones which were able to cross any sea of ocean. It seems natural that, sometimes, their crews saw a number of strange things and even sent in UFO reports. Below I will outline three unidentified sightings, investigated by Ion Hobana and Călin Turcu.

Nicolae Ştefanescu, commander of the oil tanker "Argeş", recounted: "On October 24th, 1968 at 15:47 GMT, on a calm sea, we were sailing through the strait between Madagascar and the east coast of Africa, known as the Mozambique Channel. We were ready to conduct astronomical observations, necessary to determine the ship's position. The atmosphere was quiet and the sky was cloudless. Suddenly, I heard the shout of amazement from the third officer, Ştefan Anton, who was with me on the bridge and was pointing to something in the sky.

I saw, coming from the southeast, a white bright object, travelling across the sky at an amazing speed. When it approached us it looked like a disc the size of half of the apparent diameter of the Moon, bright orange-yellow in colour and was emitting blue-green rays from the centre of the disc. After a few seconds, the object stopped, remained motionless for a moment and suddenly changed direction eastwards, almost perpendicular to our line of advance, disappearing into the vastness of the sky. The observation lasted some 12 seconds. According to the calculations with our sextant, the object was at a distance of 25 kilometres and had a diameter of about 17 meters".

On December 24th, 1972, the ship "Moldoveanu" was near Labrador, at 60° N and 62° W. Between 03:00 and 04:00 the crew noticed a shiny object heading at high speed straight towards their vessel and flying low over the waves.

Arriving just above the ship, the object has stopped and changed several times its shape and colour. After initially being round, it became an elongated oval and the colour went from red to yellow and then becoming white and bluish. According to the sighting recorded in the logbook of the vessel, after an hour of observation, the object suddenly shot into the sky; it became increasingly smaller and disappeared.

On September 17th, 1982, the "Bocşa" ore ship of 55,000 tonnes was in the Atlantic, just below the equator. Here's what the captain Ştefan Freitag tells us: "It was around 21:00. The duty officer had just had determined our exact position. To check it, he asked, immediately thereafter our coordinates from a navigation satellite. The data was consistent. We were at 11 degrees 37 minutes south latitude and 33 degrees 28 minutes west longitude, about at the limit of 200 nautical miles from the territorial waters of Brazil. As the sun had just set it was possible to observe the satellite as a bright mobile spot in the sky. When I wanted to discuss our position an officer, who had just left the bridge, yelled that he could see the satellite! I rushed out to take a look. The bright indicated spot, as viewed from the side, had a green glow. I told myself that it was probably a plane flying from South America to Africa. I intended to go back onto the bridge, when the officer exclaimed, "Look there, another satellite!"

This other "satellite" was about the size of a full moon. It gradually faded; however, beside it, immediately appeared a new, brighter, green-blue "star", that also grew in size until it became about the size of the full moon. Then it faded too and through the same metamorphosis, a third "Moon" appeared. In its centre occurred a burst of orange light, which was very iridescent and within minutes covered the entire "Moon". The apparition was surrounded by an aura, like Saturn's ring, which then also started to fade.

At that time, Captain Freitag had alerted the crew who were gathered at that hour in the ships lounge area. Fourteen crew members came up on deck. Captain Freitag had activated the video camera and the doctor of the ship and the crew chief began to take pictures.

Meanwhile, a fourth "Moon" appeared; it had undergone the same stages as the third, except that its halo was upright. Suddenly, the "star" "flared up" very quickly, apparently without moving in any direction. It was like a celestial body that could have crashed into the ship at very high speed. The terrified crew noticed that through the door into the interior of the vessel; the captain's dog was yelping and howling.

Captain Freitag remembered at that moment, a radio broadcast warning in 1981, to all vessels in an area of the ocean, stating that an American space capsule may land there. So he rushed to the bridge. However, when he arrived there, the apparition "calmed down". Now it was shining in all colours of the rainbow and was surrounded by a bright flashing halo which gradually faded away. Finally it remained there just looking like a luminous cloud.

Captain Freitag further reported: "The UFO 'show' was repeated, identically, with the fifth appearance of the object. I must emphasise that throughout the development of these phenomena, no sound was perceived and no heat radiation was felt. Only the Geiger counter – which, unfortunately, we brought on deck rather late – showed a slightly increased level of radiation. But it was far from the levels that are dangerous to humans".

A day later, on September 18th, 1982, a British ship – coming from South Africa and heading for Bermuda – observed, around the same time and only two degrees of latitude closer to the Equator, seven occurrences of the same kind. David Johanson, captain of the "Tenchbank" – this was the name of the British vessel – communicated by radio with Captain Freitag, then sought clarification from the Brazilian coast guard. But the coast guard, that usually gives very detailed information, with a proverbial efficiency and punctuality, about everything that happens or might happen, preferred, this time, to remain silent.

Over land and sea it seems that the UFO phenomenon knows no boundaries. Observed by the human eye and radar this enigmatic and complex unidentified phenomenon continues to puzzle and frustrate. The political situation in Romania at the time of the above sightings could make it 'dangerous' for ordinary citizens to report such observations but it could have been much more dangerous for those in the military to do so. The risks they took by going on the record are something that thankfully their counterparts in the west did not have to face.

AFTER 1990

Retezat Mountains – August 1991

BEFORE midnight on August 13 to 14, 1991, an IL-18 airliner, flying from Bucharest to Timişoara with crew of nine people aboard, radioed they had started to descend for landing at Timişoara airport. In the middle of the conversation with the flight control tower concerning their position and altitude, at 23:53, the aircraft crashed, hitting a slope on the Retezat Mountains (in Southern Carpathians, Romania) at an altitude of less than 1500 meters and 150 km from Timişoara. The aircraft commander was well known and appreciated in Romanian civil aviation, with more than 3000 hours of flying experience on this type of aircraft. That night, in the Retezat Mountains, the weather was excellent. After almost a year of investigations and hearings, the officials concluded that the cause was the total lack of guidance of the crew. The error was an apparent deviation of 50-60 kilometres from the course that they should have been flying on.

By a strange coincidence, the morning after the disaster, before the publication of any news of what happened with the airliner, the newspaper called "*Zori Noi*" of the nearby city of Petroşani published under the headline "mysterious phenomenon" a small article dedicated to the adventure of a group of seven people, who stated that, on the night of August 4, 1991, they had seen a UFO-like formation at a location just two kilometres away from the aircrafts crash site.

Subsequently, Constanţa Corpadea, a reporter for the "*Adevărul*" newspaper (one of the most important ones in Romania) and then the writer Mihaela Muraru-Mândrea PhD, conducted interviews with two of the group recalled: mountain rescuers Martin Domokoş, who has worked in Retezat Mountains for thirty years and his colleague, George Resiga. Using the information they gathered, Ion Hobana became convinced that we are dealing with one of the most important UFO cases in history and he wrote an article, from which I will high light the main elements.

On August 4, Domokos and Resiga, along with five hikers, had left the "Pietrele" hut (1480 m. altitude), heading towards the mountain rescue base which is near the "Bucura" lake (2040 m.), carrying the necessary food to last for a few days. They went slowly, because one of girls had a slight problem with one of her legs. During the hike and on the way toward the Bucura saddle, the highest point of their journey, a group of four hikers had gone on in advance. After nightfall, the hikers saw a bright light in behind them. They stopped and waited for those left behind and asked them why they had to signal them with a bright light. The others said they had not signalled at all. Continuing on their way together and closer to the Bucura saddle, they all observed to the north-west, a very fast moving light. Believing that a tourist was lost, they began to shout and to wave their flashlights. The unknown light, whose initial trajectory was in a straight line, now began to move in a zigzagging fashion and its speed increased. It was clear that this was not some lost tourist. The girls in the group were scared and tried to flee. The light was of a red colour and had come closer by several tens of meters. Domokos shouted at it: "Friends, come here!" Then the light was stationary for a short while and then turned afterwards towards the "*Valea Rea*" (translated: "The Bad Valley"), where it had come from.

Resuming their ascent, the group members observed, toward Valea Rea, a bright white light; and then another, this one being pale blue. After several minutes, they reached the Bucura saddle (2206 m. altitude), one of the places with the best viewpoint in the area. There they saw a multitude of lights: green, blue, turquoise (this was the dominant colour), reddish-yellow and pink. The lights, located in the upper right side of the valley, first took the form of an ovoid, which then turned into a much defined cylinder.

Then a parallelepiped form having a solid body of which each face is a parallelogram followed, all sides lit, then a triangle and a huge heart-shaped object. In the final stage of observation, the seven hikers had the impression that they were in an airplane, flying at night, at low altitude above an enchanting city, with illuminated boulevards, streets and intersections.

George Resiga remembered that in the backpack with food he had a powerful set of binoculars. He took them out and they all looked through them in turn. Each light had the shape of a disc, with a phosphorescent porthole.

The mountain rescuers had a radio and tried to contact their colleagues at the rescuer's base near Bucura Lake immediately after they noticed the red light. Unfortunately, at that moment, because of the terrain they could not establish contact with the base. Reaching the saddle, they signalled with their flashlights to those at the base and shouted, urging them to put into operation their own radio station. But when they finally managed to call them to see this miracle, the myriad of lights changed once again their configuration, turning into a kind of airport runway viewed from one side. Then it regained the initial ovoid form, which began to climb, sharply intensifying its brightness and disappearing at a high altitude. Up until this moment the weather had been good; everything was clearly visible, allowing them to observe the phenomenon in ideal conditions. But, immediately after, the area was shrouded in a heavy fog. It was not the rising mists from the neighbouring valleys because it was perfectly calm and without any breeze.

Those at the rescue base received the stories from the seven witnesses with disbelief, suspecting a hoax or a hallucination. But their emotion was real and the details provided all corresponded with each other. On the following morning the radio news announced that a UFO was seen above the Danube, at the Iron Gates area. This was the moment when they decided to send a brief description of the story to a local newspaper.

The incident of 4th of August 1991 is not the only such report from the Retezat Mountains. A friend of Domokos saw at a distance of about two kilometres in a straight line, an orange light that travelled along the mountain ridge of Stânisoara from the hut of Pietrele to the saddle of Retezat; Mr Resiga talked with a hiker from Bucharest who, located on the plateau in front of the Pietrele hut, saw a very bright light moving in zigzag motion. Sound familiar?

Ion Hobana wondered if the geometric metamorphoses of the object had a special significance, or even whether there was a message of some sort. According to him, the loss of orientation of the airliner could be caused by such a UFO encounter. "It is hard to believe that the crew began the descent, thinking they were above the airport of Timişoara, when in fact they were over a forest. Where were the lights of the airport? But maybe they could see a very bright and complex unidentified aerial phenomenon, which may have been mistaken for the city lights and the airport".

Ion Hobana noted that there are other similar stories. For instance, the crew of a cargo plane C-54 flying on February 10, 1951, at 00:55, from Keflavik, Iceland, to the air station Argentia, Newfoundland, observed at an altitude of 3,000 meters, a glimmer of light and then the lights of a small town. It was impossible, as they were above the ocean, 250 miles offshore. In 1958, the crew of an American cargo aircraft, a Super-Constellation, flying at an altitude of 6,000 meters over the Atlantic Ocean, heading towards Gander, Newfoundland, saw before them, at 25 miles, a group of bright spots, like the lights of a city.

I can add, that Goethe recounts, in his autobiographical book "Poetry and Truth" that while travelling through Germany, he saw, at the bottom of an abandoned quarry, lights as of a big city.

The Popa family case

As reported by Călin Turcu, on Friday, August 13, 1993, after dark, Costin Popa, an engineer aged 52 , from Ploieşti, with his wife, Mariana, an economist, aged 45 and their daughter, Diana, aged 22, a technical university student in Bucharest, were travelling by car to the village of Telega (25 km northwest of Ploieşti), at the invitation of some friends. They crossed a deserted area, with no houses or other lights nearby. At one point, for no apparent reason, the car engine stopped and the headlights went out. Costin Popa got out and opened the car hood. He took a flashlight, but when he switched it on his hand was hit by an "electric shock" so powerful that the flashlight fell to the ground. But after his wife grabbed it with her handkerchief, the flashlight worked normally.

Looking at the engine everything seemed to be in perfect working order. All of a sudden and without hearing any noise, they were hit, "as by an invisible fist", by something that his wife likened to "a wall of air". Then they saw what a very frightening image. At the right side of the road, in front of some bushes, at about 25 to 30 meters away was a "milky fog-like screen that seemed to be pulsating with a yellowish-white light". It was a rough rectangular shape, with a length of about 10 meters and a height of 2.5-3 meters and it seemed to float at about half a meter above the grass.

They did not stand around for long to watch this apparition. Costin slammed the hood of the engine and all three took refuge inside the car. But the car would still not start. At this point the "milky screen" pulsed slightly, the white-yellowish brightness increasing and decreasing in intensity, every 2-3 seconds. The witnesses did not hear any noise and did not feel any heat from the object either. They were waiting desperately for another car to come by and help them and they began to discuss whether they would be "abducted by UFOs", as they had recently read something about this subject.

After a period of time that seemed to last forever although in fact it did not exceeded 20 minutes, the 'screen' "began to slowly move to the left, elongating somewhat and tapering off". When it arrived in front of them, across the road, it had become a narrow band of light about 30 meters long and only one meter wide. It remained there, motionless, "for up to two minutes" and then "began to fade". In less than ten seconds, over the road remained only "an egg-shape of light that was three meters long and two wide". For a moment, it became very bright and suddenly ascended into the night and disappeared.

After a second or two, everything came back to normal. Immediately they were able to start the car as if nothing had happened. Without any hesitation they left the place in a hurry. After no more than 10-15 minutes, at 22:35, they reached their destination. Their faces were white as a sheet and they trembled as if it was freezing cold. After being told what happened, their hosts were surprisingly not very astonished by their account. In that area circulated all kinds of unusual stories, with strange lights that hung around at night, on the crests of hills or through the trees in people's gardens, with scorched circles of grass "where the fairies play by night" and with animals acting strange for no particular reason.

Interestingly, as Călin Turcu pointed out, on the same night, August 13/14, 1993, just hours later, at about 70-80 km to the south, above the Bucharest-Otopeni International Airport, were seen at lower altitude, for 30 minutes, four unidentified flying objects, which issued green and red flares and were recorded on radar systems. It is worth also to recall that the event is very much like that of Răstolița, in 1974, at the hut of Doctor Andrei Antalffy, a case presented in a previous chapter.

A secret UFO base in Vidraru Lake?

On the southern side of the Făgăraș Mountains, the highest ones in the Romanian Carpathians, on the river Argeș, there is the dam "Vidraru", 166 meters high, with a road on top of it which is part of "Transfăgărășan" highway. The dam gathers water in a lake with an area of about 9 square kilometres for a hydroelectric power plant. The construction was completed in 1966 and UFO sightings in the area began in 1968. Here I will take a look at some of these cases.

Călin Turcu obtained, in 1996, a testimony of I.A. (name withheld), then aged 49 and a technician in Craiova. He described that during the period of his compulsory military service, in March-April 1968, he was in a group of 80-100 soldiers, returning from a march from the dam to the city of Curtea de Argeș (about 25 km). At 18:00, their attention was drawn to a white, bright light, coming from the left side of the road from the area of the dam at a distance of about 1-1.5 km.

He went on to add: "We noticed a globular (spherical), bright white-lilac fluorescent body with a belt of pale red and pale green lights in the middle, which descended over the road on the crest of the dam, apparently touching the asphalt in the middle of the dam. The band of lights in the middle of the object were rotating, or lighting sequentially, giving the sensation of rotating, or the entire object was twirling in some way. I estimated its size to be about 20 to 30 m in diameter. From the distance at which we were, I did not hear any noise. The total observation time was one minute, at most. Some of the soldiers wanted to return to the dam, to get a better view of the object, but the officers would not allow it so they continued their way. Then the object was no longer visible, being covered by vegetation and the mountainous region". As long as has been observed, it stood "apparently motionless and shone around the dam and road, a cold, white light, like a halo".

Among the cases which journalist Gabriel Tudor had examined, some are located around Lake Vidraru. One such case occurred on August 12, 1978. Sorin Neacşu, a history student at the University of Bucharest, visited the area with his girlfriend. After visiting the ruins of the Poenari stronghold (from XIV century, rebuilt in 1459 by Prince Vlad Ţepeş of Walachia, "The Impaler", who was the model for "Count Dracula"), they decided to spend the night on the mountain, near the dam, which was a short distance away. The evening promised to be very romantic. The two had dinner and then sat on a blanket on the grass in order to admire the wonderful summer night landscape and the reservoir. But, as Neacşu said (then history teacher at a high school in Bucharest): "At around 23:00, from the lake rose suddenly a giant disc with an approximate diameter of 30-40 meters. We were in front of it at a distance not greater than 500 meters. I could see it perfectly and I followed its movement with my eyes wide with terror. But it did not come towards us. After it vertically rose up and gave the impression that it would head in our direction, the disc tilted sharply backwards and shot skyward at an incredible speed. In five seconds it was only one bright spot in the sky, moving away to the north, towards Transylvania. After another few seconds, it totally disappeared from view beyond the mountain tops. The object was shaped like a basin turned upside down and had an undefined colour, in any case a dark one; and in the central dome were several portholes, with green lights. I did not see beings on board, but I'm sure they were there. I must mention that throughout the period of observation I did not hear any noise coming from this giant object. Once it was gone, I noticed that the lake's waters were very rough, quite large waves were smashing into the side of the dams, which I think does not happen often in inland waters. I have visited the area several times since then but we have never again seen such occurrences".

Another incident examined by Gabriel Tudor was that of the young man I.F. (name withheld) from the town of Moneasa. He was performing his military service in a unit of gendarmes guarding the hydroelectric complex at Vidraru. The sighting happened in the autumn of 1996, when he was on guard duty. As he reported: "It was 05:40 in the morning. I'm sure of that because I looked at the clock, knowing that at six there would be a change of guard and I could get some rest. The sky was very clear but the stars were barely visible. A star caught my attention simply because it was brighter than other stars around and it seemed to drop from the sky. At one point, it stopped falling and started to move horizontally, closer to where I was and it kept coming towards me and was very bright. After a few seconds I noticed that actually it was disc-shaped, extremely bright and I thought what will I do if the UFO reaches my position. I can tell you frankly, I had my hair stand on end; I felt such a fear that my hair raised on my head and my scalp was tingling! But the object came to a halt over the lake and fell in it, sinking into the water at about five hundred meters from the guard post where I was. There was an illumination on the water that lasted for about five seconds. I believe that the UFO sank on purpose as it entered the water very slowly rather than at high speed.

I have not officially reported this to anyone. Not to the corporal, nor to any higher officers, not even to my colleagues in the platoon because of the fear that it would certainly arouse and I may not be allowed go on the leave which I was promised either. I am not a UFO enthusiast, nor did I believe before that UFOs exist; but now I have kind of changed my mind".

Another case was published in the newspaper "*Curierul zilei*" from Piteşti (the Argeş County capital). Two of its journalists travelled on the evening of 16 November 1998, to the Lake Vidraru to write an article about the wolves, which apparently threatened the life and property of local residents in the area. At 23:00, when they were approaching the lake, their car stopped apparently without cause. While the driver opened the hood to see what it is, a blast of rain overcame them, seemingly coming out of nowhere. Not long after, seen in the cars headlights, two shepherds from the village of Corbeni appeared along with their flocks of sheep and dogs barking like mad. The two shepherds, after calming down, began to talk about a light, "as big as a house" which was accompanied by the sound of thunder which rose into the sky.

Immediately thereafter, an oncoming car approached. Its occupants, a couple from Focşani claimed to have seen, near the lake, the same luminous object. The woman said that it emitted a green light and its shape resembled two overlapping dishes. Very excited, she also talked about how the object arose from the waters of the lake, pulling with it a huge amount of water. Was this the rain that had fallen on the two journalists from out of the blue?

The journalists also said that after a few minutes, when preparing to climb on the road to the dam, their watches showed that it was still 23:00, an anomaly that, after they left this area, has not been repeated. Reaching the dam, they met a soldier on guard who told them that, indeed, he heard the noise, but had seen nothing out of the ordinary.

A somewhat similar case happened in Oltenia, in the summer of 1993 in the village of Streiesti. The witnesses in question began to run away after the appearance of a "ball of light" with a diameter of 3-4 meters. Once they were at a safe distance away they climbed on a fountain from where they observed, on the dam of the reservoir on the river Olt, three bright objects, white, green and red lights which expanded and decreased at regular intervals. One of the witnesses, teacher Nicolae

Cepăreanu, said later that on another occasion, similar lights, "bright as a neon light, but with different colours" appeared over the lake, as "if coming out of the water." Although there was not a breath of wind on the lake, pretty big waves smashed against the shore in a similar way with the observation from Vidraru Lake.

Meteorological phenomena?

At the beginning of 1991, in Romania, several strange "weather" phenomena and aerial observations took place. According to the journalist Adina Mutăr, who published a report in the newspaper "*Ziarul*", "A UFO – an ovoid jet propulsion device, observed also by the Hungarian authorities – was seen over the Transylvanian cities of Cluj-Napoca, Huedin, Cugir, Tuşnad, Oradea and Arad, on the night of January 18th to 19th 1991. After that, another phenomenon was to confuse the specialists. Apparently, on the night of February 15 to 16, 1991, a giant UFO had evolved in the southeast of the country, in weather conditions impossible for any aircraft to fly with a blizzard and wind speed gusts reaching 20-25 meters per second (80-90 km per hour). In one instance, suddenly, a strong thunder clap was heard. The people who came out to see the spectacle of an unnatural thunderstorm and lightning during the winter saw a cylindrical body with a length of 150-180 meters, 20 meters in diameter and green in colour. From out of the object, were detached, from time to time, several spheres each three meters in diameter. These spheres were approaching the high voltage power lines and were producing the violent thunder or at least the illusion of thunder and lightning. Over 40 cities and villages: Slobozia, Urziceni, Călăraşi, Ţăndărei, Feteşti, etc. remained without electricity for almost an entire night. Defying the weather conditions the green-coloured UFO moved very slowly. It stopped also above Bucharest and then disappeared towards Southern Dobrogea. Institute of Meteorology gave a statement which detailed only the unusual electrical phenomena. But the radar stations in the area had no problem in tracking the object. They knew it was not a conventional aircraft as all of the airports were closed due to the adverse weather conditions.

The RUFOR magazine (1994-96)

The same UFO enthusiasts that published the samizdat magazine RUFOR from 1979-1986, took in 1994 the initiative to print a real magazine, containing UFO related articles, that was to be sold all over Romania. It had 21 monthly issues, the first 8 in a tabloid form and the rest as an A4 magazine, the numbers: 1-13 in 1994, 14-19 in 1995 and 20-21 in 1996. The magazine was produced in the Transylvanian city of Târgu Mureş and the chief editor being Peter Leb (1957-2008). Unfortunately the situation was not favourable for such publications, due to many problems with distributors.

Almost all important Romanian UFO researchers published articles in this new RUFOR magazine. Most of the articles were about cases abroad, including abductions or stories with religious overtones. However, there were also several new, unpublished, Romanian cases. We summarise here below a few of them.

Issue number 9 of the magazine RUFOR, Keresztes Ervin, president of a society of interdisciplinary studies in Sfântu Gheorghe, the capital city of Covasna County, reported the case of "Dr. A" a village physician known by the author for over 10 years, a balanced intellectual, with a library of thousands of books and who used to spend his holidays in the Danube Delta.

On October 22nd, 1992, on the "Sfântu Gheorghe" arm of the Danube, near kilometre 29, Dr. A was fishing along with his brother-in-law H.L., when they were caught unexpectedly in a storm. Amid thunder and lightning and after a powerful clap of thunder – as the author wrote – both of them "woke up in the middle of a luminous sphere, with a diameter of about 5 meters with a well-defined outline. Then they lost all sensory perception and being blinded by the bright light". They stayed there for about three minutes. Dr. A recounted that on his left cheek there was a scar of 3.5-4 cm diameter which disappeared after a few days and with another scar on his neck. This one was 9.5 cm long and lasted a lot longer before it faded away. He also experienced for several weeks afterwards an acute pain of oesophagus.

Back on the Delta, on April 9th to 10th, 1993, at the same location, "in his mind emerged a series of hypnogenetic visions which were at the threshold between sleep and reality". Consciousness being always present, the witness recorded them to memory. "He saw in this visions people with big heads, deformed, which had yellow eyes like that of a cat. They communicated telepathically or through text messages as well as by hieroglyphic texts". Dr. A stated: "According to my subjective opinion, these entities were inside my consciousness".

He tried regression, with self-hypnosis to try and unlock any hidden memories of his encounter but without any success. Ervin Keresztes was inclined to credit Jung's theories that the witnesses gained access, through trauma, to the current archetypes on UFO abductions. A question mark in his opinion, are the scars, which raises the suspicion that it was more than just an access to the collective unconsciousness. The same Dr. A found on the shore of Danube, at km 84, a metallic object, almost completely buried in the mud. It was pyramid-shaped with a height of 11.3 cm, with a volume of 200 cubic centimetres and a weight of 1.38 kg. It reached UFO investigators on July 20, 1993. By spectrographic analysis, Bulletin no.194 / December 07, 1994, the laboratory "Plasmoterm" in Tg.Mureș, determined that the object was 99.9% chromium, 0.02% vanadium, with manganese and silicon traces.

In the same area, the same people have reported also several other abnormal phenomena: the disappearance of objects from the witnesses, a wall of water 1.5 meters high which prevent the boats from passing and much more.

Other interesting UFO sightings published in RUFOR, belong to Attila Kosa-Kiss. Born in 1954, he completed a post-secondary school, becoming hydro-meteorological technician. In 1994 he was responsible for the protection of water quality in the city of Salonta in western Romania (there where he lives to this day). At the same time, it was an amateur astronomer member of the AAVSO (American Association of Variable Star Observers) and of other associations, participating in EQLP (Earth Quake Light Project) and being author of numerous articles published in Germany, France, Austria, Hungary, Czech Republic, Russia etc. The following sightings are summarised from an article published in RUFOR no. 11/1994 by Călin Turcu, based on documentation provided to him by Attila Kosa-Kiss, in Hungarian and translated by Lelia Daniel. Excerpts from the same documents were published also in the Hungarian weekly from Romania "*Erdélyi Napló*" no. 3/1994.

Kosa-Kiss reported that on June 16, 1973, at 22:15, he saw in the sky above his home in Salonta, two bright points of light side by side and both at the same height (estimated at 3 kilometres) and spaced apart about the diameter of Moon. Both had the magnitude of Sirius (the brightest star in the sky). After about a minute, the two lights increased their brightness looking like the planet Venus. After this the two lights overturned, fell to the right, keeping the same distance between the two lights and disappeared behind the house.

Another encounter took place on February 28, 1978. On the evening in question the witness observed from the city's water station, under a cloudy sky and over the snow-covered fields, two lights, at a distance of about one kilometre and at the height of the electricity poles. Periodically, the two lights became very bright and then they would fade. After around ten minutes, Kosa-Kiss decided to try and signal to them. He lit and extinguished quickly the outside light of the station, then went, with the flashlight above his head, toward the mysterious light source. He had made only a few steps when he saw that the two lights had intensified, took the colour of butter, then started rising smoothly, directly towards the witness. Kosa-Kiss wrote: "As the lights approached it was clear that it was a huge mechanism (or object) flying over me but still impossible for me to define its form. The lights, which could illuminate a stadium, seemed to come from some enormous round tubes and the air seemed to be dispersed horizontally before them.

When it arrived directly above me, at about 400 meters height, I could not see anything except the two reflectors. Probably something tied them, as very close to these tubes, I saw a dark red 'lamp'. It flew over me with a barely perceptible noise, like a fine and discreet humming. In about 3 minutes it had crossed the sky and disappeared in a south-westerly direction". The whole observation lasted between 19:05 and 19:20.

On August 27, 1992 at 22:21 Kosa-Kiss saw a slightly elongated, dull yellow, object in the constellation Pegasus, at a height estimated at around 3000 meters. It seemed to be coming toward him and a fine noise was heard, then it turned horizontally to the left, reaching in five seconds the constellation of Perseus. The humming sound grew louder and the light intensity increased. The witness looked at the object with a Zeiss telescope, which magnifies 52 times. The object, which occupied half the visual field, took the form of a capsule. "Then it became a sphere, surrounded by a kind of halo. A few moments later it had reached its peak of brightness shining as brightly as the Moon in the first quarter. Afterwards, it seemed to shrink and I distinguished on its surface 8-10 lamps or small windows". From this moment the witness watched the object with the naked eye. The brightness and the noise decreased and then the object turned 140 degrees, descending obliquely to the right.

Several hundred people in Salonta had also reported hearing a strong unreal noise and many had left their homes to see what was happening. The astronomer thought it could not be any earthly object much less a phenomenon of natural origin.

He has collected the interesting testimony of a taxi driver, also from Salonta. At 22:28, his attention was drawn to the noise. He saw then a dark red light moving in the sky. He stopped the car to take a look through the windshield to try and see what was happening. Suddenly the object made a turn of 90 degrees and headed straight towards them. The driver panicked and shouted to his passenger "It's a machine falling towards us". Instinctively he started the car and switched on the headlights. At this point the object froze and came to a stand still at about 40 meters above the ground. "Its entire surface was illuminated and its red colour was 'boiling' in different shades. The object was perfectly spherical with a diameter of 3-4 meters and it rotated around its vertical axis in counter-clockwise direction. It hovered for about two seconds (when the car had travelled just 10 meters), then it began to fade and after another ten seconds the light and the sound just went off". The driver said he spoke also with a field guard nearby who said that at 22:21, he saw "a strange flying object shaped like a hat".

The amateur astronomer also made two other interesting observations of unexplained lights at September 19th, 1992 and 29th to 30th May 1993. Călin Turcu wondered why such observations are not made by professional astronomers too. Or are they?

UFOs in Roşiorii de Vede

Ion Nuţu, former two terms mayor of the city of Roşiorii de Vede (Teleorman county), is an ASFAN member. He has observed UFOs on several occasions. One example is in 1968 he pursued a dirty-creamy "balloon" that was stationary for hours (despite the wind) above the city.

One evening in November 1996 (when he was deputy mayor) he travelled by car, at 20:30 along with two other people to conduct a survey on Urlui Lake (40 hectares) which belonged to the City. On this lake some illegal fishing activities had been reported.

Less than one minute after their departure when they were still in the street, the darkness of the night was replaced by a green light. Nuţu, sat to the right of the driver, saw through the car window, at an angle of about 45 degrees and at a height estimated later at 70-100 meters, a "necklace" or a deformed pentagon, of 9-10 red, orange and green lights, each with a diameter of 20-25 cm. Although the interspersed green lights were not dominant, everything around was coloured green!

They stopped the car and got out. They could not see an object itself but the diameter of the apparition could have been of 10-12 meters. After 4 or 5 seconds the lights suddenly went out but left behind a dirty yellow spot that moved slightly to the south with no noise. A third person, who could barely stand up, because his knees were shaking, said that when the object had moved he could hear a slight hum, like a breeze, something that Nuţu did not himself hear. The driver wanted to drive south to follow the object but the deputy stopped him because the phenomenon had disappeared and they had to reach Lake Urlui. The whole remainder of the evening was overshadowed by the excitement created by this encounter.

Returning home and before parting, Nuţu asked the other two to not speak with colleagues from the City Hall about the sighting as to him the case was "quite sensitive". However, the two others, both deeply moved by the events were unable to resist telling their colleagues about this remarkable sighting of theirs.

In the same area, there were also other UFO encounters. A UFO was seen on the night of September 3rd -4th , 2004 and in one of the last days of July 2010, there was a terrible noise that made the earth tremble under the feet of witnesses, while at high altitude, crossed a "strange plane, which looked more like a helicopter, enveloped in a sort of fog". Other reports have continued to come from there until today.

Like the rest of Romania its mountains, lakes and dams have not escaped the attention of the UFO phenomenon. Civilians, military men and amateur astronomers have all gone of the record with their accounts of some very bizarre but nonetheless fascinating UFO encounters. Some such reports do have similarities with those reported in the West, however many of them seem to have a unique twist to them that only happens in Romania. Why that is remains a matter for debate much like the UFO phenomenon itself.

Fig.9 "Admiral Vasile Urseanu" Astronomical Observatory of the Municipality of Bucharest, where are the ASFAN headquarters.

ASFAN

An Association for Unidentified Aerospace Phenomena

ION Hobana returned to UFO research in 1993 and after a long absence he published several books in this field. In 1998, three researchers: Ion Hobana, astronomer Harald Alexandrescu and myself, took the initiative of creating the Association for the Study of Unidentified Aerospace Phenomena (ASFAN), as an organisation of well established specialists in various disciplines relevant for active involvement in UFO research. It was and has remained the only non-governmental and non-profit organisation in Romania, with legal personality, dedicated exclusively to the ufology. The legal permission for the establishment of ASFAN was obtained at the Court of the City of Bucharest on September 28, 1998, taking into consideration the approval of the Ministry of Research and Technology and that of the General Mayor of Bucharest. The offices of ASFAN were established in the building of the "Admiral Vasile Urseanu" Astronomical Observatory of the Municipality of Bucharest, Boulevard Lascăr Catargiu 21, Bucharest, property of the City [Fig. 9].

For the 21 founding members (demanded by the law at that point in time), highly skilled individuals were selected: mathematicians, astronomers, engineers, specialists in radar, aeronautics, meteorology, photo-imaging, informatics, medicine, as well as interdisciplinary oriented personalities. The main aim was to have a multidisciplinary and pluralistic approach to the phenomenon. The initial elected board was: chairman Ion Hobana (1931-2011), Vice-chairman Dan D. Farcaş Ph.D., mathematician and IT specialist, executive director Harald Alexandrescu Ph.D., mathematician and astronomer (1944-2005), Treasurer Alexandru Musat physicist, speaker Alecu Marciuc, radio programs producer. Now the chairman is Dan D. Farcaş and the executive director is George Cohal.

Two of the proposals from Ion Hobana defined the character of the association: the use of the more appropriate term "unidentified aerospace phenomena" instead of "unidentified flying objects" and the interdisciplinary scientific methodology (as much as possible) in the research of this phenomenon.

Ion Hobana kept in touch with many ufologists worldwide, he participated in international conferences and invited to Romania several ufologists from abroad. Other ASFAN members maintained these contacts, making new ones too, with several UFO research organisations and specialists abroad. Some examples of this are the activity of Dan D. Farcaş with the editorial board of the "European Journal of UFO and Abduction Studies" (2000-2003), or the collaboration, in 2012, for the National Geographic Channel documentary "UFOs in Europe: The Untold Stories". ASFAN is included also in the "*EuroUfo*" network, or in "*Académie d'Ufologie*", being represented by Dan D. Farcaş.

For three years (2000-2003) ASFAN organised public conferences on a monthly basis in central halls in Bucharest. A more complex, one day UFO Conference was organised in May 2014. ASFAN members were invited to appear on all of the main Romanian TV channels and radio stations for debates on current UFO events and related issues. Some ASFAN members have or had permanent UFO columns in Romanian popular science magazines. Unfortunately, the funding and the time available for the members was always very limited, so the achievements of ASFAN were lower than had been hoped and in time most of members became inactive with no one to take their place.

ASFAN received and examined written reports, photos, video footage and other data (far from all cases). The most interesting ones are available (in Romanian) on the web site: HYPERLINK "*http://www.asfanufo.ro/index.php/raportari-recente*" *http://www.asfanufo.ro/index.php/raportari-recente*. The site also has a smaller English page. For the most interesting cases, ASFAN members made field investigation. We will look at some of the most interesting in the following pages.

The light carousel of Năneşti

On the evening of Saturday, June 30th, 2001 in the village of Năneşti, Vrancea County, about 40 km. from the county capital Focşani, an unidentified aerial phenomenon of a most unusual type appeared overhead. The case was referred to the press first by witnesses from Bucharest who had been driving on the road that connects the city of Galaţi with Tecuci, near the village Lieşti, about 8 km. away, from where they saw strange lights above the village of Năneşti.

The journalists from the county newspaper "*Monitorul de Vrancea*" made the first investigation the next day along with a local TV company. As a result the news of the sighting appeared in the newspaper "*Naţional*" from Bucharest. In quick time a team from ASFAN, consisting of Gheorghe Cohal and Alexandru Muşat were on site. They estimated that the total number of witnesses was at least 50, but they had time to talk only to a few of them: Tănăsache Agafiţei, a retired teacher of

Romanian language in the local school, his wife, Elena Agafiței, Costel Stoian, his wife, Elena Stoian, Dumitru Jujău and Ștefan Stoian father of Costel Stoian.

That Saturday night, most of the villagers were watching a popular TV shows, broadcast on public television channel TVR1. The sky was covered with clouds and during the day it had rained. At around 22:30, the electricity supply was interrupted and the whole village was draped in darkness.

According to villagers such blackouts were very rare and of a very short duration. After several minutes of waiting the villagers began to grow impatient; they went outside to see whether or not the neighbouring villages had also no electricity. But much to their annoyance all appeared normal and only Nănești had no "lights". The situation was hard to explain, since the village is supplied with power via two different lines of high voltage and through three transformers: two on the line from Vulturu and one on the line from Tătăranu.

On leaving their houses a number of witnesses noticed, in the sky above the village, a red, round, slightly diffuse spot, moving slowly. When the "ball" stopped, it began to spin, turning into a rotating segmented ring of pale yellow light. As it rotated, the ring became larger and larger in diameter, coming closer to the ground, until having a radius of 100-200 meters (some would say even more). After a short period of time the ring began to climb again, maintaining its rotation, shrinking until it reached the point where it started, turning again into a red spot. This red dot moved around the sky then stopped and started to rotate again, turning into the segmented ring, descending and growing, coming close to the ground again and then climbed back into the sky. This cycle of events was observed by a number of witnesses for about 8-9 times over a 45 minute period, while others said that nearly it performed this manoeuvre at least 20 times. Some witnesses stated that during rotation, the object had a swinging motion, like a boat rocked by waves. Mrs Agafiței saw the red circular spot disappearing over the horizon and then returning and putting on this mesmerising show.

From other parts of the village reports came in describing the object as a dark red cloud lit from inside, which spread around in a lot of squares of light, like windows, which reached to the ground and then they ascended congregating at a certain point where they then disappeared from view. When the squares of light reached the ground, the witnesses had the feeling that the entire village was enveloped in a soft, misty, milky light.

Most of the witnesses, after observing the lights for 30-45 minutes, seemed to get bored and retired in their homes. The phenomenon had stayed visible until around midnight and then stopped abruptly, as witnessed by Ștefan Stoian, who was a guard on the night shift at a vegetable oil factory near the village. There were no feelings of fear or apprehension and one of the witnesses even tried to signal with the flashlight toward the sky. No photos or videos were taken.

That evening in the "House of Culture", took place the wedding of the son of a local village householder, Ştefan Necula. After the power failure, at 22:30, all expected the blackout to last only a minute or two. At around midnight, when the wedding guests were preparing to go home, the father of the bride decided to intervene and took a roast chicken and some wine to the electricity distribution post at Vulturu. But there, they were informed that, from their point of view, everything was okay and the fault was probably in the county capital Focşani.

The power supply returned to normal at around 02:00 and without any further problems. As a result of this, the wedding celebrations were resumed and the wedding guests were no longer interested in the cause of the blackout.

When contacted later, the "*Renel*" electrical company showed that in their official records for that night there were no malfunctions or interferences recorded in the Nănești area. Some locals said, however, that those at "*Renel*" found in one of transformers a charred stork (bird), blaming it for the blackout. But, as we know, storks do not fly at night and more importantly the question remains as to why all three transformers failed and why they all came back on together after a shut down of 3:30 hours? The stork explanation would not fit regardless.

For a number of reasons the ASFAN investigation of this incident was not considered as 'case closed' and the file on the case remained open. Several researchers including Elena Agafiţei said that on other occasions strange light phenomena had been observed in other villages in Vrancea County too. For example, in 2002, another bizarre phenomenon appeared at the Coza village (Tulnici commune, 85 kilometres northwest of Nănești) when a spherical object lit up the village for seven consecutive nights. There were dozens of eyewitnesses willing to recount in great detail their story.

The Nănești case was reopened in 2012, when the UK TV production company "*Pioneer Productions*" decided to include this event in a series called "UFO Europe – Untold Stories" (in the Romanian version – "*Extratereştrii în Europa*"), which has already been broadcast in 2012 and 2013 on the National Geographic TV channel. To this end, a "Pioneer Productions" team and four researchers from ASFAN (George Cohal, Cătălin Bănică, Vlad Cohal and myself), took a trip to Nănești on 5 July 2012.

After a meeting with the Mayor, the team interviewed a number of witnesses. Tănăsache Agafiţei, a retired teacher, permitted us only a short interview stating that he felt his respectability in the village might be threatened. He remembered that the phenomenon was visible for a very long time from around 22:30 until well after 01:00. The phenomenon was not accompanied by any noise and the "patch" or "ball" was estimated to be at an altitude of approximately 500-700 meters and generated a bright circle of light which was rotating at a very high speed. When the light shone on the astonished witness he decided to awake his wife to view the phenomenon together. Being scared for the moment, she caught him by the arm fearing that the light could abduct her husband. The teacher also mentioned that just recently he had seen on the clouds a projection from a disco spotlight, but in no way did it resemble the phenomenon he observed on June 30th, 2001.

Steluţa Necula, the bride in the interrupted wedding party was interviewed along with her mother. They said that at first they thought that the blackout was a practical joke or a trick arranged by someone, but when the darkness continued and then they saw the light phenomenon, they realised that it was something bizarre and it was no joke.

Costel and Florenţa Ştefan regretted that they have not photographed or filmed the phenomenon, because they remembered too late that they had access to photographic equipment. Both agreed that the luminous manifestation lasted from 22:30 until around 24-24:15. They gave a similar description to the other witnesses: The light circle, with a diameter of 200-300 meters, was very bright, not at a very high altitude and when descending it didn't touch the ground. The light seemed segmented in curved rectangles. A complete cycle of opening and tightening the circle of light was estimated by them to take about 5-10 minutes.

Both witnesses remember that three months before this interview, they observed, an unexplainable light in the sky one evening that moved over the village. It passed over to another village and then returned in perfect silence.

Strange lights in Pupezeni

An ASFAN team composed of Gheorghe Cohal and Ion Nuţu, went on November 29th-30th, 2003 to investigate and possibly try to record luminous phenomena observed by locals around the village of Pupezeni. The trip was organised after repeated invitations from Ionel Constantinescu a producer at the Romanian public television. The TV producer was from the area in question and he accompanied the team during their investigations. The small village of Pupezeni (Bălăşesti commune, in the north of Galaţi County) is located 15 km south of the city of Bârlad and consists of about 50 houses and 350 inhabitants. It is isolated between several hills which are partially covered by forests.

The team interviewed and filmed 13 local residents. There were a lot of witnesses to the events in question, but only a small number could be interviewed simply because of the lack of time.

One of those interviewed was Dan Năstăsache who reported that on the night of November 22, 2003, he was attending a wake for his father who had recently died. Going out into the yard to smoke a cigarette he saw a red shooting star about the size of a "manhole" that fell from the sky above the forest. He believed that this was a normal occurrence as he heard of the old tale that a falling star signals the death of someone. But five minutes later he saw the red light ascending on the same path that it had fallen and disappearing into the night sky. He also noted that some red lights were ejected from this "falling star".

Roman Hotnog was interviewed while guarding the cattle grazing in the village pastures. He reported that he observed, several times, unusual light phenomena above the forest of Aciua and that this had continued to happen for several years. Headlight-size lights of a "reddish-blue" colour appear for about 1-1.5 minutes and then disappear to the left or to the right. The observations were made between 22:00-24:00 and some lights were the size of a "basket bottom". Other lights were shaped like an "arrow" pointing downwards.

Aurel Popa and his wife described that one day in October 2003, at around midnight, they saw some red lights above the forest of Aciua. On a previous occasion they noticed a bright light looking "as if the sky opened" just above the nearby "Adam" monastery. The light was yellowish in colour and looked like an arrow pointing downwards. Mr & Mrs Popa believe that all of these sightings are "divine signs".

Mircea Manole said he noticed, almost every week, strange lights over the forest of Aciua, as well as in the opposite direction. On one of the nights he observed between 23:00-24:00, opposite the forest of Aciua, a bright, milky yellow light moving southward, zigzagging to the right and then to the left. He also saw a very big and fast moving light which was flashing and he could hear a humming sound. However he believed that it could not be an aircraft of any kind.

The team also inspected the area with metal detectors and Geiger counters etc, concentrating on the forest of Aciua. An interesting connection is that Pupezeni is at 8-10 km north of the village Cerțești, where, in 1996, a Close Encounter of the third kind took place (which we will detail in a later chapter). It was verified that in this sparsely populated area there are no military bases and no military manoeuvres were carried out that could account for the sightings. It is typical that most of the villagers considered the lights as something normal and many simply ignored them, while others said they are "divine signs".

In the autumn of 2003, there seems to have been a "wave" of observations in Pupezeni. But according to Ionel Constantinescu, who visited the village several times informed us that phenomena like the ones reported above were continually observed for several years but unfortunately they were not investigated.

UFOs at Bucharest Otopeni International Airport

The International Airport "*Henri Coandă*" from Otopeni, north of Bucharest, is occasionally visited by UFOs. Such a visit took place on the night of 13th /14th August 1993. The newspaper "*Evenimentul Zilei*" no.349 of Monday, August 16th, 1993, announced on its front page: "Friday night at Otopeni Airport the radar detected four unidentified flying objects. They were moving at a low altitude" and for 30 minutes the UFOs gave off red and green light signals". The article added: "Friday night at 01:56, in the airspace over the Otopeni Airport four unidentified flying objects were reported. Two UFOs were oriented in the South-East, South-West and the other two to North-East, North-West".

According to a statement, recorded on tape, one of the operators working in the airport control tower described that the objects were first seen on the radar screens and looked like a "spot". At that time there were no commercial flights or military flying exercises scheduled. Before long the objects were observed through binoculars. A number of "parabolic movements were made by the four UFOs". The objects, grouped in this pattern, began to emit green and red light signals. The distance between the four objects and observers was estimated at 8-10 km.

We should remember also that on the same night, engineer Costin Popa, along with his wife and daughter, met up near Telega (65 km north-west of the airport) and observed a "wall of light" and four luminous spheres. This event has been covered in a previous chapter.

The Deputy Commander of the airport refused to comment on the event, stating that it was a military exercise and therefore a secret. Some members of the security forces at the airport indicated that service personnel at the control tower had reported the UFO sighting to them.

Călin Turcu observed that in the late 1980s, rumours of a similar incident circulated and was linked to Otopeni (or perhaps Băneasa?) Airport. It was alleged that troops had fired at an elongated, cigar shaped object and even that it landed at the end of the airports runway. Turcu went on to add that he could not say for sure if such an incident did indeed take place simply because if the military was involved it would without doubt remain a secret.

Another widely publicised phenomenon was observed in the vicinity of the Otopeni International Airport on the night of 14th to 15th July 1997. Ion Hobana documented the event in a long discussion with Mr.Virgil Vinersariu, shift manager at the airport control tower on the night in question.

The phenomenon was first noticed when the control tower operators directed the landing of Istanbul-Bucharest *Tarom* flight. It had the appearance of a circular

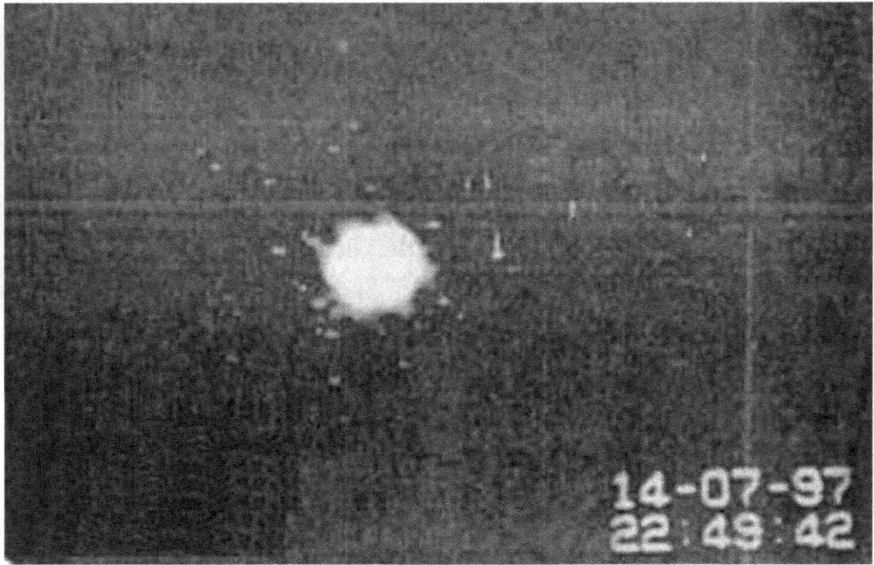

Fig.10a & 10b Light ball filmed two hours by the video cameras, placed on the control tower and on another building of the airport Otopeni in 1997.

light, west of the airport, between Buftea and Corbeanca (at about 5 kilometres). Throughout the observations the radar did not detect any unidentified target. As a result the altitude of the object could not be determined however the UFO was well below the scattered clouds at 2,000-3,000 meters.

Mr. Vinersariu asked, at 22:49, the duty officer to turn the video cameras, placed on the control tower and or another building of the airport, toward the unidentified light. As a result a recording of the sighting was made for approximately two hours [Fig. 10].

The phenomenon was observed from inside the control tower as well as from its terrace. Through binoculars could be seen in the middle of the circular light a horizontal band, coloured white, orange and red, colours that blended together.

When the airports lights were switched on, in order to land a C-130 aircraft, an operation that lasted just 12 minutes, the phenomenon disappeared, reappearing at 5 to 10 kilometres in the opposite direction over the Tunari and Ştefăneşti villages. This time the object seemed to look like two light balls of different sizes which were fixed together. This tandem of lights moved around in a strictly limited area. When the airports lights were switched off, the intensity of the light phenomenon decreased. Surprised by this, Mr. Vinersariu switched the airport lights back on in an attempt to test the reaction of the phenomenon. The unidentified lights intensity increased in apparent reaction to the airport lights. When the number of airport lights were reduced the unidentified light also seemed to dim. This game was repeated several times. The phenomenon disappeared suddenly and unexpectedly with one of the last images being video recorded at 01:10.

Ion Hobana was eager to hear what the witnesses had to say and to see what had been recorded on the videotape. He concluded that given the weather conditions and the duration of the observation, a mass of condensed electrostatic energy (plasma, ball lightning) could not be the explanation; its prolonged appearance, the absence of any noise excluded any conventional explanations such as weather balloon, airplanes, helicopters and astronomical bodies. The apparent reaction from the UFO to the airport lights being switched on and off seemed to imply some kind of intelligent control.

On May 11, 2004, 22.50-23.20, a bright red and green light was seen and recorded by two video-cameras at the "Henri Coandă"Airport. Three minutes of video film was made by the camera of the control tower and more than 30 minutes by the camera on runway 2. The phenomenon remained in much the same position and at a constant height

The newspaper Gardianul came into possession of one of the videos. Sorin

Stoicescu, who in 2004 was director of the Directorate General of Civil Aviation at the Romanian Ministry of Transport, informed the newspaper that the images were genuine and not faked. They were analysed by specialists at the Ministry of Defence and SRI (Romanian Intelligence Service). According to Sorin Stoicescu, the bright object even changed its shape while under observation and being filmed.

Spanish researcher Manuel Borraz wrote: "The video images closely resemble that of a celestial body (star or planet). I have checked if Venus was visible on May 11, 2004 and, yes, the planet Venus was very close to the horizon". Dr Richard Haines, however, comments: "When I viewed that video I was only surprised at the intensity of the point source of light. It appeared to be brighter than most planets I have ever seen on typical CCD video devices. Nevertheless, I did not notice any 'image burn' effects shown by a luminous trail behind the image due to camera motion. So the object or light source was not intense enough to cause this burn effect. I think we should not automatically brand this as a planetary IFO just yet".

In our opinion, the direction of the object was South-East, so it could not be Venus or some other celestial body.

Other cases reported to ASFAN

At this point I think it would be useful to present in short a few other examples of the reports submitted to ASFAN and/or analysed by its team.

On the 05.05.2004, at around 21:00, Luigi Chiţan, a TV cameraman was filming a few shots for a commercial which included the night time panorama of the city of Râmnicu Vâlcea, from the terrace of a restaurant on a hill named Capela (Chapel). When he reviewed his film about a week later the cameraman discovered on the footage a light phenomenon that was not observed with the naked eye during the filming. For 1.41 seconds a bright flying object was filmed moving at high speed in the sky between the cameraman and a nearby hill some 4 km away.

The local TV news showed some of the film in a broadcasted on 13th May 2004 on the private Romanian TV channel "*Antena 1*". An ASFAN team composed of Ion Hobana, Alecu Marciuc, Alexandru Musat and Gheorghe Cohal went to Râmnicu Vâlcea and held discussions at the local TV station "*VL1*" along with those involved (Mr. Cozma, the director of local television, Luigi Chiţan, cameraman and technicians who processed the images). Copies of the film were taken and given to ASFAN.

The images in question were studied, enlarged and played back frame by frame. The object appeared to be a composite body or a group of four symmetrically placed lights [Fig. 11], moving behind the branches and leaves of trees located between the

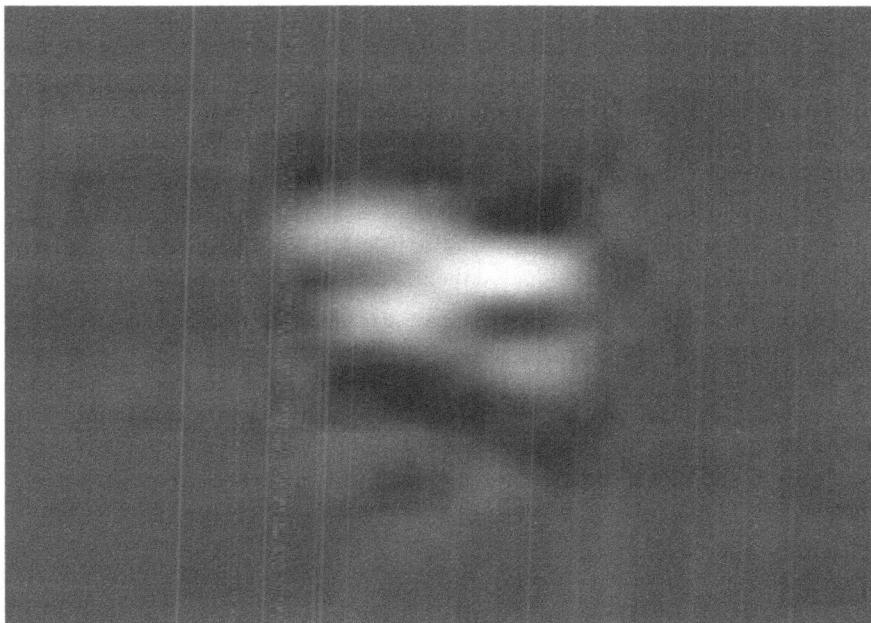

Fig.11 Strange object or formation, filmed for 1.41 seconds at Râmnicu Vâlcea.

camera and the object. The disappearance of the phenomenon occurred instantly, as if it had been extinguished or vanished without altering its trajectory and speed.

In Bucharest, on May 16 and May 21, 2005, two luminous phenomena were observed and reported to ASFAN, accompanied by the eyewitness written testimonies, videos and photos. Reporter Adina Mutăr featured the case in the newspaper "*Ziarul*" on June 20, 2005, with six photos attached.

A witness reported to ASFAN: "On May 16th, 2005, at around 20:30, in the company of several other people, I noticed an intense black object moving at high altitude, seemingly from Victoriei Square toward the downtown area. I could hear no noise and did not notice any lights on the object. The object then flew at a constant height where it remained for about 12-15 minutes. At this point it could be easily seen by dozens of people. Then it moved off towards the Militari neighbourhood, disappearing at high speed".

The UFO was observed also from the Parliament Palace, where it created some confusion. We quote from a witness statement: "On the evening of May 16, 2005, at around 20:30, watching the sky by accident, I noticed in the direction of the Ministry of Defence, stationary above it at a height which I estimate to be 80-100 meters, an oval-round object with an apparent diameter of 1-1.5 meters. I whistled to my colleague who was nearby; he confirmed the observation, telling me that he stared at it for several minutes. I must mention here that the object gave the impression that it stood still, with only a slight shift to the left. I watched it with the others who were present and then, after 20-30 seconds, it disappeared at speed, without any noise towards the Militari neighbourhood".

The two witnesses above were standing near the Parliament House. The observation was made independently of each other. Both intended, for different reasons, to ask us to keep confidential their names and their occupation.

On the evening of May 21st, 2005, when the residents of Bucharest celebrate the Saints Constantine and Helena, a luminous phenomenon was again observed in the Militari neighbourhood, in the Gorjului Market area. Lavinia Boncan, a teacher living nearby, went out on the balcony of her apartment block at around 00:30. It was a night sky without any stars and the cloud ceiling was very low. She saw "a playful bright globe", with the apparent size of the Moon; it was stationary at first but then started to move with incredible speed and then stopped again. Its

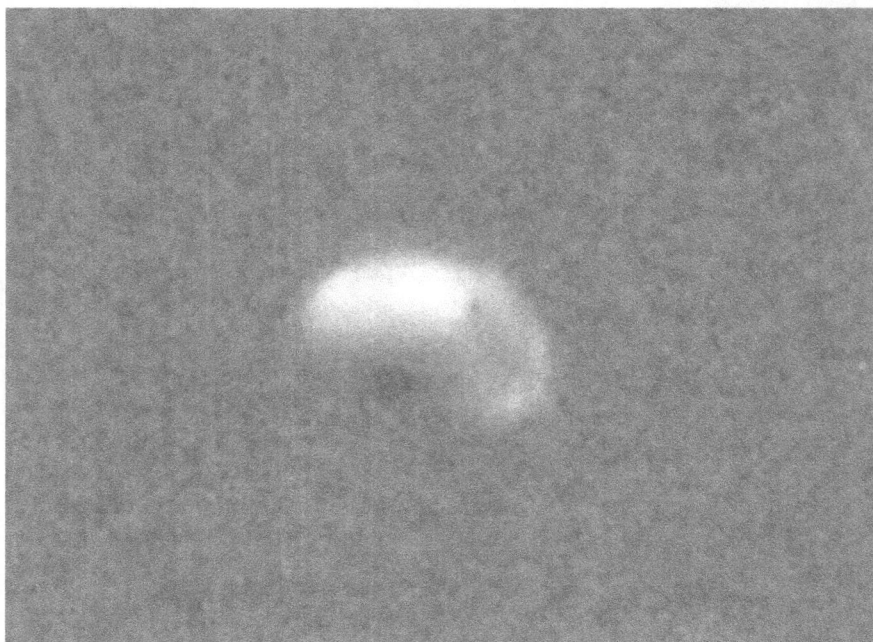

Fig.12a, 12b &12c White, hat-shaped object observed by Mihnea Mustață and other two witnesses, on April 13, 2012, north of the city of Ploiesti (three of many images).

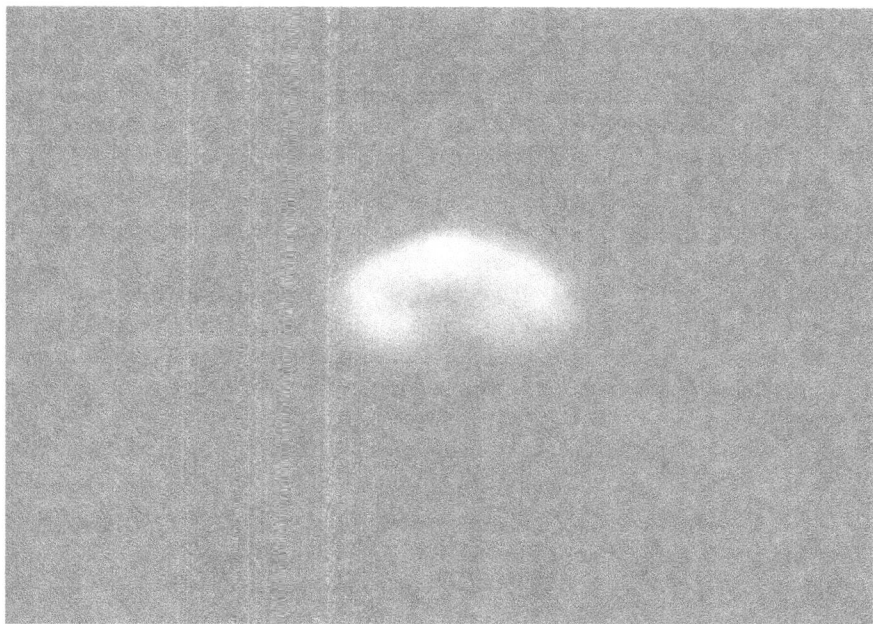

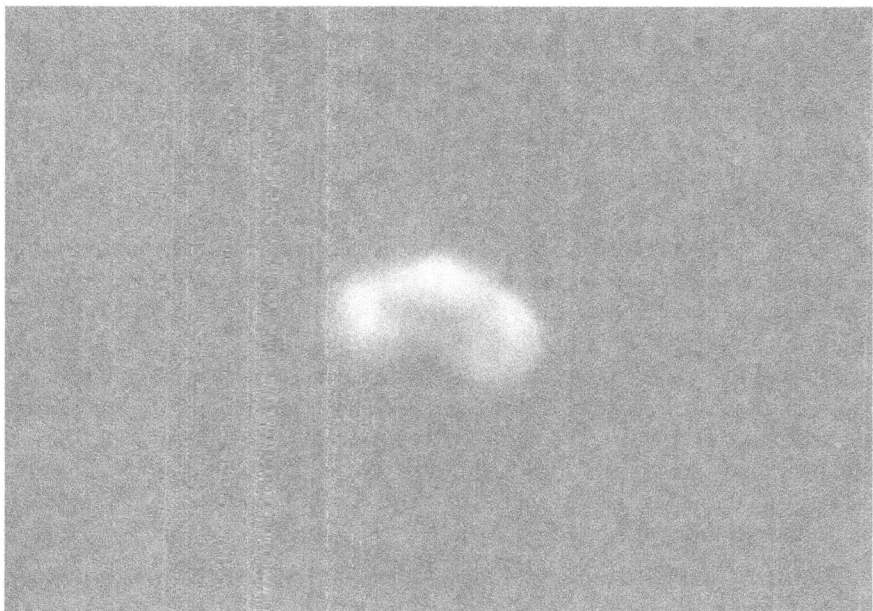

appearance lasted until around 00:50 when the apparition suddenly disappeared. Using a digital camera, the teacher took several photographs of the phenomenon.

The newspaper "*Ziarul*" asked for information from local air space control. The answer from them was that: "As for the nocturnal apparitions of May 16 and 21, 2005, nothing unidentified was seen with radar devices".

On April 13th, 2012, north of the city of Ploiesti, (60 km north of Bucharest), Mihnea Mustață observed along with two other people, a white, hat-shaped, object passing above the field, moving from west to east with constant speed estimated at 80-90 Km/h and toward the village of Pleaşa. The object disappeared from view for a few minutes and then reappeared in a different location in the sky and was moving three times faster than that of a departing airliner". As it departed it was accompanied by "several bright balls of light". Starting at 14:28 the witness took several photos of the objects [Fig. 12 a, b & c]. A few seconds after the main object disappeared, two jet aircraft passed though the same area. The distance between the planes and the object was estimated to be approximately 1500-2000 meters.

On a very serene evening, sometime between May 25th and 31st, 2012, AC and RC (names with held), both engineers working at a wind farm in Dobrogea, were on the top of a 4-5 story building in the village of Mamaia-Sat (between the sea resort Mamaia and the town Năvodari). At one point AC observed that coming from the south to the north, at an incredibly high speed was a formation of lights in a V -formation. He alerted his colleague who also the on-coming object. The lights crossed the sky, over the Black Sea, without any noise in 4-5 seconds, suggesting that the object was travelling at a supersonic speed. The V- shape seemed composed of triangular clusters of 3 or more lights [Fig. 13].

The recollection of the two witnesses was slightly different from each other. AC estimated the object was at 10,000 meters at an angle of 60-70 degrees. The colour was yellow-orange. The lights kept their number without disappearing or multiplying and they seemed to be all on the same horizontal plane. RC, who watched the lights for only 2-3 seconds, confirmed the angle of 60-70 degrees, being forced him to twist his neck to see the phenomenon. But he estimated that its altitude was not more than 200-500 meters and the speed of 300 m/s. RC saw orange-red lights. He said that the lights come on randomly, much like on a Christmas tree. He also observed between the two branches of the V shape a number of fading lights looking like dots that moved around in no apparent order. He said that these balls of light were "3D", some were in front of the others and they had a different intensity.

The case was investigated by Cezar Darac, ASFAN member, who also made the accompanying artistic reconstruction. He appreciated that the lights seen

Fig.13 Sighting at Năvodari, in May 2012 (reconstitution).

inside the "V" by RC could have been an optical effect caused by the speed and by the trajectory overlapping the Milky Way, which then was visible parallel to the horizon. Darac found a third witness, in the city of Tulcea, who witnessed the same phenomenon on the same evening. The investigator said: "He was speechless when he saw the artistic reconstruction".

Another case investigated by Cezar Darac happened on November 8th, 2013, at 16:36. He was called on the phone by a friend. Being at work at the time he could not answer his friend until about 17:10. The friend told him excitedly that when he called, he was in his car and driving along the ring road of Bucharest, accompanied by his sister, and was preparing to exit onto the A2 motorway, towards Fetești. Both of them in the car saw a light brown cylinder-shaped object which hovered over some high voltage power lines and seemed to have a slight rotation around its axis [Fig. 14]. The duration of observation was 10 minutes. The cylinder was not shaking, nor vibrating, it had no lights and no noise was heard. It disappeared suddenly, without moving, while the stunned witnesses looked on in amazement.

Fig.14 Flying cylinder near Bucharest, in November 8, 2013 (reconstitution).

Immediately Darac came out on the terrace of the 12 floored building where he was working, noting, north-westerly (i.e. in the almost opposite direction to the place where the cylinder was seen), a very bright yellow-red light moving slowly up and down along with another 2 to 3 lesser lights. The sun was still visible but it was almost at sunset. He tried to photograph the lights with camera but without success.

Out-of-place artefacts

In 1973, in Romania, in the heart of Transylvania, near the city of Aiud, workers extracting sand from a quarry, not far from the river Mureş, found three objects, "packaged" like in a shell, underneath a 10 meters thick layer of hardened sand.

For a proper study, the three items were sent to the History Museum at the city of Cluj-Napoca. Carefully removing the surrounding petrified sand layers, the specialists found a fragment of a leg bone and a tooth, both of a young mastodon. The third item was an unknown metallic object, about 20 centimetres long, 12.5 centimetres wide and about 7 centimetres thick. It had two cylindrical holes, of different diameters, so that the narrow hole penetrates the object toward the base of the larger hole in a perpendicular way. Moreover, the larger hole had in its lower part a chamber as for assembling in it a rounded axe head [Fig. 15 a, b & c]. On its

Fig.15a, 15b & 15c Age-old aluminium object found in 1973, underneath a 10 meters thick layer of hardened sand, near the city of Aiud.

lower surface and on its sides the object showed traces of repeated use. All of these details, when combined, suggested that it was once part of a bigger device.

Mastodons, related to elephants, lived from 34 million years ago and disappeared 11000 years ago. Some estimates said that the age of the bones found was about one million years.

Repeated metallographic analysis made on the strange object raised further questions. The bulletin issued by ICPMMN Research Centre (in Măgurele, near Bucharest) showed that the metallic piece was actually a complex alloy composed of 12 different elements: aluminium (88%), copper (6.2%), silicon (2.84%), zinc (1.81%), lead (0.41%) tin (0.33%), zirconium (0.2%), cadmium (0.11%) and minor amounts of nickel, cobalt, bismuth and silver.

A very unusual feature was the existence of an anomalous thick layer of aluminium oxide on the entire surface of the object. It is known that this metal oxidises very rarely in depth of the material; usually the first thin oxide surface layer limits the penetration of oxidation phenomena in the metallic body. But the aluminium was discovered in the laboratory in 1825 by Oersted and the industrial production was started only in about 1883. It was virtually impossible to be produced an oxide layer so thick in just a century.

A specialist from Bucharest who reviewed repeatedly the metallographic analysis also wrote: "It's puzzling that the aluminium has an aged structure and the alloyed elements remained also in such a good condition". None of the qualified people who saw the artefact (archaeologists, university professors, engineers) was able to identify the object or to find a resemblance to any human product. The exception was a specialist in aviation engineering who suggested that the object might be a landing foot of a small aircraft.

The information above was taken from the book of Florin Gheorghiță "*Enigme in Galaxie*" (Enigmas in the Galaxy), published in1983. A team, which included ASFAN members George Cohal and Ion Nuțu, as well as Cristian Pompei, of the publication "*Lumea Misterelor*" (The World of Mysteries) saw the object in the archives of the National History Museum of Transylvania in Cluj-Napoca in May 2007. Museum director: Viorica Crișan, along with Zoia Maxim, offered all the necessary clarifications, including copies of newspapers and some reviews on the Internet. Unfortunately, because of many different reasons, among them the fact that the museum was under a long renovation, they could not show any original documents or reports of analysis performed in the '70s. Previously, the aluminium object was the star of an exhibition in the museum, but it was withdrawn by the museum's administration of that time. The same management refused the request to show the object in an "ancient aliens" exhibition in Germany, organised by Erich von Däniken.

It's been said on this occasion that some experts estimated, by evaluating the aluminium oxide layer over a millimetre thick, that the object discovered near Aiud could have a fantastic age of 250,000 years!

At the request of the Cohal-Nuțu-Pompei research team, the "aluminium heel" was brought to Bucharest for new analyses at the National Institute of Research and Development for Physics and Nuclear Engineering, Department Archaeometallurgy, in Măgurele, near Bucharest. The results were the following: aluminium – 80.5%, tin – 6.5%, copper – 6%, silicon – 4%, zinc – 2%, lead – 0.5%, antimony – 0.5%, in addition were highlighted traces of silver, nickel, manganese and iron. A second, non-destructive, analysis of the Aiud object was accomplished in the Laboratory of the Faculty of Physical Metallography. It revealed 97.6% aluminium, 2.4% tin and less than 1% other elements. Both analyses amazed the experts, first, due to unexplainable differences and then because they were convinced that it is a metallurgical impossibility! Aluminium is not alloying with tin!

In September 2007, George Cohal and Cristian Pompei met in Iași, Florin Gheorghiță, who has the first to publish the story of the aluminium object. Among other things, he said that at that time (the 1970's), a rather large sample of the "heel" was taken and sent somewhere in Switzerland for analysis and the results should be in the Cluj-Napoca museum.

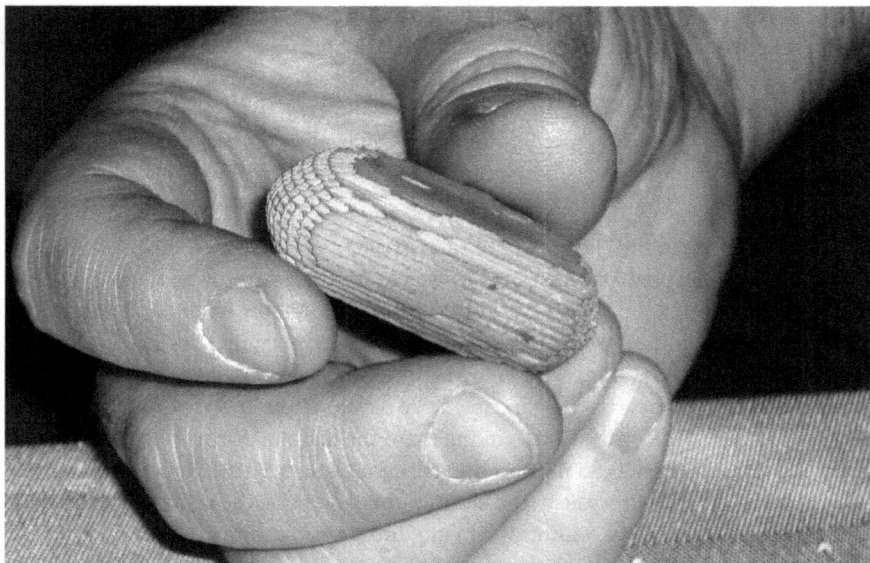

Fig.16a, 16b & 16c A strange "honeycomb" found in 1970s in a Buzău Mountains creek.

Engineers at "Alro" of Slatina, one of the biggest aluminium companies in Romania and in Europe, examining these analysis reports could not identify any similar aluminium alloys produced anywhere in the world.

George Cohal also investigated another strange object. During the 1970s, in a village in the Mountains of Buzău County, a man named A.V. was looking for a few special rocks for a friend's aquarium. Searching in a creek's clear waters he saw something that looked like a rock, yet it wasn't. It resembled a honeycomb, filled with clay and it had the round shape of a pebble. This suggested that it had been on the riverbed for a long time.

After washing this object, A.V. saw it was made out of small, square, piled up pipes, with its sides measuring 1 mm, forming a strange unnatural structure [Fig. 16 a & b]. This object was brought to Bucharest. In 1999, A.V. gave it to Gheorghe Cohal, an ASFAN member (later executive director of the association). At a first glance, the object which Cohal named "the honeycomb" was very fragile and brittle. It also looked like a silicate (the pipes' walls seemed to be made up of fine particles of sand, pressed up together in a pattern).

Under a microscope, in the "honeycomb" structure, can be seen tiny microspheres, of white, black, golden, red, green, blue and yellow colour [Fig. 16 c]. In 1999, together with Harald Alexandrescu PhD, the coordinator of the Astronomic Observatory "Admiral Vasile Urseanu" and executive director of ASFAN, Cohal visited the offices of The Faculty of Geology, Grigore Antipa Museum and the Institute for Rare Metals; but nobody could tell them what the object could be and to what purpose it served before 1970. Some suggested that it could be a catalytic converter, but this device could not exist in 1970 with the first catalytic converter was made in 1973. In addition, the micro-spheres do not resemble those of a catalytic converter.

At this point there is yet another strange angle to this story. In 2004, Romanian astronaut Dumitru Prunariu was the itinerary Ambassador Extraordinary and Plenipotentiary of Romania to the Russian Federation. In this capacity, in August 2004, he had the opportunity to meet in Moscow the famous medium Eugenia "Juna" Yuvashevna Davitashvili (1949-2015). She told the astronaut that a few years previously, one night, she received "energy information about a UFO crash in Peru" and "she sent her 'astral body' to explore the impact site". The next day, when she woke up in her bed at home, she was holding one of the fragments of the crashed alien ship. Juna showed Prunariu this fragment, who took it in hand. "It was the size of an elongated egg, lightweight, seemingly a ceramic honeycomb with a network of parallel channels of perfectly square section, which had eroded around the edges". In March 2009, Prunariu had in his hand also the object discovered in

Fig.17 Ion Hobana, Dumitru Prunariu and George Cohal, after examining in 2009 the "honeycomb".

Buzău Mountains and was at a meeting with Ion Hobana, George Cohal and me [Fig. 17]. He stressed that the object was almost identical to the one shown to him by Juna in Russia in 2004.

When speaking about out-of-place artefacts, we should remember also the famous Romanian pilot and writer Doru Davidovici (we will tell more about him in a chapter). He wrote several times about a statuette, apparently made of bronze, polished and covered with a thin, black-green, glass crust, representing a beautiful woman draped in a kind of knee-length toga and who had six fingers on both hands and six toes on her feet. The statue was shown to him by a fellow aviator, who said the father of a friend of his discovered it in the depths of a mine in the Apuseni Mountains. "He found it while using his pick hammer and when he took the statue out the shiny rock pattern was left in its place forming an outline of the figure". Davidovici believed that the statue which he called "the goddess of orichalcum" (also title of a book written by him) could be of "hundreds of million of years old". Unfortunately the statue disappeared, his friend saying that it had been stolen. Are such object simply out-of-place and by that I mean that they have somehow been manufactured in modern times but then disposed of and rediscovered in a layer of mud or rock that confuses their dating. Are they anomalous objects that hint of an advanced technology from the so-called 'ancient astronauts' who visited our planet millennia ago? As you can see from this chapter ASFAN has been involved in many fascinating and unusual reports but surely the most bizarre and fascinating of these could be the so-called out-of-place objects? We shall see.

MILITARY CASES

A UFO at a shooting range

FOLLOWING a debate concerning UFOs, on May 6th, 2008, on the public TV channel TVR 1, Doru Voloşeniuc, aged 45, a manager at an insurance company in Botoşani, reported to ASFAN an incident he experienced when he was conscripted into a military unit operating within the shooting range at Mălina, in Galaţi County. The incident in question took in early March 1985 at around noon.

He was sent to collect some compasses from a military vehicle, which was also equipped with various types of monitoring devices and which was in an area some 600 meters away. Along the road the witness felt that "something is there". He was amazed to see, hovering at about 1.5 meters above the ground, a flat, silvery, lustreless object It looked almost like a plate, face down, not very convex and having very smooth curves. The object had no portholes or windows. The witness stopped in his tracks and after about three seconds he had the impression that the object was aware of his presence. The object was shrouded, very quickly, by a blue-green mist. This mist appeared not from within the object, but simply the air around it changed and the mist appeared. The witness wondered if this change was some sort of camouflage or it was produced simply by the increasing rotation of the object. Then completely out of the blue a strong ringing sound was heard which totally overwhelmed the witness. It was a painful feeling, a vibrating noise, penetrating right into his bones. The conscript was lifted off the ground by some 30-40 cm and thrown horizontally and slammed into the road face down. Voloşeniuc expected the worst; he looked up in and scanned the area but thankfully the object has vanished.

He ran to report the incident to his commanders. Three commissioned and two non-commissioned officers visited to the site, looking for any evidence but they found nothing. The witness stated that the object was not on the ground and had neither "legs for support" nor any signs of propulsion. The military unit chief of staff asked the doctor to examine the witness to see if he had suffered from any physical or mental illness. The news spread quickly through the unit and there were many discussions about the sighting for several days afterwards. Several other soldiers declared that on the previous night they observed some strange lights and that their radios had malfunctioned.

The case was investigated by Gheorghe Cohal, executive director of ASFAN. He published an article about it in the magazine "*Lumea misterelor*".

A UFO visits an ammunition depot

Another case in which UFOs seemed interested in military objectives was investigated by Gabriel Tudor. The witness named Ioan F., who requested not to be identified, was in the summer of 1995 a conscript at a military unit responsible for guarding a large ammunition depot in the southern Carpathians, at the Teleajen river valley. The military outposts were spread out over a very large area and as the unit was on a mountain side at an angle of about 45 degrees, the higher outposts – including that of our witness – had a very clear view of the whole valley.

The witness went on to add: "on one of the nights – I no can longer remember the exact date – at around 23:00, three lights appeared from northeast. They had a particularly strong pink glow and a speed that I estimated to be four to five times faster than that of an aircraft. From where we stood, their shape looked like several 'balls', but they were very large as they were clearly visible even though they travelled at high altitude. Two of the lights headed toward Măneciu, the third went towards Braşov. My fellow guardsmen were very troubled by this event. Some said it must be a shooting star but most were convinced that what they saw were UFOs. We did not report anything to anybody simply because we were afraid of being accused of talking nonsense and instead of fulfilling our duties we were searching for flying saucers!"

The witness continued: "But this was nothing compared to what happened about two weeks later. On the night of June 21st to 22nd, 1995, at around 01:00, my attention and that of my guard comrades was drawn to a number of lights that were visible away down in the valley. Our outpost was at a very high altitude. A friend said that it was a car, a bus or a truck that travelled along on the road and to begin with we all agreed. But at some point, the lights began to rise and seemed to be heading toward us, coming from below, from a south-westerly direction. I now knew then that it was not a car, but a flying device of some sort. We began to get very nervous as the lights became stronger and stronger and were still approaching our outpost. What followed was like a dream. It seemed that we no longer living in the real world but instead we are characters in a movie with aliens. The illuminated object approached within 300 metres of us. Now we could see that it was almost triangular in shape with rounded edges. None of us could make out the details of exactly how large the object was simply because of the brightness of the lights. The lights really bothered your eyes which didn't give us the chance to view it as good as we would have liked to. This prevented us from making out clearly something that was on the top of the object. The lights were bright white, almost like neon, but with such intensity that I'd never seen before. However, inside the lights we could see a number of less bright red spots or lights. The object passed us like it was on parade, with a smooth motion over our unit, illuminating the ground as if daylight. It flew so slowly that I had the impression that it analysed or scanned us as it went by".

"We all froze and we were not even breathing. If anyone thinks I exaggerate, then he should have been there to realise what we felt during this event. Above us, maybe at just fifty meters, hovered a flat object of unknown origin, bigger then two big trucks placed next to each other and we had the impression that it could have done anything with us. It seemed to me that we were ants compared with it. It crossed the military unit straight through its middle, an area where nothing conventional was allowed to fly. Meanwhile, we all heard a kind of buzzing noise that was very loud. It sounded as if you had your ear against a metal pipe which was being hit with a hammer. The object glided beyond the unit with the same smooth ease and it was lost in the distance, in the north-east, over the mountains. Even then I could not see so clear and I could only make out a dark, elongated, poorly profiled shadow in the night sky. Its lights were still strong and, as passed over [the town of] Întorsura Buzăului, it illuminated the forest beneath it. It was only now that we started to regain our senses. Some of my colleagues began to arm the submachine guns we had. I remember that even a few guys shouted: "Shoot! Shoot!" But then I heard an NCOs voice say: "Stay calm, guys, nobody shoot, we don't know what it is!" And there the matter ended".

The next day, all of the soldiers were rounded up and ordered to keep quiet about what happened and not to speak about this subject with anyone on the grounds that a disclosure like this would adversely affect the prestige of the unit! I want to specify that the order was firm but in no way had any threatening overtones. Later, talking to a warrant officer, an old man, who spent a lifetime in the army, he told us not to worry, because such over flights were reported on at least two more occasions.

Four UFO encounters from a Romanian fighter pilot

Captain Commander Mihai Bărbuțiu, a retired military pilot, had four dramatic encounters with unidentified aerial phenomena. He only recently has decided to disclose these incidents in public.

Born in the city of Arad, western Romania, on February 21ˢᵗ, 1929, he had been

Fig.18 Dan Farcaș, Mihai Bărbuțiu and Sorin Ghilea, at "Arad TV" in March 2015.

a military pilot since 1951 and went on to fly in supersonic jet fighters, and in 1974 he became civilian pilot.

I and my ASFAN colleague Anton Vlad had personal discussions with him in Arad, on March 4th, 2015 and also on a TV show with local journalist Sorin Ghilea and me, at "*TV Arad*" (Ghilea was one of the main investigators and authors for the 1994 crop circles case in Arad, described in one of the next chapters) [Fig. 18].

The first UFO encounter of Mihai Bărbuțiu was in the summer of 1957. One evening, he was appointed leader of flight at the airport of Caracal-Deveselu, used as a backup of the main airport of Craiova, just in case any flight problems arise and an aircraft had to make an emergency landing. At one point, he was ordered to go to the "station": a flight management point in a six wheels truck, parked near the runway. At the station he heard that an elusive unidentified target was seen on radars, appearing and disappearing. To intercept it, from Craiova a MiG-17 fighter took off. This type of fighter was the first of the Romanian Air Force having its own radar. Bărbuțiu could hear his colleague, the pilot Captain Adalbert Bodiș (now retired commander, who lives in Cluj-Napoca), reporting that he had located the target and, after a while, that he could no longer see it.

The station was run by a well-trained sergeant living now in Bucharest. At one point, he and Bărbuțiu saw a flying object coming towards them, from the village

96

of Deveselu, above the railway. Thinking that it could be a foreign military aircraft, possibly with machine guns and grenades, both of them hid under the station, behind the wheels of the truck. But much to their surprise, nothing happened and there wasn't any noise and no gunfire. Looking up, they saw on the ground a circular light with a diameter of about fifty to one hundred meters. It was an unreal light, so powerful you could see every blade of grass. It was impossible to see the shape of the source of light, only the light itself, as if you were looking at a projector. The light lasted about 20 seconds. Afterwards, Bărbuțiu came out from beneath the station and observed that the object departed to the east. He could still not distinguish its shape. Then he announced by radio to his colleague Bodiș that the object passed right now over the airport, heading for the city of Slatina. Bodiș tried to find it, without success. Nobody asked Bărbuțiu to make any report but the witnesses were advised to not discuss the incident...

In 1958 Bărbuțiu was moved to Timișoara, to a fighter-interceptor regiment. Here he went through various roles until became squadron commander. It was in 1966-1967, one night; he was on a flight from Cluj-Napoca to Oradea, with two MiG-19 supersonic fighters.

At one point, Bărbuțiu saw an object in front of him. He saw the aircraft of his colleague, Colonel Gheorghiță, on radar, but not the object. Then Bărbuțiu asked Gheorghiță if he could see the target on his radar. He answered that he could see it visually but not on the radar. Then the command station asked them what they could see. Bărbuțiu said "There's an object here that we don't see on radar, but we can see it with our naked eye. We don't know what it could be". He noted later that he could only see lights (no solid object) with an alternating, red and green flash; with the red light at the top and the green light at the bottom. It could not be mistaken for an airplane; the planes have lights with these colours, but on the wing tips, they are not so strong and have other hues. Here it was a strong and deep dark red and a very strong, unnatural green.

After that incident, Bărbuțiu was called to Bucharest, where he signed an undertaking that he will not disclose anything of what he saw. In those days – he says – things were very serious with military secrets…

The next incident was during the night a month or so later. Two MiG-19 fighters performed, at 12,500 meters, a routine exercise. Bărbuțiu was the "hunter", to intercept his comrade-in-arms Dumitru Răducanu, (then major; deceased in 2015). Finishing the exercise, the two fighters headed, in formation, to Timișoara airport.

A dense mass of clouds, from 6500 meters to 10500, was below them. It was also a full moon. The moon light was so powerful that you could read the instruments of the aircraft without their internal lights, said Bărbuțiu. At one point, he saw before him, with the naked eye, at a great distance, a flying object. The pilot said nothing, because he remembered the unpleasant discussions after the previous sighting. He was only waiting to see if his colleague also reported seeing something. When Răducanu told him: "boss, do you see this target in front of us?" he answered that nothing is there. As Răducanu insisted, the command from the ground asked – "What's there? What do you see?" So, as

Fig.19 Sketch made by Bărbuţiu on giant UFO which he has met.

Bărbuţiu was commanding, he reported that it was an unidentified object. The ground radars saw only the two Romanian military aircraft. The flight command asked the pilots to try to force the unknown object to land. Bărbuţiu said he did not have enough fuel. Then Răducanu received an order to fire a warning volley which they had been trained to do as if they were intercepting an unidentified aircraft.

Bărbuţiu, curious, moved to see the object closer. As he stated now, when he passed under it, he was surprised that he flew for ten or fifteen seconds in the shadow cast by the object. He felt also an "electric pressure", as when you are close to a very strong electric field. The jets navigation devices went haywire. He declared that "It was as huge as a football field. It was grey in colour, circular in shape, had no wings and no portholes [Fig. 19]. We were trained to recognise all existing jet aircrafts of the Russians, Americans and other states, but we had not seen anything to resemble this thing. I said myself that it must be an object from another planet".

Then Bărbuţiu began his descent. He went out of the clouds at about 6500 meters, having the city of Salonta in his right and the city of Arad in front of him. Răducanu said he armed the guns and approached the object, preparing to fire a volley, to force it to follow him. But while he reported this to the ground command the target disappeared.

When Bărbuțiu, by chance, looked back, he saw that the object was now following him. As he remembers, he was scared to death. He automatically reported to the station that the object was next to him. Then he received the order to try to fall behind it and to force it to come into land. As he recounts "I said to myself that if this object had technology so advanced, that if I was now arm the cannon and shoot, then my projectile could explode in the pipe. So, I decided to arm the cannon later perhaps when I will be closer to the airport just in case".

The pilot remarked he could not fall behind the object because it remained always in the same position to his plane. At some point, however, the object passed in front of him and began to climb toward Serbia. In an instant Bărbuțiu started to climb with it. He passed Timișoara, where there were only scraps of clouds and when he reached 10,000 meters and looked down, he was just above Belgrade and the Danube. The object was in front of him but he reported that he was low on fuel and so he turned and came to land.

While he was in pursuit of the object he had taken some photographs. All military jet fighters of those times had machine-gun cameras. When Bărbuțiu landed, he told the foreman in charge of air photographs to make an extra copy for him. The next morning, the foreman said that the counterintelligence officer took the box with the undeveloped film. Nobody knew anything about the fate of those pictures. Once again, the two pilots had to undersign a commitment that they will not talk and will not tell anyone about the incident.

Another case, where there was physical evidence too, occurred in 1970 or 71. Based also in Timișoara. Bărbuțiu at around midnight was on a mission with a MiG-21. His flight was the last of the day. At an altitude of 500 meters he entered into an area of strong and unexplainable turbulence. Suddenly he felt a blow to his aircraft and saw a bright light. His first guess was that he had collided with someone or something and he reported to the command post that he would eject. But when he saw that the plane continued to fly and respond to his commands he instead decided that he would try to land. He had no idea what had happened. No object was seen on radar or with naked eyes. He landed without any problems. Meanwhile, because of the incident, there were on site: the division commander: General Puiu, the chief engineer of the regiment, the division chief engineer, a doctor, an ambulance etc., as happens in such situations.

The pilot descended as usual, on the left hand side of the plane, where he was expected. General Puiu remarked that the additional, large, fuel tank, already empty, which should be under the belly of the plane, was missing. It could be released only using pyrotechnic cartridges. "It's not a big problem", said the General, "you put your finger in the wrong place". Bărbuțiu relates now that he retorted that such a thing would not have been possible. It is the same sealed contact, as for the gun and the rocket. And the seal was not broken; everything was intact.

The General and the chief engineer of division left the scene. Bărbuțiu remained with the regiment engineer, Gigi Grasu (who lives now in Bucharest) and with the flight technician. The latter, controlling the airplane, said: "Boss, come and see something".

The right and the left wing of a MiG each had two rocket launchers. On the right hand side, the rocket launcher from the embedding of the plan was bent about 30 degrees and the other at about 15 degrees. The launcher had no rockets, because they were used only in real flying missions. Everybody was perplexed; the launchers are not some ordinary metal pipes; they are steel girders, a meter and a half long, made of a special alloy of chromium-vanadium, since you need extraordinary strength to resist to the departure of the rocket. It should have been a huge shock to bend them, probably the same shock that produced the release of the extra fuel tank.

When the incident occurred, nothing was seen on radar, or visually and nothing was heard. The Russians, Hungarians and others were asked if they had anything in the air. Over the next days the pilots waited, but nobody offered any explanation as to what had collided with their plane.

In the autumn, the fuel tank was found in a sunflower field, nestled in the ground, without a scratch. So the hypothesis saying that the tank had struck the launch pad was not true. Then the whole thing was forgotten.

Commander Bărbuțiu commented, in 2015, that he understands that such encounters are kept secret because "They don't want the world to know that we are not the only ones here in this Universe, that we are visited by extraterrestrial beings and that the alien ships come to Earth and are controlling our airspace. There are also, certainly, actions from the authorities to not arouse fear and adverse behaviour by the general public. That is the main reason. You see if people would obtain the proof that these visitors swarm among us, they would kill each other; but people are now starting to get used to this idea".

Doru Davidovici and his colleagues

Air Force Lieutenant Colonel Doru Davidovici (1945-1989) was in the 1970's and 1980's, one of the most beloved fiction writers in Romania with over 10 books published. He was active in the Fighter Regiment 86, at the base Borcea, near Fetești, with a break of five years, when he was inspector for fighters at the Air Force Command [Fig. 20]. On April 20, 1989, returning from a training flight, the

Fig. 20 Doru Davidovici, fighter pilot and writer.

plane MiG-21 which he was flying, along with a student of his, crashed for reasons that have remained unknown. Because of his books, profession and how he passed away, he was compared to Antoine de Saint-Exupéry.

His book "*Lumi galactice*" ("*Galactic Worlds*", with the subtitle "My colleagues from the unknown"), published in 1986 and dealing with the UFO phenomenon, was a bestseller in Romania. At the beginning of the book he explained what he had personally observed. As a pilot, he knew that "regularly, the air traffic controllers and the crews of major airlines reported observations of unidentified flying objects, unresponsive to transponders" and which performed unexplained manoeuvres. "Nowhere was there a specified military instruction on what course of action we should take if you encountered a UFO, but this had not bothered me very much. I had a fast plane, there were radar stations with long range detection and I knew that when one of these bizarre devices would be detected, I will be directed towards it and things will work out, fine one way or another. In fact, I was not convinced it would be something I had to deal with; such encounters were sufficiently rare and the official reports were uncertain and confusing".

"Then, however, two of my comrades, older pilots with more experience, had a direct encounter with UFOs; and things, instead of settling, have become more bizarre. One of my comrades said he observed a ball of white light, like a basketball. "I had it on the radar at 15, 12, 10 km, but I could see it also with my eyes. When they were 6-7000 meters I raced at full speed and the size of the sphere had not changed at all. I had a sudden feeling that something was going very wrong. It suddenly became hot in the cabin, the airborne radar was jammed, I had parasites in the headphones and then neither radio nor radar worked anymore. It was getting warmer, I was sweating under the anti-g suit, the oxygen in the mask had the taste hot metal and when the dashboard started going crazy and I became dizzy and thought I was going to black out. Then I relaxed and I came around I gained control and after I turned my aircraft towards the airfield the radio and the radar worked again. The radar operators on the ground told me that they have had an image on the screen that looked like an airplane, standing still and then disappearing at high speed. They said they had never seen a target disappearing at such high speed"".

"Of course – continued Davidovici – I did not like to find out that the sky of our planet is haunted by unidentified flying devices much more advanced than my jet fighter, bizarre devices operating on principles that we don't even suspect. And there was something else. This time it was not a story I read in a newspaper but from a trusted colleague. It was not hard to see myself in the tight cabin with a jammed radar screen and I felt the taste of hot metal in the oxygen mask. I realised that I had no idea what to do if I were to encounter a UFO. At the same time, it was exactly the kind of situation that makes you act, insofar as this can be an action: I started looking and reading everything I could find about UFOs. I found myself in a very vast field, with unsuspected implications, unsuspected deep roots and far beyond simply encounters between our earthly aircrafts with those unidentified flying objects which act freely in the atmosphere, in space, on water and under water".

"Then I saw my UFO, on a December night; only that it was viewed from the ground. I saw an oval body, with the apparent size of a MiG-21 fighter, viewed at 3-4000 meters, flying perfectly straight, parallel to the ridge of a roof. It traversed in 45-50 seconds 50-60 degrees of horizon and disappeared beyond the branches of some locust trees between the buildings. It had a shiny white-violet colour and left a long trail behind, narrowing as it departed the object. There were actually two thin intersecting streaks of light and at the intersection, the light grew stronger, then it became thin, narrow, melted into the dark sky and looked like a white-violet egg and before it disappeared it changed its colour to red-orange. In that winter of 1972, I had nine years of flying and I was familiar enough with silhouettes of civil and military airplanes, zeppelins, rockets, meteorites, ball lightning, Venus, temperature inversions, flocks of geese, or ducks and anything else might be misidentified as a UFO. I knew what a missile or an artificial satellite entering the atmosphere looked like, but what I saw resembled nothing I had even seen before. I knew a lot of things that fly and can fool a professional, taking him by surprise: helicopters at night, or an airplane flying at low altitude with the headlights on, but that oval body there was not a helicopter or an airplane".

"I ran to the routing point; one of the boys there laughed and made a joke about the UFO. So I got radar confirmation of the object I had seen, it was still crossing the screens of the radar station, in a perfectly rectilinear flying, from north to south and moving at about 6000 km/h, at a height more than 70 km. In the period 1960-1968, the Americans experimented – launched at 11,000 m height, from under the wing of a B-52 bomber, the plane-missile X-15, flying at 100 km altitude, with 6,000 km per hour, but that happened on the other side of the globe, four years before and the X-15 had a rather ballistic trajectory. Its size was much closer to what we call a normal plane, while my UFO was huge, judging by the apparent size, it was 300-400 meters on the major axis and 100-150 meters on the small axis; but the violet white outline was not very clearly defined, that egg flew as if enveloped in a cloud of bright light so the actual size could be smaller. The UFO was seen by several pilots and no one could tell what it was and I believe that none of those who had seen it that night will ever forget it. And we thought about our colleagues from the unknown, beings likely to be in command of that light-coloured egg. We tried to think about what might be the reasons why they are visiting us but we found no answers to this question."

The opinion of Davidovici was that, with the UFOs, we face a real phenomenon, apparently controlled by intelligences which have advanced knowledge. The pilot noticed, for instance, the mimicry of visitors, writing: "It's remarkable that they have adopted our system of signalling the presence of an aircraft flying at night, using on discs, spheres, cylinders without wings, the same green, red, white lights

– even if placed absolutely crazy". That reminds me of the report of pilot Bărbuţiu, described above, about the UFOs he encountered.

Davidovici wrote that perhaps there are supercivilisations, watching us passively; an official contact by the aliens with us was refused by them because we are self-defeating. As a conclusion, he speculates about the visitors: "I think they can do whatever they want; but they will not. I think, in fact, they want to leave us in peace as much as possible".

He offered me his book, with these ideas, with a special dedication that says: "On the essential basis that we are thinking alike". After 30 years, I still agree.

In a documentary dedicated to Doru Davidovici, edition of May 3, 2015 of the newspaper "*Evenimentul Zilei*", journalist Mihnea-Petru Pârvu mentioned the statement of the two-star general Ştefan Ion, former Acting Head of Staff of the Romanian Air Force, a man with 2,500 hours of flight and former supersonic flight partner of Doru Davidovici. He said: "I have also seen UFOs! In '79 -'80, I was flying over Brăila and Galaţi. Brăila is the most beautiful city seen from above; it has the shape of an amphitheatre. I was chasing a colleague; he was my target. We both saw a UFO, translucent as a jellyfish with tentacles. My colleague, 40 kilometres away, returned to the base; he cut the mission! I landed too. We have not reported. It was shameful, back then, to talk about such things. And now, I say, how not to believe Doru, when I saw a UFO myself with my own eyes!"

The Alexeni Case, 1984

During the communist era, the Romanian national day was 23rd August. On this day in 1944, Romania, overnight, switched, with all its administration and army, against Hitler's Germany. 40 years later, on the afternoon of August 23, 1984, the aircraft (type MiG, IAR, AN etc.) who participated in the military parade in Bucharest, had returned and landed at the Alexeni Air Force Base (50 km northeast), in Ialomiţa County, not far from the city of Urziceni. At one point, the Otopeni radar station (near Bucharest) asked Alexeni station if they had left any aircraft in the air, because they saw something "swinging over the Alexeni airfield, at an altitude of 4000-4500 meters". Later the Otopeni centre stated that the object appeared from out of nowhere and was seen by 4-5 different radars from different locations, working with different frequencies. The radar signal received was comparable to that of a small plane or a helicopter.

Back then, Emil Străinu, (now retired general, PhD in geophysical war and founding member ASFAN), was working at the radar complex command at Alexeni. He described the following story summarised below.

The sky was clear, the temperature was 28 degrees Centigrade and after 15 minutes, the unknown object was observed visually as well as on radar. When observed through various optical instruments (telescopes, theodolites) the object had ovoid shape and it was estimated to be 2-3 meters long and 1.5 meters wide, seeming to be made of a shiny material, like aluminium. It moved silently and did not have any lights or jet engines. It did not seem to be bothered by the wind of 7-8 m/sec. During its appearance a strong interference was noticed on VHF and on short wave radios. The officer on duty alerted the Alexeni radar station, but they did not notice anything unusual simply because this radar unit had no way to see an intruder in the overhead area, which was to them a "dead zone".

Subsequently the object descended to 2200 meters. Moving westward, it eventually was under Alexeni radar range. At one point it was lost and found again, after five seconds, at an altitude of 22,000 meters. After this, the object (now located about 20 kilometres from Alexeni) climbed and descended, about 7-8 times, between 2000 and 55,000 meters with speeds from zero to 12,000 km/h, making zigzagging movements and turning at sharp angles that no earthly aircraft would have been able to do.

According to General Străinu, the crews of several civilian aircraft flying over that zone at the time also confirmed that they too had seen something that looked like a balloon with a metallic appearance, but declined to make any official report, claiming they did not want to compromise themselves.

As he states, the object was under observation for 40 minutes, being lost at a height of 100 km, when it disappeared into space at a speed of 1000 km/h. The radar operators, all with over 10 years experience in this field, specifically chosen to assist the military parade, confirmed it was not a balloon or any other known object.

When details were reported, verbally, to Otopeni, the answer was that it is better to forget the incident as being the national day; nobody wanted "news bombs". The magnetic tapes that recorded the event had been carefully considered, but after 24 hours they have been erased. Given that this happened on Romania's national day, nobody took the responsibility of sending a report "upwards" and the case was consigned to history.

The Mihai Kogălniceanu Case, 1989

At the Mihai Kogălniceanu military airport, north of Constanța, Romania, 18-20 supersonic fighter aircraft pilots of the Romanian Air Force Regiment 57 [Fig. 21], had witnessed a huge unidentified aerospace phenomenon. The event took place probably in the second half of March 1989 (there are differences reported of

Fig.21 Pilots from Regiment 57, at "Mihai Kogălniceanu" AFB.

the exact date). At ASFAN we obtained the testimony of four of the witnesses and partial statements from some others.

Between 15:00 and 21:00, the unit executed a shooting exercise in two sets: day flight and night flight. "At one point, it was announced that the training flights were halted, although the weather conditions were excellent and the visibility was very good" said one witness.

Around 21:20, the pilots were all ready for go home. Some of them were in the "alarm cell", a room located in a building, planning the next flight, scheduled over two days. Among them were the Commander and Colonel (now retired) Platon Streja [Fig. 22],

Fig.22 Colonel (ret) Platon Streja, at the 2014 UFO Conference.

flight inspector in the Air Force Command in Bucharest, delegate to attend and participate in flights that week. The other pilots were talking on a bench outside this building. The technicians were preparing the aircrafts for parking during the night. The sky was "crystal clear" and the visibility perfect.

Colonel (now ret.) Aurelian Dobre [Fig. 23], when I visited him along with my colleague Anton Vlad, remembered: "I was talking

Fig.23 Colonel (ret) Aurelian Dobre in 2014.

with some fellow pilots in front of the 'cell'. I was facing the take-off terminal. At one point, I saw many lights, appearing above the trees. I immediately entered the 'cell' to alert those who were inside. When I went outside the lights were already on top of us."

Colonel (ret.) Paul Oţelea, commander of the second group, then flying a MiG-23 [Fig. 24], says: "At one point our colleague Aurelian Dobre entered, calling us:

Fig.24 Colonel (ret.) Paul Oţelea, in 1980s.

Fig.25 Colonel (ret.) Dan Aioanei, in 1980s.

Come out quickly! We all went outside and we looked in to the sky and saw a triangular formation of objects at an equal distance from each other all bathed in a white matte silver light, strong but without spreading around. They moved from south to north. I appreciate that they were located at an angle of about 20-25 degrees and at a height of about 7,000 meters". He also heard "a noise that resembled the rustle of a flock of birds in flight over the forest at night. I knew that sound from my childhood, when I was wandering the woods". "From the first moment I saw them, until they disappeared, several tens of seconds passed, then the lights faded out towards the Ukraine". He added that it is a great mystery and there was no "sonic boom" or shock wave.

Colonel (ret.) Dan Aioanei [Fig. 25], who at the time was flying a MiG-29, said: "From Medgidia [south-west], a formation of 7, 8 or 9 flying objects were approaching. They looked like neon tubes, several kilometres each in length and were positioned relative to one another which formed a 'V' formation. From the distance, the tubes looked to have a diameter of 15-20 cm, so in reality they were 2-3 meters in diameter. The speed must have been at least supersonic. They were flying very high, at an altitude of over 3,000 m but may have been well over 10,000 meters. Even for us, acquainted with the sky, it was hard to estimate simply because the reference points, i.e. clouds, were missing. As pilots, we know what shape, texture and dynamics the clouds have, depending on the altitude at which they are. The formation left no trace behind, no light, no vapour trail, nothing. The 'tubes' disappeared over the horizon, somewhere east of Tulcea".

Unlike his colleagues, Colonel Dobre believed it was a single ship, but of an almost impossible size which was equipped with lights. "I think it was the size of a football stadium. Back then there were no such large aircraft and the largest now is only half the size of that ship" said the Colonel.

The pilots involved had a heated debate about the event. While some, including Colonel Oțelea, felt that they saw several UFOs, others argued that it was a single ship, but a very large one. All agreed, however, that, whether it was alien or a secret project, they had never seen anything like it before.

In 1989, the Regiment 57 of Air Force, now disbanded, was rated among the best in Europe, in terms of the professionalism of the pilots and the prestige of the unit. The pilots who witnessed the event were both well qualified and trained to distinguish an airplane, helicopter, balloon, and flock of birds, or satellite from whatever. "I flew at the altitude where we saw everything; satellites and weather balloons, anything. But I can tell you that regardless each others ones opinion, we all felt the same feeling: that of being very small and insignificant", said Paul Oțelea.

This made Aurelian Dobre believe that it was a UFO, but not one of extra-terrestrial origin, for he did not believe in such things. When the object passed overhead he heard that fizzle and had the same feeling: "We thought we were flying down some fucking pipes and others have such superior things", he recalls.

Colonel Streja reported to the Deputy Flight Commander of the Air Force. Initially they were told that no radar had registered anything. They said also that the whole story could be a collective illusion. The next day however, representatives of the higher hierarchical structures and of the Ministry appeared. All the witnesses were asked to provide written reports about what they have seen and heard. Apparently this was because at the same time UFOs were sighted at Cape Midia and by Romanian and Soviet border guards too. Some sources said later that the object(s) had been detected also by military radars, both of the aviation and navy. A report was made, but as nothing could be done as the UFO was gone the report then remained buried in the archives.

There were some other retired servicemen that were also contacted by ASFAN, who although admitted that they witnessed these events, refused to talk about them and asked us not to reveal their identity.

The Buzău Case, 1992

In 1992, during a November night, three military helicopters were recalled from the military exercise when they encountered an unidentified aerial phenomenon, near the city of Buzău. The helicopters had to accomplish a night flight in triangle, from Buzău to Urziceni city and to return after passing over Mizil town. The weather was ideal for flying, with an unusually clear sky. At first, they were flying at an altitude of 100 meters and at a speed of 150 km/h. All seemed to be running smoothly and the pilots of the three helicopters occasionally looked out to view the cars circulating at that time on the European road 85 to Urziceni.

Retired Colonel Marcel Smoleanu [Fig. 26], today deputy chairman of Buzău

Fig.26 Colonel (ret.) Marcel Smoleanu, at the 2014 UFO Conference.

branch of the veteran pilots association ARPIA, led the first helicopter. He reports that: "It was an easy task for training. The helicopters had no weapons. On each helicopter was a pilot, a co-pilot and a technician. We left at around 22.00, expecting to return at around midnight. It was an uneventful flight which allowed us all to relax. We listened quietly to some soft music playing on a radio station".

"At one point I froze with my hand on the stick, when I suddenly saw approaching from the left a bright red sphere. It was huge, with an estimated diameter of nearly 20 meters. There was no change of colour, no flickering, no noise and no trail of smoke. The object began to fly in parallel with the helicopters".

"I tried to explain to myself what it could be and, at one point, I thought that it was possible that this strange object was not manufactured on earth. I also asked my colleagues if they could see the same thing and they have confirmed they could. I was so shocked by what happened to us, that I could not speak", said Smoleanu. "I was mesmerized. Later I thought it must be a UFO, something from another world". The pilot did not look at the helicopters instruments, so he does not know if the object interfered with them or not. However, he said, the engine was not disturbed in any way and worked perfectly.

Frightened by the unusual experience Smoleanu asked the pilots in the other helicopters: "Do you see what I see?" They confirmed they did. Then, although they knew, before leaving, that there was no other flights scheduled in that area, Smoleanu called for an explanation from the military base at Urziceni which also had helicopters, asking: "Do you have something in the air?" He was told that there was nothing in the air, not from their base, nor from Otopeni (near Bucharest).

After tens of seconds in which the pilots did not know how to react, the object made some unusual manoeuvres. "At one point, our unknown object had accelerated sharply and reached an incredible speed. It went suddenly from flying next to us and – making an impossible turn, at an angle of 90 degrees, without reducing speed – It cut across our path. It entered our flight path so I therefore made a turn to the left and I slowed almost to a hover. After this manoeuvre our object disappeared" adds Smoleanu. "As suddenly as it appeared, it was gone". It was there one minute and gone the next.

The flight exercise was stopped immediately. Arriving back at their base, the pilots reported the incident to the commander of the Boboc aviation school, near Buzău. Smoleanu commented: "There was no way they could think I was crazy as there were still another eight witnesses beside myself. All of us had passed the medical examination, including psychological tests, which is not a joke in aviation. Therefore, they did not question our story. The school Commander reported to General Alexandru everything that we had seen that night. The next morning, we were called to report to the commander's office, where the General expected us. He said only – gentlemen, watch what you say, because you have not seen anything last night! Do you understand? You have seen nothing... and made a gesture as though he would pull zipper over your mouth. From this I concluded that we must keep quiet about this incident which I did up until now", said Colonel Smoleanu.

The former fighter pilot decided to break his silence about this incident in an interview in 2012 with journalist Florin Mitu, from the news organization "Ştiri de Buzău" (News of Buzău) and after a while, telling the story to the investigators at ASFAN.

Colonel Smoleanu is accustomed to unusual sensations while flying and knows what kind of optical illusions can do, but he cannot explain the phenomenon he experienced. He is convinced, after more than 20 years, that he still took a risk when he decided to talk about the incident. After his first stories appeared in the press, he received "some phone calls". These phone calls were not pleasant, but he refuses to discuss this any further. He went on to add: "I cannot give you the names of my former colleagues because I cannot take any risk to them. I have chosen to speak up because I still do not understand why there was so much secrecy regarding this incident."

In the fall of 2013, Florin Mitu identified and interviewed a second key witness, Lieutenant Colonel, now retired, Doru Drăgoi [Fig. 27], who was shift manager that night at the command point at the military airfield Buzău. He remembers that he

was called in on an emergency by a Captain who was "at the tube" (radar screen), when he saw an unidentified target very close to the three helicopters. "That object appeared different from our helicopters and much bigger. After I saw that the UFO was close to possibly colliding with our helicopters, we informed the flight leader with the order to bring the helicopters in to land". Initially, he refused, saying "Mind your own business; they are helicopters from Alexeni or from Bucharest", although he knew that no flight was scheduled from those

Fig.27 Lt. Colonel (ret.) Doru Drăgoi in 2013. airports that night. However, he contacted a helicopter pilot (not Smoleanu) and said: "Be careful as you have on your right hand side a large object". The pilot replied, "It's not on our right; it passed to the left and it's huge". After also speaking with Marcel Smoleanu, the flight leader agreed to bring the helicopters in to land.

Doru Drăgoi reported further: "After the helicopters landed the radar operators called me to come and look again at the radar screen. I saw a lot of targets on the screen, more than ten. They made strange movements in the Mărăcineni – Săpoca area (several kilometres north-east of Buzău). They flew as if they were helicopters in a line until they reached Săpoca, then, one by one; they each made a 180 degree turn and then disappeared as if they had hot the ground. "Witnesses later joked that they had a UFO base at Săpoca".

There was yet another surprise. Another call came from the radar area asking the officer Doru Drăgoi "to come out and see them in the sky". Drăgoi says: "When I came out of the command post, I saw the clear sky, the stars and bright objects crossing from east to west at an amazing speed. I knew from the flight information that no earthly object was flying there at that time. Foreign aircraft were unable to fly here because we are in the centre of the country and the objects would have been detected at the border. Then I realized that we are dealing with a large scale UFO phenomenon". Doru Drăgoi added that speed, acceleration and the manoeuvrability of the UFOs led him to believe that the objects "did not originated on earth".

The radar tapes were kept normally for 48 hours under a military aviation rule, but Doru Drăgoi retained the ones from that night for much longer. He was right to do so as a few days later a Major from the higher Command came and wanted to see them. Then he said that if something similar happens in future, they should immediately report directly to Bucharest, "Because these objects toy with us too much and try to simulate our helicopters movements". He was well acquainted certainly with other similar incidents. However the hypothesis of such 'simulators' is hard to be accepted both because they appear on radar as having the same size of a helicopter, but mostly because of the observations made with the naked eye. The objects simply did not look like helicopters and were much bigger. Marcel Smoleanu also commented that other fighter pilots at the Boboc base were telling him, privately, that they saw above them, on various nights, unidentified objects moving at high speed. "But they were very high-up".

Florin Mitu, the journalist who was the first to investigate this case, found some other strange and unexplained phenomena that occurred in the Mărăcineni – Săpoca area, in the same period. These phenomena are still under investigation.

Romanian fighter hit by "UFOs"

On the afternoon of October 30th, 2007, six kilometres from the town of Gherla, near Cluj-Napoca (in Transylvania) a "MiG-21 LanceR" fighter, from the Air Base 71 at Câmpia Turzii, was performing a training flight. Apparently an unknown object hit the plane during this training flight. The case was widely publicized, including in the spring 2008 issue of the UK magazine "*Flying Saucer Review*".

As Marin Mitrică, military pilot since 1991, recounted: "Suddenly, from my right, I was hit by an object of some kind. The collision broke the plastic window covering the cockpit. The splinters punched a hole in my helmet and wounded my face. At first, when the object struck I ducked as much as I could, over the console, as the air-stream was powerful and the temperature was -30 Centigrade. I reduced the speed of my aircraft from 850 km/h and descended from 6500 meters in order to avoid hypoxia. Fortunately I had the oxygen mask on. The biggest danger was the hypothermia".

The fighter landed without any further problems, directed, by coincidence, by the pilot's wife, who was in the control tower. The aircraft was immediately investigated by a military commission. They had no idea of what had caused the damage. Each fighter has a video camera recording the flight, but the speed made the images unclear. The recording showed two triangles, the size of an A4 sheet, seen approaching from the right hand side. General Ion Avram stated that the images were delivered to the "*Serviciul Român de Informaţii*" (Romanian Intelligence Service) to be analysed, "as, they have the relevant laboratories and analytical equipment".

Lt. Commander Nicolae Grigorie investigating the case (himself a MiG pilot and graduate of the French Institute for Aeronautical Security) stated in the newspaper "*Gândul*" that all conventional scientific explanations were ruled out. First off they had excluded any and all natural causes. The aircraft had not been hit by a bird, as they do not fly, at end October, at the height of 6,500 meters and no traces of organic mater were found on the body of the plane. Nor was it a piece of ice, because the sky was clear and there were no weather conditions which would cause water to freeze. Nor was it hit by a meteorite, because no astronomical data confirmed an entry of any such astronomical bodies in the atmosphere on that day.

Then they excluded causes due to any human activities. There were no civilian flights at any hour at the location where the MiG-21 LanceR was, no exercises with artillery, or missiles, no incidents reported to police involving fireworks or weapons and no weather balloons had been launched.

Data collected by Lt. Commander Nicolae Grigorie has been supplemented by a survey of the National Institute of Forensic Expertise. The conclusion of analysis performed by Cătălin Grigoraş, expert at this Institute, is that one of the two unidentified objects was ascending and the other had a descending trajectory and that the object that struck the aircraft was in motion, rotating around its own axis. The Radar in Câmpia Turzii has not recorded anything at that altitude so it is almost impossible for the object to be launched from Earth. In addition, the objects caught by video camera had very irregular shapes.

Nicolae Grigorie stated: "We can say with certainty what it was not, but not what it was. An object struck the MiG, but we don't know of what material it was made of and what its origin was", refusing to speculate about a possible "extraterrestrial origin". He confirmed that during the 67 milliseconds when the "UFO" was caught in view by the camera, two objects passed before the aircraft "just as something would pass in front of a car, without it being hit".

Neither has any European experts found an explanation. The incident above Cluj County has been discussed by the Air Forces Flight Safety Committee (Europe) (AFFSC E) However, none of the experts on military aircraft from other European countries have added any plausible alternative hypothesis to those discounted by the Romanian investigators. Finally, as a participant in this body of experts in military aviation safety, Nicolae Grigorie is of the opinion that in Romania incidents involving unknowns are on par with those for other Air Forces, not more, not less.

A specialist opinion in the paranormal field, Adrian Pătruţ PhD, professor at "Babeş-Bolyai" University of Cluj-Napoca, president of the Romanian Society of Parapsychology, said that such phenomena have been reported in the area of Cluj, during the years 1990-1992, but also in the Timiş region. There were UFOs recorded on radar and also seen with the naked eye. They were, however, never confirmed or denied after an information embargo was imposed in 1992 by the Romanian Army.

Access to the Romanian aviation UFO data

ASFAN organized, on May 10th, 2014, the first edition of the "UFO Conference" in Romania, in the main room of the Museum of Bucharest Municipality, in Suţu Palace historical building [Fig. 28]. In the first part of the conference, three cases of Air Force UFO encounters were presented (all described above): the Alexeni Case, witnessed by General Emil Străinu, the Mihai Kogălniceanu Case, witnessed by Colonel Platon Stceja and Colonel Aurelian Dobre (recorded on video), backed by statements of other witnesses and the Buzău Case, presented by Colonel Marcel Smoleanu and Lt. Colonel Doru Drăgoi (recorded on video). I made a presentation

Fig.28 Suţu Palace, historical building in the heart of Bucharest, where the 2014 UFO Conference has been held.

Fig.29 Dan Farcaş speaking at the board of the Romanian UFO Conference in 2014. Next to him Emil Străinu (left) and Marcel Smoleanu.

Fig.30 George Cohal and Cristina Aldea presenting the Ooparts section of the Romanian UFO Conference, 2014.

about declassifying military UFO data worldwide and in Romania [Fig. 29]. The second part of the conference featured out of place artefacts, with George Cohal, ASFAN executive director and Cristina Aldea [Fig. 30], President of the Cologne (Germany) branch of the SSA (Society for Research in Archaeology, Astronautics and SETI, led by Erich von Däniken). She is also a member of the Italian National Ufology Centre (C.U.N.).

In preparation for this Conference, ASFAN asked officially several institutions to provide access to the data on unidentified aerial phenomena: encounters of military aircraft with "unidentified phenomena", "unconventional helicopters", unknown objects which passed very close to aircraft or hit aircraft, radar targets that were not identified by usual procedures, or unusual phenomena observed visually, which could not be identified, as well as other occurrences of the same category. In particular, ASFAN asked for access to documents and records of some widely publicized cases which occurred in Romanian airspace. The request was made under the law No 544/2001 on free access to information of public interest, with particular reference to Article 11, on studies and research of public interest. ASFAN also proposed its expertise to help elucidate some controversial situations for better flight safety, complying with the existing legal framework.

At the request made on March 5th, 2014 to the Romanian Aeronautical Authority, Department of Security, their response issued on March 24, 2014 stated that "the point of contact designated by regulations, by which you can request for information on civil aviation occurrences is the Centre for Analysis and Aviation Security" (an institution located at the same address.). At the request made by ASFAN, immediately, to this institute, no reply was received.

Another request was made on March 5, 2014, to the "CN Bucharest Airports", for data on two specific cases (Otopeni Airport, July 14, 1997 and May 11, 2004). The response, received on March 14, 2014 stated that the "the volume of transactions involved to research information from 1997-2004" is very high and the human resources to do so are very limited, but "you will receive this requested information as soon as possible" was the answer. ASFAN responded immediately, saying that there are just two events, also asking for a contact person. No answer was received.

Again on March 5, ASFAN made a similar request to ROMATSA (Romanian Administration of Air Traffic Services), receiving no response.

To the request, on March 3rd, 2014, to the Ministry of Defence, the response, on March 18, 2014, stated that: "The Ministry of Defence has no data and no information on unidentified aerial phenomena" but "for future cooperation" a senior officer was nominated as a contact person. ASFAN members had a first discussion with this person, who showed interest in further cooperation. On March 27th, a collaborative proposal to the General Staff of the Romanian Air Force was handed to that contact person. But, after a while, we received some excuses that the international situation, especially that of the Ukraine, put other priorities before military aviation.

The attempt by ASFAN was not isolated. Some newspapers have tried, earlier, to obtain access to military data about UFOs. The answer was that the defence structures in Romania have no resources even for much more important tasks, than those to find such kind of data.

The opinions of a Romanian astronaut

Dumitru-Dorin Prunariu, a retired three stars air force general, was the first Romanian astronaut who flew in space, during the period May 14th to 2nd 2, 1981, with Soyuz 40, along with Leonid Popov. Prunariu earned a degree in aerospace engineering from the University "Politehnica" of Bucharest and a Ph.D. in the field of space flight dynamics. Prunariu is a co-author of several books on space technology and space flight and he is Doctor Honoris Causa of several higher education institutions from Romania, Republic of Moldova and the USA.

Prunariu is one of the founding members, in 1985, of the Association of Space Explorers (ASE). From 2011 until 2014 Prunariu was the elected president of ASE International and since 2014 serves as president of ASE Europe. Since 2005 he is also a member of the ASE Committee on Near Earth Objects (NEO). He was the elected chairman of the United Nations Committee on the Peaceful Uses of Outer Space (UN COPUOS) for the period of June 2010-June 2012. Since 1995 Prunariu is also acting as the Vice-President of the European Institute for Risk, Security and Communication Management (EURISC), from Bucharest. Since 1998 until 2004 Prunariu was the President of the Romanian Space Agency.

Starting with 2004, Prunariu was, for almost two years, the itinerary Ambassador Extraordinary and Plenipotentiary of Romania to the Russian Federation. He is a full member of the International Academy of Astronautics and since 2011, an Honorary Member of the Romanian Academy. In 2012 he was appointed as one of the 15 experts of the Group of Governmental Experts on outer space transparency and confidence-building measures (TCBM), established by the UN General Assembly Resolution 65/68.

Prunariu was an indirect witness of the UFO observation, at the Mihai Kogălniceanu AF Base, described above. He was present at the Air Force Headquarters in Bucharest, at that time when flight inspector, Colonel Platon Streja, reported the passing of the UFO.

At a meeting, on February 24, 2009, with ASFAN members, Prunariu recounted that, during his astronaut training in the USSR, he was in no way instructed regarding the UFO phenomenon and he soon realized that it would be considered unseasonable to discuss or ask about alleged ET, artificial, objects or phenomena.

He later learned, however, that there are some astronauts (cosmonauts) confirming that they were accompanied in space more than once, by unknown objects (possibly alien ships), but they were reluctant to talk openly about these topics, as long as they were still on active service. Prunariu told us that, at a press conference, during the 1994 Congress of ASE in the Russian Federation, the journalists asked the astronauts and cosmonauts if they have noticed "something special" during their flight. They of course denied it, but – said Prunariu – in the bus carrying them back to the hotel, he stood by Vasili Tsibliyev, the commander of the Soyuz TM-17 spacecraft, recently returned (in January 1994) from the *Mir* space station. He confessed that he saw two objects in the outer space, with the shape of a hat, which flew parallel to the space lab. He tried to talk about them with his superiors, but they told him to mind his business, because he was sent into space for scientific experiments and not to make a fuss about this UFO nonsense. He was afraid that if he would talk more about that his superiors would not let him fly any more and he really wanted to fly into space in May. However, in private, he allowed himself to tell the story to a few others.

Donald Herod Peterson, who spent 4 hours and 15 minutes of extra-vehicular activity within the mission STS-6 Challenger, launched on April 4, 1983, declared to Prunariu that by 1970, he led a committee at NASA to examine unknown aerospace phenomena. For 2% of observations, they have not found any earthly explanation; but it was considered that this low efficiency of discoveries did not justify their activity and the committee was disbanded as a result.

"Although I have not seen UFOs, I am convinced that extraterrestrial life exists", said Prunariu. "It is impossible and even absurd, to deny the existence of extraterrestrial life and of other civilizations. It is impossible that, in billions of star systems in the Milky Way, we are the only planet with life. If other civilizations were only 100,000 years ahead of us (an insignificant period of time, for the scales of the Universe), imagine how they would fly in outer space, compared to us who have only been flying in space for just over 50 years. I appreciate that the intentions of other civilizations that have evolved near to us are peaceful; if they wanted to attack us, or to destroy us, they would have done it a long time ago. It would not be inconceivable that the Earth is monitored by an advanced civilization, but in an unobtrusive manner in which they do not want to interfere with our evolution".

CLOSE ENCOUNTERS AND ALIENS

Old testimonies

AS data accumulates, it becomes increasingly difficult to separate the classical "close encounters of the third kind" (as outlined by Dr J.Allen Hynek) and other occurrences of the same category, such as encounters with strange humanoids without the presence of a UFO, including here also folklore or religious stories. As a result we now understand that such events have always taken place throughout our history and therefore the phenomenon is far more complex than just "nuts and bolts" and the theory that we are being visited by ET (ETH).

Ciprian Ardelean and Marius June published in issue No.7 of the journal RUFOR, a story that happened at the beginning of the twentieth century. Among the witnesses was an old woman from the family Târsală, who died in 1992, aged 102. In the Păiușeni village, located in western Romania, about 60 km east of Arad, several villagers had gone up into the mountains to work. When they returned home at night, at one point, they observed a very bright light in the valley which the old lady had described as "the most powerful light bulb I have ever seen". Coming from the direction of the light, rhythmic metallic noises could be heard. The villagers became frightened and tried to avoid the area in question. But upon arriving at just a short distance from this location the witnesses saw a number of humanoid beings who were milling around an object whose outlines were lost in the glare of the light. The following day several people went through the forest, on the same path but the object was not there and there were no marks on the ground where it had been.

Another oddity occurred in May 1935, near the river Olt, not far from the Drăgășani municipality. The witness Radu Popescu from Bucharest told Călin Turcu the following story: "Together with my cousin (then both 16-17 years of age), we descended towards Olt, near the mouth of the creek Reșca, when I saw something that looked like a covered wagon. I said it must have been some travellers who have come to sell plum brandy. The 'travellers' had one person near the wagon, two a bit further away and two others were standing next to a boat on the shore of Olt. When they saw us they began running toward the 'wagon'. As they embarked a black cap of some sort covered the vehicle. Above it we saw an antenna. With a slight hum, the 'wagon' raised itself up and flew over Olt. It began to change colour to white and we lost it out of view in the distance. I told the locals about the incident and no one seemed to be surprised. "The Flyings" [*Zburătorii* in Romanian] were known to appear in this region long ago. At that time they have been appearing quite often, in a clearing in the northeast of the village of Comănița, Olt County. In those days (1935) nobody was talking about UFOs".

A close encounter in 1939

George Pârvu, PhD, born in 1930, had a remarkable career in geology and is author of more than 15 books. He had, in 1939, at age 9, a strange and dramatic encounter in his native village, named Armășești, in Ialomița County, about 5 km north-west of city of Urziceni and 50 km north-east of Bucharest. He decided to make public the incident in 2011 in two books that were published simultaneously in Bucharest. Ionel Grama published an account of the case in January 2013, in the magazine *"Lumea Misterelor"* (World of Mysteries). I talked with George Pârvu about this case in 2015 and 2016 [Fig. 31] and I have no reasons to doubt his sincerity.

Fig.31 Geologist George Pârvu PhD, in 2016.

As he recounted to me: On a bright sunny morning, at the beginning of August, he was, together with a group of five primary school colleagues, at the public pasture. Given the level ground of the site, they could run here freely and when they became tired, they could lie on the grass which was always kept fresh thanks to a creek nearby.

Lying on their back, one of the kids pointed to a bright

star in the sky which was moving up and down and moving in a zigzag fashion. Then the apparition, as if it had located them, circled a few times and then descended towards them. As it approached, it increased in volume and grew brighter. At an altitude of 70-80 meters, it stopped, hovering silently above them. Suddenly it lost brightness, became dull and turned a coppery colour. At the bottom of the object there was a hollow, circular inward 'bump'. Two of the children were scared and fled, hiding behind the wall of a fountain. The other three, including George Pârvu, stood up and gazed in amazement at the apparition.

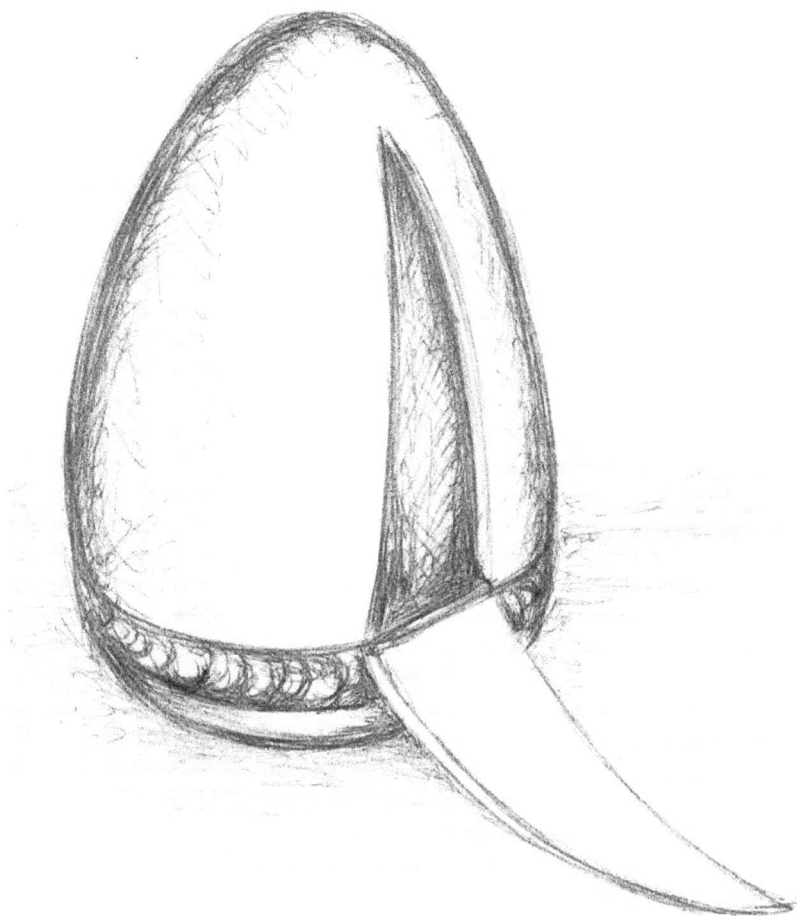

Fig.32 UFO that was seen by George Pârvu and his friends in 1939. Sketch made in his presence.

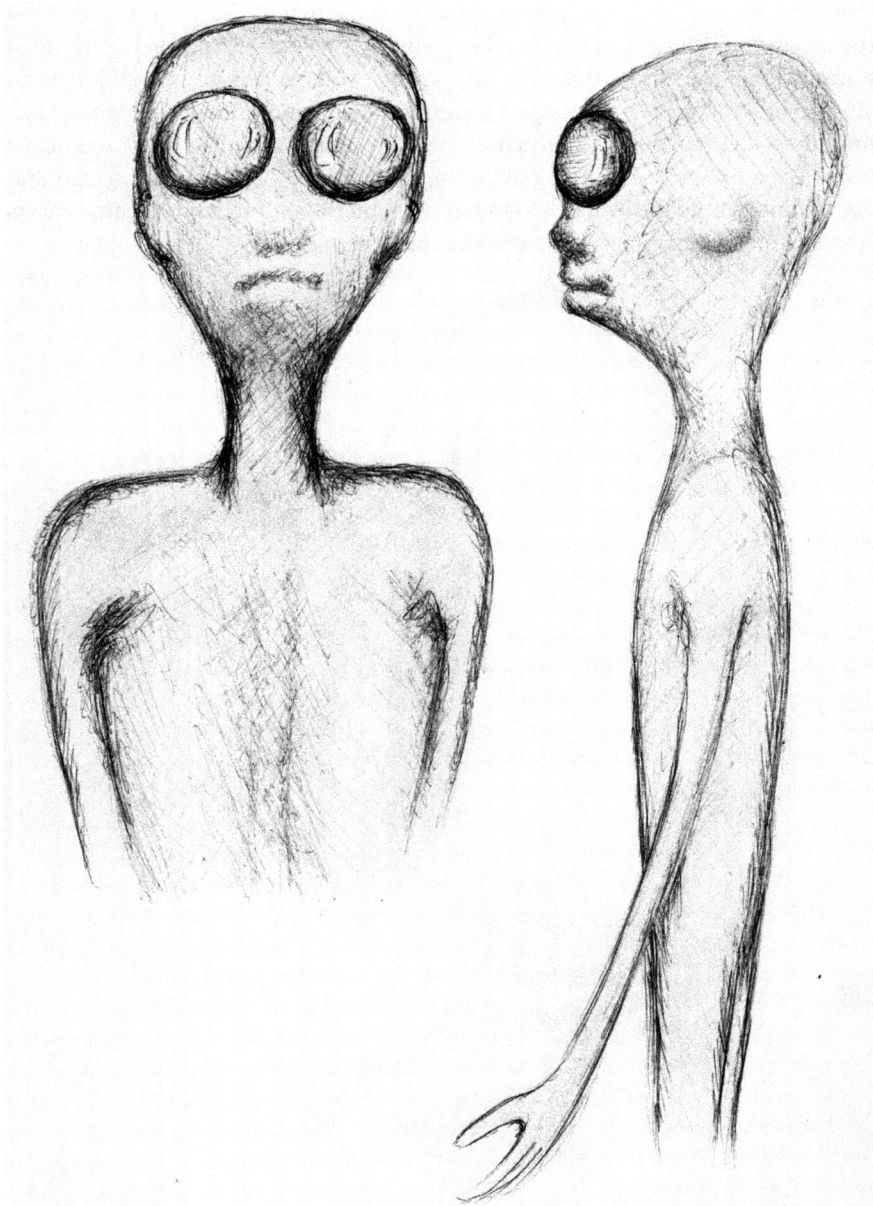

Fig.33 Aliens met in 1939 by George Pârvu and his friends. Sketch made in his presence.

The witness went on to state: "Ultimately, the object touched the ground, 40-50 meters from us. At about 20 cm from the bottom, the UFO was surrounded by a 30 centimetres wide belt, consisting of kind of small turbine blades, looking like the curved paddles in a water mill. The UFO was an oval shape, like a tulip with closed petals. According to my assessment, the object was about five meters high and three meters (or a little more) in diameter".

From the "tulip", a hatch opened [Fig. 32] and two little men came out both of whom were dressed in a sort of diving suit, coloured grey and moulded perfectly to their body. The witness said that "they were taller than us children and had a human head", so "kind of from 1.30 to 1.35 meters" [Fig. 33]. From the hatch, the little people jumped nimbly to the ground. Then they came towards the children, "side by side, walking as we do. Their legs were articulated like ours but moved rigidly and their arms were thin and knee-length. One of them carefully examined the ground pointing at it a rectangular box which was the size of a flashlight. The other was holding a stick as short as a police baton, but much thicker" [Fig. 34].

Fig.34 Alien device used to install the invisible wall. Sketch made in presence of George Pârvu.

The children approached the visitors all holding hands with each other. The friends of George were called Fănică and Marcel. When they were at about seven meters from the visitors, "the little man with the stick raised it horizontally and pointed it at us, but not in a threatening manner. From that moment on I could not move forward, because before us appeared a kind of invisible wall, hard as rock. We were kicking out and we connected with something hard. I had the impression that little people were having fun on our account".

The visitors looked at us children for a few moments after which "they greeted us by bending their heads forward, waist-deep" similar to how the Japanese bow in greeting. "Then they turned around and they walked side by side, like two soldiers. The little man with the recorder whispered continuously in to it. When they reached the ship, they jumped up on the hatch, entered and the door immediately closed behind them". The ship took off suddenly, keeping its matte colour, up to an altitude estimated at 70-80 meters. Here, "it became illuminated, almost incandescent and gushed into the sky like a fiery arrow without noise or flame".

The witness wrote: "The departure of the ship filled me with a sense of regret, a feeling of inner emptiness because they had left without asking us or telling us anything".

Left alone, the children looked at each other, surprised and they rushed to where the "flying monster" had stood. Now the invisible wall was gone. Here, both grass and soil seemed, at first glance, intact. But examining them more closely, the witnesses noticed a circular area with a diameter of about two meters, within which the grass, though unaffected, had a more yellowish colour to it when compared to the rest of the pasture. Two years after the event there was still evidence on site and, after more years, the wheat grown at that location was shorter than the rest of the field.

As the witness wrote in his books and also told me, the three children, dazed and bewildered by the strange incident, rushed back to their homes. George decided to go to his father, who worked at the railway station of Armăşeşti as a store keeper for grain purchase. The distance from the pasture to the station was about 2.5 kilometres. The witness remembers he covered this distance in eight to nine minutes. He says he was full of energy and he ran like the wind. He could not sit still at all and was feeling vibrations throughout his whole body. When his father saw him he tried to comfort him and put his hand on the boys head, but he quickly pulled his hand away as it had been stung "feeling like he had grabbed an electric wire". George told his father in detail what had happened at the pasture and saying he believed that they had encountered two devils. The father, somewhat distrustful, threatened to beat him if he was found to be lying at all.

On the way home, the boy met the local priest and told him of the incident. The clergyman tried to suggest that he saw two angels and suggested that he might like to tell the story on Sunday at church. The boy did not accept the offer, saying he did not want to lie (they were not angels in his opinion).

When he got home, his mother was waiting for him with lunch. His mother also found it difficult to believe the story so he decided to go, together with her, to see his friend Fănică, who lived on the same street. But when they arrived, they found the boy to be very sick, with his head in his mother's arms. He barely mumbled a few words. Shortly after that – said George Pârvu – he died.

George recounts that he then ran to Marcel, one of the other eyewitnesses, finding him also sick, with his head bent over a sink, vomiting green bile. George, in an intuitive impulse, took him by the hand, pulled him out and forced him to flee. They ran together for about two kilometres and then stopped. Mysteriously Marcel was feeling better now. They ran back home and his illness had gone completely.

George Pârvu attributed the dramatic consequences of the encounter to a sort of energy which the alien device gave them. He wrote: "if that energy was kept in our body, without consuming it, without turning it into mechanical work (running), it would have overloaded the heart, lungs and liver and consequently generated a fatal dysfunction of the body. If I had not run long distances perhaps I would have suffered the same fate."

The other two schoolmates, who were hiding behind the fountain, remembered later: "only vague scenes, glimpses of the event", as if they had become amnesic.

George Pârvu writes that after five years had passed, on August 10, 1944, he encountered once again the strange craft in a place, far from his village, where he slept in an elevated wooden cabin, to tend a plot of grape vines. On that night he saw a star zigzagging up and down. The star came closer, circling at a distance of not less than 150 meters and then departed. It reappeared the next day, "as a bright 500 litre barrel". Out of fear, George hid for a few minutes, with his dog, in a cornfield. The object, after making several tight circles, "suddenly went up into the skies like a flaming arrow". After a while he once again heard the noise of the UFO, the same as the one seen back in 1939. "I will never forget this noise; it is something you cannot forget". Again, he tried to hide. The object approached, made a few circles and then departed.

A third encounter happened in August 1949, when George had big problems with the conditions required by the communist regime to be admitted to University (because his father was 'wealthy'). This time, in a clearing in the Sărata forest, located near the western border of the Armășești village, he saw in above him, "walking and swaying in the air a kind of oval shaped huge buoy, like a closed tulip, which at the thick end had a concave hollow and in the centre of which was a kind of porthole, this time brightly lit". He thought then that the object gave a sign, to encourage him.

He again saw a UFO in the summer of 1954, in the centre of Bucharest. George Pârvu had now graduated and was working in a geological research institute. It was a sighting with a large number of other witnesses, who had watched a luminous apparition that slipped through buildings over Edgar Quinet Street, between the

University and the "Dunărea" building. Having the size of a huge cauldron, it made some zigzagging movements, after which it disappeared in the sky at a fantastic speed.

The next day, the witness bought the official newspapers, hoping to find a note about the event. But there was nothing. Some residents of the capital city were whispering and commenting about a rumour that an "alien", unknown, object was seen over the University building but there were no reports in the press about the sighting.

George Pârvu told of this last observation, as well as his older UFO incidents to one of the leading teachers of the geological faculty, a member of the Romanian Academy and allegedly the head of a Masonic lodge. He listened carefully and calmly. Finally, he said that he believed the stories, but asked him not to say anything to anybody about these events. He took his index finger to his lips, undoubtedly the sign of silence. The witness remembered then, that during the war, he had reported the 1939 encounter to a German officer stationed in the area, who did not believe him, but he put his finger to his lips too, advising him, with the same gesture, to keep quiet.

These events have marked him for life. He believes also that the encounters gave him some unusual capabilities, loaded him "with extra energy and bio energy", giving him, in his childhood, a physical strength and an academic power far beyond his age and helped the miraculous healing of some wounds.

At the beginning George Pârvu suspected that he had assisted in the testing of some new secret weapons, maybe by the Japanese, because of the behaviour of the two aliens. Now he accepts that this could not be correct. At the same time he is very distrustful of what is said today about UFOs and aliens especially by the media. He states also that he does not know "whether religion is hiding the truth of such events in order to preserve its dominance". He only knows for sure that in 1939, on a pasture in Romania, a "tulip"-shaped ship landed, about fifty meters away from three children, one of whom was he.

A bell-shaped visitor

In issue No. 6 of RUFOR magazine, university professor Adrian Pătruț PhD recounts a case of strange nocturnal visit in Cluj-Napoca. Iuliu Marian (I.M.) lives in a private one storey house with a paved yard. One night in May 1974, at around 02:00, he was awakened in a very strange way. Usually he struggled to wake up, but this time it was very abrupt and he was very aware, as if somebody had force opened his eyelids. His eyes involuntarily looked towards the window. His wife was awoken a few seconds earlier and she too looked out of the window.

Near the front door, they could see a strange, illuminated, bell-shaped, silhouette, which the witness could not compare with anything they had ever seen before. I.M. had the distinct impression that this figure was waiting for him. He is absolutely sure that, from the moment he woke up, he was subjected to a force field, because, as an electronics physicist, he was familiar with all things electronic. Interestingly, this feeling offered him an unusual kind of inner peace.

The witness had observed the bell for about 10-15 seconds. It had in its middle a light tube in the centre of which he was able to distinguish a kind of very thin filament. The cross section of this assembly was a perfect circle. The brightness was weak and a very white colour. The consistency of the bell silhouette (and its layout), was like that of "backlit cumulus clouds". The silhouette did not cast a shadow and left no traces on the ground.

I.M. pulled out from under the bed a real sword (he is sports swordsman) and despite the opposition from his wife, he walked out to greet the apparition. When he walked out of the door, the bell silhouette was already 4-5 meters away from him, departing at a speed of about 1 m/sec. When the witness, following it, rounded the corner of the house, the strange object was no where to be seen.

The temperature was about 10 degrees C; the weather was dry, with a very clear sky and many stars. Without any fear, I.M. has searched the area for about 5-10 minutes, trying to relocate the bell. He felt that it was still there, in some form, since the feeling of force field was still very distinct. As I.M. reported at the time, he was well aware that he was acting against his will, he couldn't resist an "impulse" that sent him back to the house as though his legs had a mind of their own.

With sword in hand, he returned to the bedroom where his wife was waiting for him. He went back to bed and the force field sensation disappeared immediately. He fell asleep almost instantly. Next morning everything was back to normal. There were no further after effects.

His wife said that she had already looked out of the window before I.M. woke up. When he wanted to go outside with the sword she tried to stop him. After a brief dispute I.M. managed to get outside. Suddenly she became relaxed and while I.M. searched the courtyard, she sat very quietly, without thinking about anything in particular. When he returned, they did not speak at all. Both fell asleep immediately. Their child, aged one year, continued to sleep peacefully in his bed throughout the incident.

Bâlea Lake – September 1978

Bâlea Lake (Romanian: *Bâlea Lac*) is a glacial lake with a small mountain resort nearby, situated at 2,034 meters altitude in the Făgăraș Mountains, in central Romania, on the scenic "*Transfăgărășan*" highway [Fig. 35].

Fig.35 Bâlea Lake mountain resort, at more than 2000 metres in the Făgăraș Mountains.

On September 23, 1978, when the highway was not yet finished and accessible, at 24:00, two technicians from the upper station of the cable car were awakened by a reddish, circular light, which was visible through the dense fog, occupying their whole field of view. The witnesses estimated that something was at about 5-10 meters from their window. It was a perfect silence. Initially they thought that the Bâlea Lake main chalet was on fire, but this idea was soon eliminated when the light disappeared.

In a two storey wooden barrack, not far from the cable car, a number of military conscripts (between 12 and 20, according to various sources) were stationed, unarmed, being assigned to work there.

Around the same time, the "fruntaș" (equivalent to "lance corporal") Ioan Dörr came out of a bedroom of the barracks to get a drink of water. On the way to the tap, at the corner of the building, he spotted, at just 6-8 meters away from him, a dark, motionless silhouette, 1.90-2.00 meters high, illuminated only by a bulb above the door. Because of the fog, the military man could not distinguish any fine details. He shouted "Who's there?", but did not receive response. He therefore thought it was a better idea to return back inside the barracks. Five minutes later the figure was still there, closer to the wall of the building; but, after another ten minutes, it was gone.

On the following evening, it was a clear sky and without any fog. At around 21:45, in front of the building, sergeant Ion Radu drew the attention of the soldiers Dörr and Vulpe towards a mound some 15-20 meters away on which was standing a dark silhouetted figure. Its height was estimated at 2.5 meters. This was done by comparison with a two meter high diesel tank which was next to it. Dörr said the silhouette was like an astronaut making slow movements. According to the other witnesses it had hands with long claws. Meanwhile, the soldiers from the next bedroom began shouting that someone had opened the shutters of their windows. These were fastened shut with wires twisted with pliers and with a cross chain (the shutter locks were at 2.5 meters from the ground). Other soldiers began throwing stones at the strange being, which had moved slowly across the mound. At one point, sergeant Radu grabbed a club and moved towards the mound ordering soldiers Dumitru Sibu and Gheorghe Stan to follow him. Arriving at 1-1.5 meters from the creature, Radu raised the club to hit it. There was a blast like the "breath of a tiger" and the sergeant fell backwards into the snow, as if struck by lightning, with his arms stretched out and his head downwards. The other two, who were some 3-4 meters away, remained paralysed for a few seconds. The entity apparently 'examined' the sergeant and then disappeared. The two other witnesses watched the scene from just a few meters away. One of them said that the entity was moving "like a man walking on water, leaning over to one side and then the other. It was floating first on one leg and then on the other". He stressed that there was in no case a bear.

The two soldiers that accompanied the sergeant went to pick him and with the help of two other comrades, they carried him into the cottage. He was unconscious, but has not unclenched his hand which still held the club. He recovered after ten minutes of repeated resuscitation attempts. He did not remember anything from the moment he picked up the club. Meanwhile, at the location where "the shadow" had stood, five soldiers saw, above the ground "a wreath of lights", with a diameter of about half a meter. Four lights were smaller and four larger, "about the size of an egg", which "danced in a circle" and "jumped from side to side".

The soldiers barricaded themselves in to one of the rooms. Over a period of about an hour and a half, they heard someone scratching at the window shutters. Two witnesses said they heard a deep voice that apparently uttered the words: "*sergend, sergend.*"

A sleepless night followed for all. The next morning they noticed that on the shutters, which had been freshly painted only 2-3 days before had four parallel scratches on them each spaced about 10 centimetres apart. At the location where Ion Radu had fallen into the snow the soldiers found nothing unusual. All that was there were the traces of the soldiers and nothing more.

The next night, the soldiers were so frightened that, except for the sergeant and a corporal, they all left the place and went to the resort of "Bâlea Cascadă" (1200 meters elevation), the lower end of the cable car. They returned only on 26 September along with a commissioned officer.

The case was investigated by a group of members of the organisation "*Univers*" from Sibiu, led by Gabriel Pal and George Buțiu, along with engineers Justin Capră (the famous inventor) and M.T. from Bucharest and subsequently by Călin Turcu. They collected written statements and sketches of the events, as well as drawings of the "silhouette", as the witnesses had perceived it.

After several years, sergeant Ion Radu confirmed the events to Călin Turcu, adding that in the barracks were 20 military men and the entity was "like a thick tube of metal with a diameter greater than 50 centimetres without any other characteristics" and it was not much taller than him. The officer who accompanied them on September 26 carried a firearm, in order to raise the morale of the soldiers, and he stayed on at the cottage for a number of days. The soldiers were all terrified and could not understand why the entity had left no ground traces behind. Approximately two months after the event, a committee of military investigators visited the area. They concluded that "it was a phenomenon of electrification, or magnetisation, of the air" which caused an "electric shock" which knocked the sergeant to the ground. Sergeant Ion Radu did not, at least in public, disagree with this explanation.

A flying saucer in Ciucaș Mountains

Cornel Alexandru Olteanu, a peasant from the Izvoarele village, Prahova County, well known locally as an honest and hard working man, recounted that he had, in October 1979, a most unusual experience. The case was investigated separately by Călin Turcu and Gabriel Tudor.

Olteanu waited for the rain to stop before he went to a forest in the Ciucaș

Mountains, to pick mushrooms. He left his motorcycle where the road ends and embarked up the path that climbs up *Valea Berii* (Beer Valley), advancing to the *Fântâna lui Ioan* (Fountain of John), where the river Teleajen has its source. While gathering mushrooms, he saw in front of him, at about a hundred meters distance, in a sort of clearing under a high cliff, a grey object resembling a car. But a car could not reach this location as there are no roads. Curious, he approached the object and now saw that it was a metallic disk, "with a turret in the middle, a bit like a military tank". "It was round in shape, grey in colour and did not exceed 3-4 m in diameter". The disk was supported by three or four legs.

Near the object were two little men who seemed to be "working on something". They looked almost like children, about 1.20-1.30 m tall, had large, round and completely bald heads and their skin was a "dirty yellowish colour". "They had very large eyes like those of a cat and a head twice the size of that of a man. The nose was small and flat and their mouth was barely visible". The witness did not notice if they had any lips or not. "Their body was frail, puny, like that of a child. Their arms were knee-length and thin as sticks". "They were dressed in a sort of one-piece suit".

Olteanu reported also that: "I think I was within twenty meters of them when one turned and as soon as he saw me, the other also turned to face to me. When I looked in to their eyes I do not know what the hell happened to me, but I could no longer move. I stayed there, stuck like glue, although I wanted with all my heart to get away from there but I could not move a muscle. I felt as if I had been tied up. I could not even move the tongue in my mouth, nor my hands or feet. One of the little people began to walk towards me but the other one grabbed hold of him looked him in the eyes and he changed his mind, remaining where he was instead. They both turned around, climbed up a small ladder in to the saucer. The ladder then was raised up and a door closed behind it. After a second or two, a number of white lights came on looking like a belt around the disk and they flashed like the warning lights on a police car. However, I could not hear any noise and as I blinked my eyes five or six times, this bizarre object arose from the earth and ascended into the sky at a great speed. Meanwhile, I still sat there, I was conscious, but I could not move. When the object was at a certain height it leaned to one side and then it took off through the trees. I can honestly tell you, on my honour, that as this object passed over the trees they all bent over as if they had been hit by a hurricane. Fir and oak trees, as thick as a man, were bending over like twigs as it flew over them. In less than a minute this huge piece of flying machinery was just a white spot in sky and was lost in the distance over the mountains. Once it had departed I realised that I could move again. I ran to where it had been on the ground and could see only a yellowish stain, the size of an egg and nothing more. When I returned to this location in the years that followed, I found that there were no longer any traces of where the object had landed."

He also said that, following this event he had no ill effects whatsoever. Turcu asked him if he had been afraid during the incident. "Not at all! Why should I be afraid?" "They could kidnap you" – replied the ufologist "So what? I would have been curious to go with them and see how the mountains look when viewed from above".

When he returned to his village, the witness tried to tell some friends about the experience he had gone through. But he gave up after they made fun of him. Fortunately, while working as a guard at a high school in Vălenii de Munte, he met Călin Turcu, who accepted his statements as truthful and remained convinced that the man was not lying. The witness had a poor level of education; he had never read anything in his life about UFOs and had little knowledge of the subject. It was hard to believe he could concoct such a complex and bizarre event as he had nothing to gain by doing so.

The Chiraleş-Lechinţa case

Adrian Pătruţ investigated a possible case of a UFO landing on the "Bobeica" mound next to the Chiraleş village (Lechinţa commune, Bistriţa-Năsăud County). A number of witnesses said that on the evening of Thursday, November 15, 1979, around 17:00, a group of children, seventh and eighth grade school students, while playing at a place called "Cripta Grofului" (The Crypt of the Count) had observed a milky-white illuminated body, shaped like a "mace head" with pointed excrescences, with a diameter of about 1 m, which was moving from south to north, at about 15 meters from the ground and was not making a sound. While in the air, the object looked to be self luminous. The children had the impression that it crashed at a place called "Bobeica", a mound covered with vegetation and trees.

The first observation occurred at a distance of about 300 m, with good visibility, amid clear skies. After the object had disappeared from their sight, the children ran in the direction of the mound. Having travelled about 200 meters, they stopped, astonished by the spectacle that unfolded before their eyes. From behind the mound appeared not one, but two glowing objects both of the same size. They made a "lap" around the mound. They then landed on the ground, between a walnut and a plum tree on the western part of a steep slope. On reaching the ground, the lights went out and the surprised witnesses saw two little people of about 80 cm tall, dressed in bright white costumes, as made from tinfoil, with a kind of antenna on their head. The objects were now black and resting on the ground upon three tripod legs. The children stated that the little people came out of the "ship" through a "door" which was located underneath the objects. They were walking along in a 'bouncing' motion and went up to the top of the mound where it appeared that they had made something.

The children took a deep breath and approached a little closer with the intention of going right up to the objects and the little people and were now only at a few meters from them. The little people seemed to have guessed their intention all the all quickly climbed back up into the ships. The objects again became two bright-white spheres, moving at about 5 m distance from each other and at about 8 m height above the ground and departing without noise they sped over the village of Cristur-Șieu.

At the moment of objects landing, jet-flames were also observed by Anica Câmpean. She stated: "I had just drawn water from the well. Bobeica was in my view at about 80 meters distance. When I pulled up the bucket of water from the well, I saw three or four long 'flares' of red-orange colour. At first I thought some fishermen may have made a fire or perhaps that is was a car. I entered the house after being called by my smallest granddaughter. I realised afterwards that it could not be a fire or a car. The flames were higher than the Bobeica plum tree and were thicker at bottom and thinner at the top. I do not know what they could be. I felt no cold, no heat, no smell and even I was surprised that those flames did not produce any smoke. Nor did I hear noises".

Adrian Pătruț investigated the case and examined the scene with the natural sciences teacher Teodor Foșlui and the children who had witnessed the event. "I found on this occasion – said the investigator – imprinted in the ground, traces of an almost circular shape with a diameter of about 8 cm and depth of 3-4 cm, blurred by the curios children, who have arrived earlier and have trodden on the traces. However, it had preserved a very revealing trace: a large round spot, slightly oval, in the grass, right where the children had observed the objects landing. There the grass was bent pointing downhill and the colour was clearly different from the grass nearby, which was green and stood tall in all directions, while at the place where the objects had landed it was like blown in one direction by a powerful jet or blast of air. There were also some burn marks, but they were not conclusive as the grass could arguably have been ignited by some children. What was conclusive was the shape and the colour of the faded portion of ground where apparently the grass was burnt". Pătruț also realised that the Bobeica mound was the only place within a radius of several kilometres where such a device could easily land. The mound made for an ideal landing spot.

The Cerțești case – 1996

During the night of July 8 to 9, 1996, in the centre of a village named Cerțești (pronounced *Tchertzeshty*, Galați County, in South of the Moldavian Region (ten kilometres south of the village Pupezeni, presented in a previous chapter), a police sergeant and a guard had a close encounter of the third kind [Fig. 36].

ALTERNATE, MOVING
RED-BLUE LIGHTS

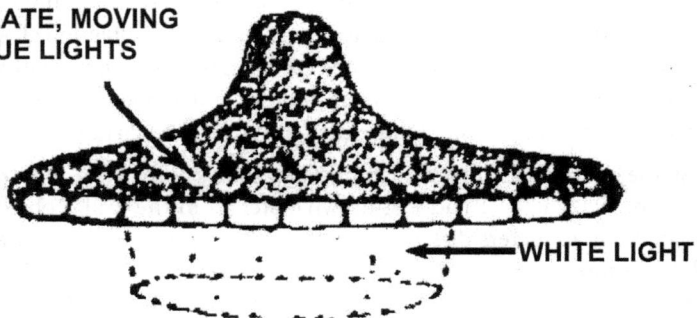

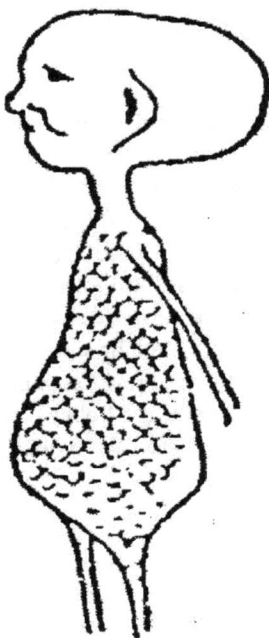

WHITE LIGHT

Fig.36 UFO and alien at Cerţeşti in 1996. Sketch made in face of the witnesses.

Fig.37 From left: Dan Farcaş, Mihai Bădescu and Călin Turcu, the team to comment, in August 1995, the Cerţeşti case for the Romanian Public TV.

Initially, only newspaper and tabloid reporters investigated the case. The TV producer Mihai Bădescu with Călin Turcu went to Cerţeşti, on August 5 for preliminary investigations On August 12th 1996, they returned with a bigger team, to make a short film about this event for TVR1, the main Romanian Public TV channel (The film was broadcast shortly afterwards). The producer invited Călin Turcu and me to comment the case [Fig. 37]. During the day we had detailed discussions with the witnesses of this encounter and with other people including many sceptics. The main findings are as follows:

The police sergeant Marian Mancu and Maricel Rusu, a voluntary guard, were patrolling on the main road passing through the village Cerţeşti, on July 8 to 9, 1996, at night. At around 00:30 when they were in front of the police office, Mancu told Rusu that he would go home for ten minutes in order to get something to eat. In this location, on both sides, between the road and the sidewalks, there are deep ditches, with small bridges across them. The houses are behind the fences, in the middle of orchards and gardens, except – opposite the police station stood a two-storied house, with 12 apartments, one of them accommodating the policeman. The entrance is behind the building. The moment the sergeant passed the corner he heard a whistling sound from the street and sensed a current of air. He immediately turned around and saw on the road something "splashing with blue and red lights and making a sound like *voom-voom*".

At first glance the sergeant had the impression that a police car from the county capital Galați had arrived on a routine patrol. Getting closer he soon realised that the object was hovering half meter above the paving and a small and very strange person was moving around outside of it. He cried "Guard"! He saw the horrified guard, emerging out from the ditch were he was hiding just below a bridge. He whispered: "Mister Marian, it is Satan!"

Maricel Rusu declared later that immediately after the sergeant disappeared behind the apartment house, "a fluttering from the above appeared". The neon lighting of the street seemed to change in intensity. The object descended smoothly, without making any noise and came down just behind him. For a brief instant he was convinced too that it was the police car on a patrol. However, when he turned around he became frightened when realised that the object was hovering just above the ground and that three small human like creatures were moving around outside of it. As he stated: "when I saw what they looked like, their very ugly faces, I told myself they are not human. I became afraid and I was hiding myself in the ditch just-in-case something might happen because I have never seen any such beings in my life before."

Both witnesses agreed that the object had the form of a flat hut, 5-6 meters across and 2-2.5 meters high and was hovering and balancing half a meter above the ground. Around the edge it had a continuous girdle of light "like a rainbow". The colours: red and blue (or green in other statements) changed from each other and were very bright. At the bottom of the object was a bright white light and none of the witnesses saw any doors, portholes or other marks of any kind.

After about two minutes the UFO rose vertically. At that moment its lights became much brighter and the streetlights went out. When the object reached around 30 meters, it changed direction and turned north-west, toward the village of Pochidia, with a tremendous speed.

The guard Rusu had a better view of the humanoid creatures. Sergeant Mancu noticed only one and only from behind. Their height was estimated to be around one meter, maybe even less. Rusu said he heard some noises made by them, "like the rain in the drain pipe". The visitors had a big head, very elongated behind and covered with bumps, with no hair. Their face was white and they had big eyes and big pointed ears. Gray scales with a metallic sheen like fish scales, covered their body. Their belly was relatively big and limp. The arms were "not thicker than two fingers". None of the witnesses remembered the nose, the mouth or any footwear. The witnesses could not tell for sure if the creatures were walking or floating above the ground, but accepted as more likely the second possibility. Rusu said they moved, "as if they were drunk".

The physical traces were weak. A huge sweet cherry tree nearby, had around 15% of its leaves affected by an extreme heat on the side where the object was seen. The damage was visible even after one month, when we were at the site. Some people from the village told us that on the next morning, after the encounter, many leaves and broken limbs were spread on the road on the site. Some others were convinced that this debris was the result of human activity or of the wind. No other signs were recorded. Nobody measured for radioactivity or took any samples.

Sergeant Mancu declared that after the object disappeared he had to help Rusu to come out of the ditch. The guard told him that he was sick and he had to sit on the grass for a while before he could stand up and start walking again. He remained convinced he was seeing Satan. After about a quarter of an hour a tractor was came along the street driven by Nicu Chicoş. The two asked him if he had seen anything unusual. The tractor driver finally admitted that he and another countryman Emil Bugeac, of the nearby Cârlomăneşti village, had seen a bright light, with some coloured blinking lights in the evening, before at 22:30 or 23:00, three kilometres away from Cerţeşti. But it could have been an aircraft of some sort.

On the following day, Mancu told a few villagers of what they saw. One of them contacted the news agency *Mediafax*. At the beginning, Mancu refused to say anything to the journalists, but later on he obtained the approval of his superiors who allowed him to go on the record.

A countryman, Gheorghe Ghenghea, from Cerţeşti, was watching that night, along with his daughter a song contest on TV. While watching the TV the image on screen deteriorated, extinguished, came back on for a moment, extinguished once again and, after a short while, it came back and the program continued without any other problems. No other lights were on in the house; so it could be a short electricity blackout thought Gheorghe Ghenghea. The witness went outside to ask a neighbour about it, but apparently everybody was asleep. The TV set was new and he had no problems with it until that moment, or after. The local inhabitants told us that some other electrical appliances in the village were disturbed too on the same night. Unfortunately we did not have enough time during our investigation to verify these allegations.

Another interesting witness was Ştefan Dumitru Cârje, 62 years of age, from the village of Cotoroaia, 4 km Northeast from Cerţeşti. He woke up, on the same night, because of some barking dogs; at 01:12 (he remembered seeing the watch). The backyard was lit up by "a very powerful and extended yellow through red light" coming from above. Going outside, he could not identify the source of the light. "The sky was

Fig.38 Sergeant Marian Mancu, in front of Cerțești police station, 1996.

red and the ground was red as well. It was so bright you could read a newspaper". He told us he had three years of military with the Air Force but it was a light that he had never seen the likes of before. The witness noticed that "all the animals were awake but they did not seem to be scared. The birds were not croaking or cackling. It was only the dogs that were barking". After a while he re-entered the house. While considering whether or not to wake up his wife and two grandsons in order for them to be able to see this phenomenon, "the light became thinner and thinner and maybe it lasted for a further three minutes until the powerful light disappeared and all returned back to normal". He added later: "I saw something like a 'haze' rising up to a certain height and then it disappeared slowly in to the air".

The witnesses to this event are very credible. The police sergeant Marian Mancu (30 years then) [Fig. 38] was, for a while, a veterinary technician, before graduating at police school. He was healthy and sane and was married with two children. The majority of the village population, including the village mayor Gheorghe Nechifor, considered him a serious person, not capable of lies or hoaxes. Mancu was more interested in the historical events of the region. He led an initiative to build a monument for the heroes of the village who had died fighting in the two world wars. He had a personal library of several hundreds of books, but nothing about UFOs, paranormal or connected issues. The sergeant told me that even when he had heard something before about UFOs, he did not believe in them and was not interested in them.

The guard Maricel Rusu (41 years) [Fig. 39] had graduated only six classes, but his education was not even at this level. He could read with difficulty and was only interested in local events that appeared in the newspaper. He had never heard anything before about the UFO phenomenon. Maricel Rusu is an Orthodox Christian, believer but not practicing. This explains his first hypothesis, that he had met Satan and the fright he endured as a result. He has no recorded psychiatric disorders and he served in the army as sapper. The villagers could not remember any lies or tall tales from him in the past. Even if he drinks sometimes, he has never been seen drunk. Before the close encounter his arm was badly injured by a horse bite and he was taking antibiotics so he was not allowed any alcohol.

It is unlikely the witnesses could invent all the very peculiar details and to go public with them in such a highly natural and convincing manner. It also is unlikely that it could be a delusion staged by someone else. Unfortunately we did not have the means to conduct any psychological tests, or lie detectors, but we did not discover anybody with any kind of motivation to invent such a story.

Not all the villagers gave credit to the witnesses. A mathematics teacher contested the story stating that she was awake at the same time and was living in the same

Fig.39 Guardian Maricel Rusu; in background the small bridge underneath which he was hidden.

apartment house as the sergeant, but she heard and saw nothing. Another person said that his "Mercedes" was on the street and that it was misidentified as a UFO. Another person objected stating that the location was too narrow for a landing because of the telephone or electrical wires on both sides of the road. This objection was rejected, the distance between the wires being comfortably wider than the dimensions estimated for this UFO. More interesting, the "debunkers" were mainly people that had legal problems with the policeman or people related to them.

With all of the data above, we consider that the Cerţeşti case could be qualified as a close encounter of the third kind. But was it more than that? Was it, maybe an alien abduction account? Our first argument is that, in the following days, sergeant Mancu felt sick and powerless and he was of the opinion that he was suffering from some kind of radiation poisoning. The guardian Rusu had repeated nightmares. As he informed us: "I was dreaming for several nights about how I was hiding myself in the ditch and then I woke up frightened mainly because the beings were so ugly".

I questioned both of them about the possibility of any loss of recall or a "missing time" period during the encounter. None of them had any such impression. But when I tried to establish more precisely the time line, I found that none of them was wearing a watch. The sergeant said "I did not have my watch with me because the bracelet on it was broken". Rusu did not own watch at all.

Trying to establish the succession of the events, we found strange discrepancies. Not one of the witnesses remembered seeing the humanoids descend from the UFO or re-enter it. More than that, the witnesses could not explain how the visitors re-entered the UFO, because no doors or entrances were visible. Maricel Rusu declared "I did not see how they descended". The situation was the same when the UFO was rising up – the creatures simply were not there anymore and nobody saw them get in to the object. The same witness declared: "they disappeared, but I didn't how they disappeared. I don't know where they entered the UFO and I did not see them entering. Maybe they entered from behind?" Sergeant Mancu also recognised that he could not explain how the little men disappeared. His impression was that he observed the small creature for only four or five seconds in total.

It would have been interesting to use regressive hypnosis, or something similar, in this case. Unfortunately, in Romania we face a lack of professionals practicing hypnotic regression and willing to apply it in such situations. Also, even the expenses to arrange such sessions are a real problem.

Călin Turcu also remarked that on July 8, at 21:28 pm, in Vălenii de Munte, Daniela Mihalcea, aged 37, had seen, for 5-6 seconds, two reddish glowing round objects, half the size of the Moon, laterally spaced, going up and down over a hill. On the same evening, in the city of Tulcea, teacher Felicia Constantin, sitting with her

Fig.40 At the house of Călin Turcu (first from left), in Vălenii de Munte, July 1999. From right to left: Dan Farcaş, Marian Mancu and Gabriel Tudor.

father in their yard, observed a strong, incandescent red, circular light on which were distributed a number of slowly moving spheres.

As a peculiar but not unique sequel, we can mention that after two years, sergeant Mancu was fired from the police. It is rumoured that he was fired, among others, because "that's the guy who sees UFOs". Călin Turcu tried, repeatedly but unsuccessfully, through letters to the authorities, to obtain the reinstatement of Mancu. In July 1999 Turcu had even convened a meeting, in this regard, at his home in Vălenii de Munte [Fig. 40].

I would like to add here an additional remark. In our short and busy visit to Cerţeşti, while talking with the villagers about what happened, I discovered that many villagers, or from nearby, claimed they also have seen UFOs in recent times and obviously their cases were not reported anywhere. In the following, I make a brief note of a few such cases.

H.I. from Cârlomăneşti recalled that on September 19, 1995, he returned from Galaţi, in a car in which there were five people. At 21:00-21:30, just 50 meters before the crossroad where the road to Cerțești comes off the country road to Cârlomănești, a number of flying lights appeared behind them, like reflectors, two in front and one below, "casting on our car a light so bright you could see the whole forest around you. I am 54 years of age and I've never seen anything like that". The occupants of the car completed the distance to the intersection in a panic and have turned to Cârlomănești. The car became unstable and they feared they may lose control of it. They felt an extreme heat. H.I. said "We turned to the left into the cornfield because we feared that otherwise the car might catch fire". The three lights passed them at short height, along the road, toward the village. The witnesses did not remember any engine failure or other effects on their car.

A young man, A.D. on patrol one night in Cerțești with sergeant Mancu, the date was 6th-7th August 1996, saw at around 01:00, over a house, "a round object, the colour of fire" yellow to red, which was the size of a football . "It passed, moving quickly down the road". Interestingly, in the press it was mentioned that, on the same evening, a UFO was also seen in the city of Roman, about 100 kilometres to the north.

Two women villagers: LU. and D.A., left in the morning of July 30, 1996, to herd their cattle. When they arrived at around 06:30, there was another woman already there. Sitting down they noticed in the sky "a white, bent, oval-shaped object". It was so bright that you could barely look at it. "It looked very nice and had on it some kind of candles". It moved very slowly swaying with the front up and down "as a boat on the water". They sat there and looked at it "for about half an hour, until it faded away with nothing more to see". In the meantime, other people came to help herd the animals, witnessing the phenomenon. Many of them made jokes about the sighting.

The villager A.D. told us that he recently observed, at 09:00, passing smoothly "in diagonal plan" a cylindrical object, with sharp ends and was a metallic grey colour, resembling aluminium. A former artilleryman, who was also a witness to this, considered that the object could be at an altitude of 7,000 to 8,000 meters.

Another villager said he owned a field of melons not far from the village. Recently, one night, sitting there with a boy, they saw above them, very close, a luminous flying object. They had also seen the same thing during the previous year. It could not be confused with planes or helicopter so far as they were concerned.

I had only the opportunity to note these cases in brief detail as I was not able to investigate them as fully as I would have wanted to. All of these incidents happened in one small location and over a very short period of time. We learned about them only because of our visit to the site. The witnesses considered the sightings not interesting enough to be reported officially or to the press. They would have remained completely unknown if the main event had not happened. I wonder how many similar situations are in the villages of Romania (and of other countries too).

VISITS, CONTACTS AND ABDUCTIONS

Hunted from the sky

THE abduction of people (often called "close encounters of the fourth kind"), in the context of the UFO phenomenon, is a controversial field, even among ufologists. But the research done by Dr Leo Sprinkle, Budd Hopkins, Dr John Mack, Raymond Fowler, Dr David Jacobs, Karla Turner and many others can not be overlooked and the amount of evidence is increasing. If you have the patience to examine it, you will understand that the phenomenon exists and has a wider spread than one might think. The victims of abductions are, mostly, normal, healthy people, who are all from different walks of life and are just like you and me. Simplistic explanations such as "temporal" or "frontal lobe epilepsy", or "hypnagogic or hypnopompic paralysis", not to mention some sinister military experiments, are totally unsatisfactory when trying to explaining all the richness and variety of these incidents. They include not only kidnapping in "nuts and bolts" UFOs, but also visitations of strange people or lights, haunting and even some unexplainable dreams and other phenomena.

In Romania there are also a number of cases that can be considered as "UFO abductions", in that broader sense; unfortunately they could not always be seriously considered, given the absence or the lack of involvement of specialists. But judging at least by the cases that I know personally, the witnesses of these cases are sincere people, not interested in publicity, to whom something inexplicable happened and who desperately seek someone to listen, to believe and to provide even a fraction of an explanation.

To begin with I would like to mention two incidents that occurred in 1991 in the Pătroaia Vale village and were investigated by Gabriel Tudor.

One night, in the autumn, at around 23:00, two people were returning on a bike, from a gravel pit located about three kilometres from the village. Suddenly, when they were only two hundred meters from their house, they heard a whizzing sound overhead and both of them saw, wide-eyed in horror, a blinding light, coming directly towards them from out of the sky. Scared to death, the two witnesses began to pedal like mad and they were bathed in light as they rode along. As Ion Petcu, one of the witnesses remembered, it was a globe, about the size of a big car. The apparition stopped falling and began to pursue them for about 30 meters, without making any noise except for that whir. Ion Petcu said that "the object was made of light". Once they entered the village, the globe left them in peace, taking off and looking like a beacon above the fields outside of the village. The witness arrived home in a state of extreme excitement. He took his wife, who was scared of his appearance, in to the yard, to show her the light in the sky. When he discussed the incident with Gabriel Tudor, he said that the only thought that was bothering him in those moments of panic was: "If this thing shoots a beam down here and melts us then no one know what happened to us". The man was known in the village as a very healthy and down to earth person. He had no interest in UFOs but became convinced that "the orb just wanted to have fun with us" and that it certainly "was not from Earth".

Another inhabitant of the village, who wished to remain anonymous, saw, on the same night, something "like a cloud of flames" coming down near the railroad, located just two kilometres away from the village. That person, convinced that the flames are signalling the existence of a buried treasure (an ancient popular belief), started to dig there, with his wife. It must be assumed that their treasure hunting was all in vain.

One evening of the same autumn and year, in the same place, three young commuters – two men and a woman – were returning to the village from the railway station, along the track. The woman, Stela Andrei, recounted to Gabriel Tudor: "We were walking in a single row, I was in front, Florin Florea came after me and the last was Cătălin Cobianu (a vigorous, well-built young man, 1.85 m tall). I heard Cătălin saying that he was feeling ill. I turned to ask Florin to check and see what was wrong with him. Then, Cătălin started shouting that something was pressing down on him. When Florin went to help him, he found him lying between the rails, trembling and with his face contorted by pain. He kept repeating that he could not get up and that an unseen force was holding him down. Florin wanted to lift him up, but the moment they touched, he was shaken by something and was thrown back as if being hit by a powerful electrical discharge. At exactly the same moment there was a very loud and strange noise. It was similar to the one made by water dripping into a sink, but amplified hundreds of times. This noise came from above, over a nearby cornfield, but I could not see anything to cause it and it was completely dark. Cătălin said later that he noticed a ray of light coming toward him but the others had not noticed it".

"Horrified, Florin and I lost our temper and instead of helping Cătălin – who screamed constantly: "Don't leave me here! Don't leave me alone!" – we ran away. We ran to the quarry and there I asked a dumper truck driver to come with us to help our friend. At first, the driver agreed and took us into the cabin, but after a few hundred meters, when we asked him to go towards the village – the road to the rail is shorter there – he became angry, believing that we actually wanted to get a lift home for free. We swore that it was not so, we begged him, claiming that our friend needed help but all to no avail. He turned the truck around and headed back towards the quarry, but here we met a guard, a very good friend of the driver, who was terrified to death and asked if we had heard that infernal sound. At that moment, the driver no longer doubted us and headed at full speed toward the railway. But to our amazement, Cătălin had vanished! We looked, we shouted but all to no avail. Horrified, but feeling guilty for our cowardice, we turned toward the village and here, much to our relief we met Cătălin! He was coming from the opposite side of the village; he was visibly confused and told us he did not remember what happened to him or how he got there. He was more than two kilometres from where we abandoned him".

Cătălin Cobianu also told Gabriel Tudor that he could not remember anything about what happened after his friends left. He said that, when they were walking along he had the impression that "someone" was behind him and he suddenly felt very ill. Then, just above him, there was an incandescent globe, from which sprang a beam of light, that was projected on him. In the next second, he fell down to the ground and could no longer to get up. As he stated: "I felt that my body was being held down by something much stronger than me. It was as if an invisible person had pushed me down and had nailed me to the ground. I could not make any movement, I was paralysed, shaking involuntarily, but I could not control myself in any way. I was aware of my surroundings and I was very afraid and when I saw Florică and Stela leave me, I thought, I'm going to go crazy with fright. After that, I don't know what happened and I cannot explain how I ended up in the village. I found myself walking down a street and I was wondering why I'm actually there. I thought even then that I was dreaming". The unexpected arrival of the others showed him that the incident was not a dream.

Following this event, Cătălin Cobianu began to show an increased interest in UFOs. He confessed that "I dream sometimes that I am in a different world. I know that I am not on Earth but I don't know where. There are two suns, big like our sun and they exude a beautiful, soothing light. At other times, I dream that I get up and fly and I see the Earth from above".

From the time when the two friends ran off towards the quarry, to their reunion in the village, about an hour had elapsed. In that hour of "missing time", Cătălin was alone and he does not remember what happened. In his opinion he was somehow "contacted", but we can not exclude the possibility of an abduction experience followed by a "loss of memory". Unfortunately, said Gabriel Tudor, there were no other means available in order to investigate this case more thoroughly.

The case of S.C.

Among a few abduction cases that I have investigated, the most typical is that of S.C., a person to which I have a family relationship, but who does not want to disclose his identity.

He was born in 1946 in the northeast of the Danube Delta, in the village named C.A. Rosetti, in Tulcea County. He graduated in 1975 from the State Institute (University) of Fine Arts "Nicolae Grigorescu" in Bucharest, specialising in scenography, a profession he practiced for a while in the cinema. Currently he is living in California.

He recounted to me the encounters that happened quite a while ago and in April 2013 he narrated once again his strange encounters, adding some further details. Below I will summarise his case.

After finishing high school in 1968, he failed at his first attempt for admission to the Art University. As a result, he decided to stay a year in Constanţa city, to improve his level of preparedness. He rented, during this time, a small and cheap apartment without access to any sanitation facilities and heated only by a wood burning stove. One winter night, at about 22:00, just before going to bed, he took a few steps outside in the courtyard. There was a layer of snow of about 20 centimetres deep. Suddenly, the courtyard was lit from above by a blinding light. The next moment, S.C. felt he was being raised up into the air going higher and higher. He could not move, but he could see the adjoining courtyards which were all separated by tall fences. He could see them all, for the first time, from above and not from ground level. Among other things, he saw a vintage car of his neighbour a tailor by profession.

He then saw himself in a big room, "indirectly illuminated". He recalled that around the edges of the room were a number of grates, suggesting to him some kind of air conditioning and, on the floor, slabs like those of a chessboard. He heard "telepathically" voices from 3-4 people, but he did not see them. He thought there was also a bizarre "translation system" of some kind because when he heard any words he received a twinge in his head and then he understood the meaning.

He tried to speak with these voices. He asked: "What do you want from me? Why did you bring me here?" The answer was: "We want to test you; we heard that you failed the admission to the university and we want to see why. We want you to make a model here on the floor". After this, a sort of robot, with rubber tracks, brought some thin square coloured plates of about half a meter in size and with a spongy and sticky underside. The same robot then placed them on the floor, as S.C. thought of how best to position them. Unfortunately, there were only four metallic colours, including yellow and green. As a result he could not make anything spectacular with these plates. He tried, however, to propose two or three models. "Interesting", said the voices and then advised him to apply for admission in to decorative arts rather than painting division of the college for which he had been preparing. After this advice from the voices he was released.

When he recovered, he was lying face down in the snow. The cold snow on his face soon woke him up. Just for a moment, he could not remember what had happened. Remembering only that he was out in the courtyard, but now he was a few meters away from where he had stopped and did not see any footprints showing how he had got there. Even if it had snowed a little more in the meantime his footsteps would still have been visible. He returned to his room, not knowing what time it was, but the fire had died out long ago, a sign showing maybe that several hours had passed and not just a couple of minutes. Back then, he did not smoke or drink and had never taken any drugs. He could not understand what had happened to him. Trying to remember, he returned to examine the traces in the snow. Then, gradually, the details of his abduction returned to his conscious memory.

The following morning he thought maybe it was just a dream. However, walking along the street, in front of his neighbour's house, he could not help but look over the fence which he had never done before. There he saw the vintage car, just as he remembered it. He decided then, for the first time, to climb into the attic of the house where he lived, in order to get a better view of the neighbouring courtyards. Here again, the details he had remembered of seeing the courtyards from above had been confirmed

He did not have the courage to tell the story to anyone, lest he be regarded as mad. The first person to which he has confided was his mother, which he visited during the Christmas holidays. She listened and then she said that he was, for sure, kidnapped by devil and begged him to swear that he would not tell anyone else about this.

She then told him that it was not the first time he had gone through such an ordeal. One summer's day, while S.C. was only a month or two old, his mother was weeding in the garden somewhere in the Danube Delta, near the Letea forest. She had three children; S.C. was the first. He was sleeping in a basket, which was hung from a tree branch and covered with insect gauze. From time to time she came to check that everything was in order. At one point, she saw, from the distance, near the basket, three black apparitions (i.e. three devils – she said – they had even horns) and nearby a large object which was the shape of a hat, resting on three legs. The mother rushed towards them, but a blast of light hit her and she fell to the ground. When she recovered, both the visitors and the baby were gone. A search followed and then she thought that somebody must have killed the child.

A few days later, while the mother was still grieving for her missing baby, at around 04:00-05:00, while she slept, the grandfather of S.C. saw a fire coming down from heaven and when the fire was extinguished, standing at that very place, supported by three legs, was a "big hat" and some "divers". They put the basket back, in the same place from where it was taken. The grandfather called the mother immediately, but in the meantime the visitors have gone. They both found the child sleeping peacefully in the basket without any evidence that something bad had happened to him.

Following the advice received from the visitors, S.C. applied for decorative arts and his application was a success. Apparently there were only 6 places available and about 200 candidates applied.

It was in his third year at university, when he had his next encounter. Back then, he had a steady income which came from restoring old paintings, giving private drawing lessons and also whitewashing and tiling a number of buildings. He rented an attic that he used as a workshop. One night, staying here, he felt the need to barricade the door before going to bed, as he heard unusual footsteps on the stairs. When he woke up, after a short while, he saw a figure sitting on a chair, not far from his bed. It seemed to be studying him. At first he thought it was a ghost. Then he saw that the visitor was wearing a helmet like that of a diver. A telepathic conversation followed, accompanied by the same twinge in his head with every word. When asked how it got through the barricaded door, the response was "this is not a problem". S.C. asked him to take off his mask, but the apparition said that he cannot do this because of "earthly environment", primarily the atmosphere. He then said: "We are old acquaintances; we know a lot about you". "Are you, maybe, those who took me from the cradle when I was a baby?" asked S.C. The visitor confirmed, adding that "we are interested in you for our experiments. We will find you everywhere you go; you are ours".

But when he asked: "why me?" the answer was very confusing. "It was an accident; we actually had another target, but we did not recognise the landmarks we were looking for. Then we found you". S.C., remembering his mother's allegations, said: "Are you devils!"

"What are devils?" asked the visitor. "Those who make only evil", replied S.C.

"Oh, yes! That means you have remained with all those old superstitions". S.C. insisted: "Why do you conduct such visits, what's the point?" Further explanations from the visitor became even more confusing. In fact, the visitor was not one of those who kidnapped him in the Delta, but only "representing those who were there all those years ago". They are all "migrating" and our Earth is just a stopover. Those who pass around here transmit information to those who are to come. Not by radio but telepathically. More extraterrestrial civilisations migrate and in time, Earthlings will have to do the same. "You have an advantage as you live near the periphery [of the Galaxy?] and not in the centre, where we come from".

S.C. admitted that maybe he had not understood some words or expressions, or they were not "translated" properly. The two were communicating telepathically, which may have caused some confusion. In addition, as in many other cases, the messages conveyed could well have been purposely misleading?

The witness had not been interested in UFOs before these events. Around a week after this incident, he heard that a UFO had been seen over Bucharest. There were newspaper articles and images. He then thought, well maybe he had met a UFO?

In the fall of 1987, he immigrated to California, where he still lives today. He earned his living as a "handyman". By the early 90s, he lived on the fourth floor of a building in San Diego. One day having just returned from an exhausting job and being past midnight, he was preparing to go to bed, when he saw a bright light through the window.

He went out on to the balcony. Out front was a garage, the roof of which had been made into a tennis court. Hovering over it, he saw a round flying saucer, with a colour reminiscent of a military camouflage. From under the disc there was a small round platform and on it were standing two people. Then the platform rose and brought the two entities directly level with his balcony. S.C. withdrew immediately but continued to watch what happened. The two beings walked from the balcony into the children's room and from there, going from room to room, they arrived in the small room that S.C. used to sleep but also as kind of storeroom/workshop. The room was full of tools and spare parts for all kinds of things.

S.C. pretended to be in a deep asleep, but watched the two beings out of the corner of his eye. They had transparent globe-shaped headsets, through which could be seen a perfect human profile and they wore 'scaly' costumes, smeared with some kind of oil that smelled like "the ocean". The witness at first thought that their outfit was their skin, but then he saw the fine joints of a perfectly moulded tailoring. One of the men was wearing a bulky backpack; the other, who appeared to be the chief, or doctor, had, linked to his arm, a device with buttons on. Clicking

153

one of the buttons, a rod came out and shot thin beams of green light down on to the ground.

S.C. "played dead", but the visitors were not fooled. "Good boy", said the chief and with every word S.C. felt a twinge in the back of his head. They pulled the blanket off of him and then made him float, rigidly, in the air above the bed, being rotated occasionally around the shaft, "like a roast animal". The rod with the beams was moved along his body and this time some meaningful information seemed to have been obtained. The beings were particularly worried about his kidney and spinal column. "He is terminated; we can not do anything longer" said the chief. Nevertheless, the deputy tried to persuade him to try something, asking him "to call the station" as to ask for "more power". Finally it seemed that this procedure had succeeded and the two beings declared themselves satisfied and then disappeared. S.C. could see through the window that the disc was rising, leaning to one side and then springing upwards like lightning and becoming invisible.

Immediately afterwards, two employees from the buildings security team appeared on the terrace, searching the place with flashlights. S.C. dressed quickly and went down to ask them if they had seen the object. Unfortunately they were not been willing to discuss this with him.

The next morning, his daughter, then 12 to 13 years of age, said she saw two men entering her room during the night. The light on her personal computer came on by itself and she could see figures that looked at her and at her younger brother and then they went into the next room. S.C. reassured her that it was just a bad dream. All day that day the news media announced that a UFO was seen in the area. For a long time after this incident, S.C. felt in excellent physical condition, healthy and full of energy, having previously been tired and exhausted all the time.

There was also another encounter that he remembered. It happened not long after the 9/11 terrorist attacks. In broad daylight, S.C. was taking a rest and worked on some drawings he was making for an invention he was trying to work on. Suddenly he had the feeling that he was not alone, although he could not see anyone else nearby. He heard a man's voice instead, translated in his mind, as in the previous encounters. "Do you want to build a flying saucer? Try this model". A series of tips for his sketches followed, as well as some operating principles for a novel type of an electric engine. He still hopes to build a prototype even today.

He also discussed on this occasion other topics with the invisible visitor. From what he learned, the aliens do not believe in a God, like the one in the monotheistic religions. His invisible conversationalist said: "You have always felt the need for a supreme power to protect you. Maybe for earthlings a supreme god would be the sun, without which nothing could exist". Concerning human life on Earth he said:

"It's an evolutionary step. The evolutionary process happens in steps. There is no reincarnation but only a record". When S.C. asked how much he should believe in everything the visitor told him, the reply was confusing: "That is not important, neither for you nor for us".

I have known S.C. for a long time. He is a very down to earth person and he is not in the habit inventing fanciful stories. In addition, he has had no reasons to do such a thing. He was not willing to tell anyone about these incidents apart from me. Detailing his experience to me he made every effort to clarify the details, even if they did not always fit logically into this strange series of events. All of the details were remembered consciously by S.C, and there was never any suggestion or attempt to use regressive hypnosis.

Crina C.

Crina C. was born in 1970, worked in journalism and was, for a while, a member of ASFAN. She had been interested in UFOs since she was 4-5 years of age. She was pretty much interested in all things 'mysterious' and suffered from a deep fear of the dark, having a permanent feeling that some unseen entity was chasing her from within the shadows.

In January 1980, living with her family in Bucharest, she had a very strange experience. As she recounted: "I remember that I had dreamt of something nasty. I remember clearly that two or three little men, with an overly large head and huge hypnotic eyes, moved around me. I did not know what they wanted from me, but I instinctively felt that they were looking for something and could only find this by experimenting on my body. I was really horrified! I woke up and I realised that I was actually in bed with my grandmother and even when I calmed down, saying to myself that it was just a nightmare. I suddenly to look at the window and could see a silhouette of a figure around 1.30 m in height. Looking closely, I realised that it is one of those creatures that had appeared in my strange dream. I started to scream; waking my grandmother and my parents. I do not remember precisely how the silhouette disappeared, but I know that I felt terrified".

When I woke up on the following day, I noticed that the left side of my face was completely immobile: my eye stood out, my mouth remained closed shut and I could not move my facial muscles at all. Mum, whom I had told everything, looked outside through the snow in the yard, for any trace of anyone or anything but the snow was undisturbed with no footprints of any description in sight. My mother's attention was now drawn instead to the unusual behaviour of our dog: who barked and whined as if to warn her that something was not as it should be".

At the local doctors Crina was diagnosed with "left facial paralysis". But the doctors were not able to explain what had triggered the paralysis in a girl just ten years old. Despite the treatment that followed, which removed many of the effects of the paralysis, she said her facial muscles remained affected for the rest of her life (but I did not notice anything about that).

Gabriel Tudor, who examined her case in detail, wondered whether someone had interfered with her nasal passages which in turn caused the nerve damage. Crina had unexplained nosebleeds, not very intense but quite regular, a condition that has been reported in other claims of alien abduction.

Another puzzling fact is that Crina had, since birth, just above her navel, a small oval sign or mark. The day after the strange experience, her family members noticed, barely able to believe their eyes, that this mark above her navel had vanished without a trace, just as though it had never been there. At the time, the girl, impressed, she put the entire incident down as an encounter with evil entities (perhaps inspired by the religious atmosphere in her home).

Meanwhile, the girl grew up, got married and gave birth to a child. One day in early July 1996 another encounter happened, having some common features with the Certesti CE3, which occurred during the same period. Crina C. was in the country house of her mother in Spineni village, Olt County, with her daughter and mother. As the evening approached, an inexplicable uneasiness surrounded them. When night fell, her mother went to sleep in another room, Crina and her daughter then aged six, stayed up to watch TV. As she told Gabriel Tudor: "In the evening my mother always allowed the dog to sit on the doorstep, as if to guard us. What surprised me was that on that evening, the dog did not come out of its kennel. Clearly, he was afraid of something. We did not really pay any attention to this. Later, after I turned off the TV, we went to bed and fell asleep. At around three in the morning, I was in a strange state between sleeping and waking. I was perfectly conscious, but I could not move. In that state I saw a flying discoid craft, like UFOs, with a small turret on top, descended slowly over the road opposite our gate and three grey little men of very small stature with huge heads emerged. The next thing I remember is that I had my eyes wide open but I could not see anything, being in total darkness, outdoors and in a room, as if someone had pulled some black curtains around us. I was awake, but I could still not move. I stood there, paralysed and my child was sleeping next to me, when I felt the presence of those beings beyond the wall of the house in the corner near the window. I remember distinctly I heard thoughts that were not mine and sounded like: "We came for the baby and for you. We want the child first!" Terrified, I tried to move towards my daughter, but I could not make a move as my body did not react to my thoughts. With great concentration, I managed to stretch out my arms and held the child tightly to my chest. I was determined not to leave her in their hands; I knew that they would do something bad to her, something they had done to me in childhood. But they continued to demand, downright commanded me, I felt this commandment in my mind. It was not a request, it was an order. I had to do what they said. But I did not. I stood there, with the baby girl in my arms. The child during all of this did not wake up at all and I resisted their commands as hard as I could. Aware of their power, yet I knew, I felt that if I did not allow them to approach, they could not do anything. Again I felt that those entities beyond the wall were not truly living beings, but rather like robots, programmed to do something and not knowing what to do if their program could not be completed. In the village, the dogs barked, howled in despair, only our dog remained quiet, as if it was asleep! At around five, at dawn, I suddenly felt that the visitors had gone. I felt like a heavy weight had been lifted from my shoulders.

In the morning, at around eight, when I wanted to tell my mother what had happened, she took me aside and told me she'd had a strange dream. It was with a neighbour who had died. He made a big fire in front of our gate (i.e. exactly where I had seen the alien ship!) and tried to enter the house, "to hurt us". I told her of my experience and we went together out into the yard to see if there were any traces of anything unusual. To our surprise, we found near the windows, in the damp earth, a number of rectangular marks, about 10 cm long, 2 cm wide and 2 cm deep. They were parallel to each other and gave the impression that the beings that made them did not walk normally but rather jumped – the traces were two by two, at a distance of 20-30 cm. I am sorry I was too bewildered to think about making a photo or a mould of them".

Corina has also observed on several occasions, lights moving "in an intelligent way". She felt that they came to see her, or her daughter. Added to this her young daughter also had a particular interest to these balls of light. Once she said: "Look, Mummy, they have come to do their duty!" Her daughter also had nightmares, like the ones she had had as a child.

Other cases

I suspect that in Romania there are no fewer cases of alien abduction accounts or alien visitation experiences than there are in other countries. However, while in other countries there is a large degree of public interest in this topic this is not the case in Romania. Techniques such as the use of hypnotic regression are almost unheard of when investigating such encounters. There are a number other differences too. To show them, I will now look at a number of other cases that we may label as 'close encounters of the fourth kind'.

In issue 10 of the magazine RUFOR, Călin Turcu related that, in the spring and summer of 1991, he corresponded with Mrs M.M., from the city of Mediaş, a teacher, and then 33 years old and unemployed. She had a series of UFO sightings and night visitations that began in 1968 (starting when she was 9-10 years old). In October 1980 when she was a university student at Cluj-Napoca, she was awakened by some loud noises that sounded like something heavy rolling along the ground. Her roommates checked that the windows and doors were all locked and then went back to bed and fell asleep. After a while, she alone woke up and saw along her bedside "a being who I thought was female. It seemed to be dark haired with a bandana around it or had a helmet that covered its forehead. Her face was smooth and pale as if she had no mouth. I felt paralysed". The witness heard in her mind: "don't be afraid, the one who sent me did this to help you".

Then she felt like the visitor injected something into the vein of her left hand and then fell asleep. In the morning her face was red as if sunburnt. She discovered also, on her left arm, traces of three bites which were still visible in 1991.

Several other visitations followed, usually after midnight, with: "a huge foul-smelling monster", "two large phosphorescent bulging eyes", "a face shining like a golden mask, with big, glowing and deeply set eyes" and "a black shadow that she fought with and defeated". Between 1982 and 1987 she recorded the exact dates when she was awakened by these same noises, or heard footsteps, voices, flickering wings, doors slamming, when saw a strange light or felt a foreign presence in her house. On November 26, 1987, she saw two silhouettes of men in the bedroom; on November 10, 1988, she felt that someone was sitting on her bed near her right leg. During the same period she observed a number of strange lights that could have been UFOs.

On March 2, 1989 she dreamt that she was going to work by bus and a UFO abducted her from the middle of the terrified passengers. She was flying through the air with a sense of euphoria, "to the gate of an Establishment" after which she woke up. On several occasions she used the sign of the cross to try to chase these apparitions away. After several letters, Călin Turcu lost contact with her and therefore could not investigate these incidents any further.

In the first issue of RUFOR magazine, Csaba Borbáth, an investigator from Târgu Mureş, reported the case of Mrs. B, aged 53, a well-known personality in Târgu Mureş, which is why she asked for discretion regarding her personal identity.

On the night of March 15, 1993, she woke up and saw just a meter away from her bedside, a shadow, about 1.5 meters high which was stretching towards her. When it was to reach her arm, she said "stay and I will catch you", making a vigorous movement to try to catch the "shadow". What she caught was "something triangular, elastic and dry, like the edge of a quilt". She tried to light the lamp but it was not working. She got up and turned on the light in the room. Nobody was there or in the adjacent room. In the morning everything was back to normal. A bit later she discovered on the wrist of both her arms, an oval bright spot next to which was a bruise. In addition, on her right hand, which she tried to grab the apparition with was a large red stain. All these signs had appeared inexplicably. During these events she was wearing a cotton nightgown with long sleeves, which did not have any unusual marks or stains upon it The marks on her arms and hand were visible for eight days, but they did not cause any discomfort. After they disappeared they reappeared again in August but were not precluded by any unusual incidents that she could recall.

Electronics technician I.D. was born and raised in Teleorman County, then was employed in Bucharest. Participating in ASFAN activities, he sent several reports of UFO observations, before telling me about his own experience and that of his family members.

One a Saturday evening in 1988 or 1989, the extended family of I.D. gathered in the parental home in a village in Teleorman County. The house was full with someone sleeping in almost every room. He slept in one room, near the window with his eldest son, their four year old, next to him, then the younger son and his wife. She asked if they could open the window shutters but I.D. was not in favour of this.

At one point during the night, the eldest son began to squirm and to cry very loudly. I.D. woke up and tried to calm him. But when he focussed his eyes in the gloom he saw near the child's feet, a dark human figure, "even darker than the darkness of the room". The figure was bent over the child and was doing something in his lower body, with what appeared to be his hands. The body contours seemed to be human and the only other detail that I.D. noticed was a hat, "like those from which circus illusionists pull out small animals". He could not distinguish eyes, nose, mouth, feet, clothing or any other details.

As soon as realised that he was not dreaming, I.D. he tried to move the intruder away by kicking out with his feet but they got stuck in the blanket. Then he jumped up and tried to hit him with his fists. Instantly, the figure straightened and began to shrink and at the same time to depart towards the wall opposite the bed looking like the image of an old TV set when it was switched off. The witness could not say that the visitor departed through the wall; he rather disappeared into the air in that direction. Now his wife also woke up and asked to turn on the lights. I.D. tried to reassure the boy, who was still crying and asked him what he had been dreaming about, but could not learn anything from him. In the morning he recounted to the other family members what had happened during the night.

A similar episode happened at least once more, at the home of I.D. in Bucharest. It was on February 29, 1996. He knows the date because he has the habit to record in a notebook when something strange happens. His eldest boy, who was then ten years old, told him he had a disturbing dream. He saw a child, dressed in a yellow jacket, beside him on the bed. When he awoke, he saw, near him, a figure with a black-brown disk on his head. It also had an oval face, slanting eyes, a small nose with three nostrils, two normal and the third in the middle, underneath them. Its mouth was small just like a line. On the body were lines, with bright dots of different colours. The boy also saw two shadows, beside his brother, at the other end of the bed. One was taller, the other shorter. He also gave a detailed description of these two shadows.

The visitor standing nearby was moving above him "a triangle, with two squares at the bottom and with kind of writing on it. The triangle had blinking red lights on the sidelines". Then there was a blinding flash and in this light emerged a door through which the two shadows disappeared. The visitor next to him put the triangle on his right hip and then let go of it. Then he ascended, took a horizontal position and entered headlong through the bright door. Afterwards, the door had disappeared and the light went out of the window and then over the moon shining in the sky as it departed. Only now the boy woke up for good, turned on the light and woke his brother to tell him that "the extraterrestrials had come to see them".

I.D. also had several "dreams" that are not detailed here. In one of them, strange beings tried to teach him an unknown language or alphabet, in another he was in a room that was inside a flying disk. It was a dimly lit and to his left were three unearthly beings. One showed him "a plasma globe of white light", of 40-60 cm diameter, floating at about 50-60 cm off the ground and about 2-3 m away from him. The globe exercised a power over him which forced him to bend at the waist. On another occasion, he woke up with the impression that he was surrounded by numerous alien beings. He felt someone touch his head. It looked like a hand reaching out but was "fluffier than a human hand". It was feeling for something on his neck. He even sensed the touch of fingertips. He was very scared, wanted to jump out of bed, but he found that he was paralysed and was in a state of absolute terror. When he finally managed to move everything was back to normal. The next day he even asked someone to examine his neck, but there was nothing out of the ordinary to be seen apart from a small red mark which disappeared in no time.

One night in 2008, the wife of I.D. woke up, very agitated, shouting: "What are you doing here?!" after that, she said to I.D. "Didn't you see the two who were on the balcony?" Then she got out of bed and went to the balcony door, which was left open because of the heat. Later she said she saw (or dreamed?) that in the bedroom, near the bed, were two tall men, both dressed in black, who, when she woke up, ran to the balcony. In 2010, I.D dreamt that he came into contact with some entities who were the shape of the number "**8**" and with whom he had a conversation. From what they told him he remembered that "truth is beyond us, in the place from where they come" and that they abduct and carry earthlings to a "base" for "a particular purpose".

His mother also saw some unusual objects moving in the sky; in one case she said it was likely to be "a *zmeu**, as they said in the old days" and in another that "she believes that it is a divine power".

C.N., 42, from Teleorman County, is another correspondent of the association of ASFAN. He recounted to me, in 2013, several unexplained encounters he had. In 2006, one night he was visited by a ball of green light about the size of a handball, which hovered near the bed, then went through the wall.

On another occasion (in a dream?), he met some entities. He asked them who they were and what they want. Only one said, that "you must learn to shut up ... and you know well who we are, but you don't remember". Then he woke up. He was paralysed and sensed that someone had got out of his bed and had stepped on the mat but he saw no one and was terrified.

He began to write down his "dreams". In one of them, he was abducted. "I flew fast and very high. Then I saw those ships ... there were many of them but I went to the nearest". Then he saw himself lying on a transparent table with no legs coming out "as a drawer" from the wall of a strange room. Two men were hunched over his body. He tried to escape but could not move. One of entities reassured him saying that they would not hurt him. The other then "scanned" him with a "light beam". Then they put something in his nose and they checked something in his mouth. "I do not know what they did but I know that it was not evil, otherwise I would not speak to anyone about this". At the end, "a third – kind of chief – appeared in a doorway and told them let me go".

After he woke up, he took it to be a nightmare, but he noticed later that part of his beard had turned white; he felt a strange dizziness, found blood clots in his nose and became afraid to go out at night. When sleeping, he lit the lamp and always checked for something under the bed. He made some medical investigations too but without revealing anything unusual.

As he declared, it was a relief for him when he read later, on the Internet, about similar cases. However, he would prefer to be wrong, because, as far as he understood,

---

*The "zmeu" is an anthropomorphic being of the Romanian mythology: ugly, monstrous, strong, stupid, greedy, lecherous and sometimes capable to fly without wings.

if the contact was real, it is possible to be repeated and it is also likely to have happened during his childhood. Added to all of this he also reported to me a few other strange experiences.

At ASFAN, many other similar cases were reported. I mention briefly only one more, the case of T.I., now living in Italy. He was a career military man up until 1998 when he retired. He declared that, in 1995, he saw himself inside an alien ship, where upon it was explained to him this ships propulsion system. He also learned that these objects do not all have the same shape as not all of them come from the same place and do not use the same principles of propulsion. T.I. also said that, in 1996, in the area of Crişul Repede Valley he was one of many witnesses of an alleged UFO landing, which stayed on the ground for about 4-5 minutes and then took off.

A genetic experience with a MIB?

Eugen Delcea is the founder and owner of the Publishing house "*Obiectiv*" from Craiova. I don't know him personally, but his work and his cooperation with Călin Turcu makes it worthy of inclusion here.

Delcea states that two people he knows, a mother and her daughter, told him that they had been abducted by aliens, but asked him not to reveal their identity. The daughter had some remarkable abilities, incredible memories and from the age of one the apparent ability to turn on and off remotely, just by thinking, any nearby electronic devices.

In September 2002, the girl, who was preparing for bed was hit by a bout of restlessness. She could not keep still. Prompted by an inner voice, she went to the window and noticed, over the houses, two "flying saucers", standing motionless, with lights flashing along their sidelines. While she wondered how she could get aboard them the voice faded and that was the last she remembered. When he awoke the next morning in bed, she remembered how she had walked along a corridor illuminated by a white glow. A door opened and she entered a room in the middle of which was a table. Around it, seven people, with humanoid figures dressed in black suits and ties (a somewhat unusual appearance!), were standing. They were tall, had four fingers on each hand, a pale face and big round eyes.

She was invited to sit on a chair. Communication was done telepathically. They said they came to Earth to save the planet and she has a mission in this respect. One of them asked her to put her hands on the table. As a result, she felt a strange warmth spreading throughout her body. When she tried to remove her hands, the alien at her right grabbed her pyjama, which was torn. The one who was holding her hands calmed her, assuring her that nothing bad will happen. Furthermore, he said she would become a doctor and he also said that she would become a specialist (when Delcea wrote this text, she was already student of Medical University). In the morning, when she woke up, she noticed the torn pyjama.

Later, she had two other such experiences. In neither one of them was she medically examined or man-handled as it has been reported in similar cases in different parts of the world.

The "alien contacts" of her mother (at least those she remembered) had started four years earlier. In the autumn of 1998 her menstrual cycle had been delayed for 4 months and at the end of this period, she woke up one night and was lying on a table in a completely white room. Alongside her were two people of medium height, with big, bulging eyes, with no eyebrows and pale faces, dressed in something that moulded perfectly to their body. One spoke to her telepathically telling her to keep calm. At first via telepathically she was given several orders, which she has executed promptly. One such order was to remove her pyjama. When she was lying on the table, she felt an examination of her vagina. Being paralysed, she could not react. After a few seconds, she was shown a tube of 4 cm and was told it was over. She remembers no more of the event after this point. The next day her menstrual cycle returned to normal.

She and her daughter went through other strange experiences, but they recall only fragments of them. For instance, in the spring of 1999, while walking down the street, the mother saw herself as if in another dimension. Everything was the same, the buildings, the streets but there were no people and cars and she could not hear any noise! She walked on, but felt that someone was behind her but could not hear any footsteps. When she turned around, she noticed a man in a black suit, white shirt and black tie (like those who kidnapped her daughter) with a loose cloak, standing motionless and with a pale face and slick combed back hair. Then everything returned back to normal: people hurrying about, cars driving along and the usual noise of the city. She felt on other occasions too that she was being 'observed' by characters, reminiscent of the so-called "Men in Black". On another occasion she saw herself in a room with a dome-shaped ceiling, intensely illuminated and with soothing music being played. On two walls were shelves with a number of containers. In them, floating in a liquid, were human embryos at different stages of development. The sight of this made her feel sick and she could remember nothing more of this experience.

The tall visitors

From 1996 right through to 2000, I tried to examine the extremely complex case of M.C. I will summarise below only the key elements of her story.

Born in 1962, in Bucharest, she married in 1980 but divorced in 1996. During the period when I investigated her case, she lived with her two children, born in 1981 and 1983, in an apartment with three rooms in Bucharest. The children slept together in one room and she had her own 'multifunctional' room

On November 5, 1991, at 23:30, she watched, with her husband, in north-westerly direction, a light "like a flashlight" that climbed through the sky and then it fell and then would climb again, bobbing from the left and to the right. The sky was cloudy and the light seemed to come from behind the clouds. (At the time there were no "Chinese lanterns", but it could be a spotlight from a night club). The husband said, at a time, that he felt afraid and went back into the house. She watched the light until around midnight then when she went to sleep. That night she had a strange dream. She saw herself in a cave. In the middle of the cave, sitting on a stone was Jesus, washing his feet in the flowing water of a creek.

At the same time, she began to have telepathic communication with various entities, which she knew by their names and some of which were visiting her home. They transmitted to her different teachings. At first an entity know as "Fedbian", who was about three meters tall, conveyed to her, for example, information as "the role of neutrinos in the differentiation of living by not living", about "masculine flavoured water" and "feminine flavoured water", or bizarre formulas of organic chemistry, combined with complex and intricate graphics, forming a so-called "chemistry of caves". He also said her that, "God evolves through our thoughts. Our experience counts, but not as much as thoughts. God is inspired by us but he is far ahead of us". Fedbian also told M.C. that, 10 years ago, her body was taken and possessed by an etheric entity ("walk-in") sent to earth on a mission. First she had "to make contact with the Cosmos, through the collective unconscious, to bring to Earth, via this route, a new means of treatment and protection for the people". The same collective unconscious will allow people to understand her and to accept the information she gives them. She learned that, to this end, she will be endowed with paranormal powers such as "a wall of protection through which no one can pass".

M.C. enrolled in 1992 as student at a private law college but in 1993 she moved to the "Faculty of Cognitive Sciences and Parapsychology" of the Ecological University of Bucharest. After two years, she gave it up due to lack of funding and remained alone with two children to support. In 1995 she worked for several months in the laboratory of one of her former professors, Marioara Godeanu, as a researcher in the study of biology.

As M.C. recounted, in November 1993 she began to be obsessed by the name "Cevul", which will prove to be another entity that transmitted messages to her. He suggested her to use, to this end, a conversational "Ouija" board with the alphabet and other signs around it and a loop or a pendulum with a pebble. This way, she received messages "from astral" by dictation, at the beginning in a "state of possession". After a while, she was capable of stopping this dictation at will. Some of the messages came from "entities who would not give her peace until she wrote down their messages". At other times, she asked the entities to answer certain questions.

From "Cevul", she has received information about past mythical civilisations such as Mu and Atlantis and of entities that are looking for human women willing to accept them as partners in order to create a new race of beings on Earth, "through love and free will".

In June 1994, while relaxing on her sofa, at home, at around 19:00, in her mind appeared a tall man of at least two meters, dressed in a sort of silver-white suit, with a white cape over her shoulders. He had a slightly olive mongoloid face, black hair and dark bright eyes, penetrating "like lasers". Seeing him, M.C. jumped to her feet and remained in a state of fright for a number of hours. A few days later she "gained enough courage to get in touch with her spiritual guides". They notified her that the apparition was called "Riham", giving her some other details as well.

She told the story to her husband. On the night of August 7 to 8, 1994, it was very hot and with no air conditioning, both slept scantily clothed, with the windows open. Her husband, who considered that was better for him to sleep on the floor, woke up somewhere at around 02:00-03:00. Through the west-facing window an unusually strong light shone, projecting shadows of objects on the wall of the house (it is unlikely to have been the Moon because that day was a New Moon). He wanted to go out on to the balcony in order to see what it was, but he could not move because a huge unknown pressure pushed him to the floor and held him there. He stated that the pressure he felt was so great "that he felt that soon he would explode and the house too". He turned his eyes towards the door of the living room. There he saw a being some 2.00-2.10 meters tall. He had black boots, shiny black suit, black cape and long black hair. He could not make out its face due to the pressure that pushed him toward the floor. The entity was heading for the bed and at this moment the husband had acute sense that this entity was "Riham", the one his wife had told him about and it had come to rape her. After trying desperately, for about five minutes, to get up, he was surprised to finally see himself coming out, in spiritual form, from his material body, to stand at the head of his wife, opposite the door, while seeing his body lying on the floor. The apparition in black turned back and went towards the hall. After taking several enormous steps, he turned his head and said: "I came, I saw, now I know what I have to do" after which he dematerialised from the bottom up.

Their son, who slept in another room, told them on the following day that during the night, at 02.30, he heard an unusual, intermittent, whizzing noise, coming from a direction that he could not specify. He felt the need to go to the bathroom, but, because of the noise, he was afraid and stayed in bed for about half an hour, until the noise ceased. During this time, M.C. slept like a log, not remembering anything the following day.

The day following the incident the husband was extremely confused. He would see Riham again on other nights, in the same place. He initially refused to believe in such phenomena but now he started to be frightened of it. He avoided, as far as possible, to sleep with M.C. in the same bed, usually preferring to sleep on the floor. He told M.C. that he always felt the presence of the intruder and that sometimes he "wakes up thinking that, when the time comes, M.C. will leave with him".

Subsequently, M.C. received, on several occasions, more visits by Riham. She even had the feeling that the entity wanted to have sexual intercourse with her. At one point, when trying to reject him, the visitor disappeared, but immediately she found herself in the middle of a desert full of rocks. Here she saw many disk-shaped alien ships, spaced 10-15 meters apart. A lot of individuals, of both sexes, with the same mongoloid appearance as Riham, some taller, others shorter, were carrying something from one ship to another. Riham held her hand and led her to a glass panel in front of which was a desk with buttons. As she got closer, she felt a growing sense of dread. When she put her hands on the panel, she felt a kind of energy entering through the palms of her hands and a pressure travelling through her arms.

M.C. also had other "telepathic contacts" with Riham, receiving from him "erotic images". She stated that "the pleasure she felt was not sexual but erotic", adding that during all this she had a normal healthy sex life with her husband, so these symptoms were not due to sexual frustration. Riham told M.C. that "He loved her and wanted to breed with her". Those in his world "want to create on Earth a new, far superior, race of men". Her role would be "to facilitate contacts between the two worlds".

M.C. showed some of the data that she received through this channelled communication to Professor Marioara Godeanu. As M.C. stated, the professor was surprised that it contained information that she had recently discovered and had not yet made public.

In 1995 and 1996 she had several dreams that she considered important enough to record. She saw herself travelling through the Cosmos and saw prophetic images, about events that actually happened some time later in her life. In September or October 1995 she dreamt of lying on an operating table, naked, covered only with a thin sheet, in the middle of a room. She saw nearby her mother, but at about the age of 35 and in her hand with a huge syringe with something sticky inside it.

She said "my daughter, show me where you got an appendectomy" (M.C. had indeed had such an operation at the age of 17). Her mother pulled the sheet aside and jabbed the needle into her abdomen. She felt a terrible pain and she then woke up. After this dream, at the spot where she was injected an itchy rash appeared which took quite a while to go.

On the night of September 4 to 5, 1995, she watched TV until around 01:00. After going to bed, she put the pillows to her ears as usual in an attempt to bock out any noises. She had the impression that she had dozed off for only five minutes. But when she looked at the clock, she noted with astonishment that it was five in the morning. The pillows were in another corner of the room and the sheet she was wrapped in, was on the floor. She had a strong feeling that something had happened and that an alien presence was or is still in the room, but she could not find any tangible evidence to support this.

In another dream, she saw herself in a huge hangar, of at least 100 meters in length, with walls of masonry and metal. Here were strung thousands of incubators, glass bells, supported by legs. In each incubator was a female foetus, aged about 3-9 months, inert but alive, having tubes placed in the mouth, head, navel, vagina, etc. She did not notice where these tubes were connected, nor other devices, such as a control panel, oxygen source etc. The entity that accompanied her said they will become "mould-women" to produce a particular type of biological bodies, desired by the visitors. The experiment would be conducted entirely with human genetic material.

Her daughter also had strange dreams and feelings. On October 14, 1995, the husband of M.C. finally left the house following their divorce. From April 1996, she had begun to use esoteric techniques, acquired by channelling, on her first patients from outside of her family. She subsequently assembled a sizable clientele and began to teach courses. This had now become her main way of earning a living.

I had the opportunity to look through a stack of notebooks in which she wrote from cover to cover, endless strings of data and drawings, at a first glance meaningless, dictated by the entities (including many others than those mentioned above) with which said she was in contact. I have not made copies and at one point she asked me, very concerned, to urgently bring them back her.

I was eager to examine this case in more detail, using, for the beginning, hypnotic regression. Unfortunately, a well known hypnotherapist, that I asked, refused at first to get involved, saying she suspected that these phenomena are "devilish". When she finally accepted, M.C. had changed her mind and would not participate in any such sessions.

M.C. has compiled parts of her stories in reports that she sent to several well known ufologists: Florin Gheorghiță, from Iași, Peter Leb, at the magazine RUFOR in Târgu Mureș, Călin Turcu and Adrian Pătruț, but they probably considered her case too strange to be made public.

A pregnancy with temporal anomaly?

Finally, I want to present another, atypical, case of apparent abduction, having a sexual component and possibly genetic engineering, but also a strange temporal anomaly (or a false memory, or even an invention). The case was reported by psychologist Lucian Iordănescu to the TV producer Elena Lasconi, in a TV show, in which I also participated.

In the summer of 1978, the psychologist was working in Mangalia – a city near the Black Sea. Next to him, at the same state owned clinic, was his cousin, a gynaecologist by profession, who took the opportunity to have a chat when they were not attending any patients. At one point, a mutual friend, from the town of Băile Herculane (in Banat), rang to say that his daughter, whom we call Alina, had graduated from the faculty of Arts and was coming to the seaside for a couple of days holiday.

Upon arrival she said her hello's and then went to Vama Veche, nearby, where she found a place to sunbathe alone. As she recounted later, at one point, an individual appeared, that she fell in love with and he took her to a miraculous realm. Here they spent nine months and at the end of which she bore him a child. Then, one evening she fell asleep and when she woke up she was lying on the beach at night. It was still the same day when she arrived at the seaside, and nine months had not passed. She now felt ill so on the following day she went to the medical clinic in Mangalia. There she told her strange story and the gynaecologist confirmed that Alina had all the signs that she had given birth within the last 24 hours.

As the psychologist Iordănescu said, this experience radically changed the lives of all three. He began to study esotericism with the gynaecologist putting everything down to a divine miracle and Alina left the country to roam the world looking for answers. She was in Tibet, then visited the shamans of Siberia and then went Africa or Mexico. Apparently she currently lives in Canada.

There is no other evidence to support this story. This narrative; however bizarre it may seem, we found was told to us in good faith and we could not find any reasons why this story was a deliberate falsehood. Moreover, I know that, in some cases labelled as UFO abductions, you often find sexual intercourse or artificial insemination by the visitors with the claim that the hybrid child that has resulted cannot remain with its mother because it would die and also temporal anomalies. Also, in folk tales, there are, in many places, references to unknown realms where time has a very different speed, or it is even suspended. These tales could be distorted memories of similar ancient events or they could be real alien abductions. What is certain is that these types of cases are the most difficult of all to try and research and investigate which is why many UFO researchers simply avoid them altogether.

THE FOLKLORIC DIMENSION

"The flying"

UFOs, or more correctly "unidentified aerospace phenomena", are not restricted only to light balls, "nuts and bolts" objects, or close encounters. Jacques Vallée, M.Sc. in astrophysics, Ph.D. in computer science, having a remarkable scientific background, is considered today one of the leading experts on the UFO phenomena. In his book *Passport to Magonia: From Folklore to Flying Saucers* (1969), he stated, perhaps for the first time, that the power attributed to flying saucers today, was once the exclusive property of the fairy world and that the visitors are denizens of another reality. His view is that the UFO phenomenon is perennial and the encounters have been systematically recorded and adapted, as oral stories, in the memory of human collective consciousness. Thirty years after him, Prof. John Mack, psychiatrist from Harvard University, in his book *Passport to the Cosmos* (1999) also opined that the UFO abduction continues an amply documented tradition of extraterrestrial communication, which is maintained, in some places, still today, by a small number of individuals know as shamans.

In Romania, as everywhere, strange events that took place down the centuries, entered into folklore and from them were born legends and myths. But, what is more interesting, it seems that such occurrences are also happening today at certain locations where unseen forces haunt people and, even more surprisingly, there is some evidence that now labels these incidents as being connected to UFO sightings.

A known character in Romanian mythology and early literature is "*Zburătorul*" ("The Flying"). It usually takes the form of a young man who descends by night among people in their homes, torturing girls and young women. She sees "the flying" as a real, material, powerful and beautiful being. She wakes up from sleep and is always overcome by strong emotions. Popular beliefs also provide several methods of protection against this apparition. Clearly, it is the local sequel of what in Roman antiquity and in the European Middle Ages was called "*incubus*" and "*succubus*". But the earliest mention of the phenomenon is probably in that: "The divine beings saw how beautiful these human women were, so they married the ones they chose. In those days divine beings and human daughters had sexual relations and gave birth to children. These were the ancient heroes, famous men" (Genesis, 6; 2, 4). In the Book of Enoch (Chap. VII-XI), even more details are given. And the heavenly visitors are, obviously, "flying" beings. The character "Riham", mentioned above for M.C., is undoubtedly such a character. Many parallels could be found in all cases with a sexual component in them that we have covered previously in this book.

Another, related case could be the story, transmitted from mouth to mouth, picked by Ciprian Ardelean and Marius June and published in the No.7 (1994) of the RUFOR magazine. It is said that the incident would have occurred sometime between 1818-1830, about 60 km east of Arad in the Păiușani village, as told to them by Macrina, the oldest woman of the family Târsală, whose grandmother was an eyewitness.

On the second day of Easter, the locals were at the "*hora*", a traditional collective round dance in the middle of the village, organised on some special days everywhere in old Romania. Two young men, over 2 meters tall, dressed in normal clothing, appeared in the village. The villagers pointed out immediately that they must be foreigners. The two young men chose two girls with whom to dance. During the dance, something white came out from under the long fur coat of one of them. The legend says that this was the tips of his wings. When villagers saw this, they began to become quite agitated so the two foreigners let their coats fall to the ground revealing a set of large white wings. They ascended into the sky with the girls in their arms, under the gaze of dumbfounded people. The girls struggled and numerous items from their garments fell out of the sky and remained hanging in the trees. For many years nobody touched those clothes, considering them unclean and they were left there to rot. The flyings crossed the valley and headed toward a hill in the west, where there was a cave. Young people from the village went there to look for the kidnappers. Near the cave, they found part of the girls' clothes. No more was heard of the two girls nor the two 'flyings'.

The myth of "Iele"

In Romanian tradition, much more important than the "Flyings" and also much closer to the UFO phenomenon, are the "*Iele*". They are a kind of wicked fairies, or elves, magical creatures with supernatural feminine powers of seduction, living in the air, or in forests, swirling in dance in out-of-the-way places which burns the ground and the grass there grows no more.

As Victor Kernbach (1923-1995), writer and specialist in mythology, said in his "*Dicționar de Mitologie Generală*" (Dictionary of general mythology; București,

1995), the Iele "live in the air, in forests, or in caves in the mountains, on cliffs, or on the shores of waters, in the weeds, or at crossroads; they often bathes in pure springs; are believed to appear mainly at night by moonlight, they rotate in dance in remote locations and their place of dance remains burnt as by fire, the grass can no longer grow at this place and the tree limbs nearby are also scorched". They can fly "without wings and can move at fabulous speeds, covering 'nine seas and nine countries' in just one night". "all those who have managed to learn to sing the songs of the fairies are abducted and disappear without a trace".

Historian Nicolae Densușianu (1846-1911) gathered a lot of legends and folk beliefs, through an impressive number of questionnaires distributed all over Romania. According to his research, the Iele are "spirits with female faces, walking at night, playing and dancing". At the place where they walk, "the grass no longer grows", "a red horseshoe shape remains in the grass", or "the grass becomes a black circle". The Iele "bring with them musicians" who particularly play the "bagpipes". They "light candles" and play and dance in a circle in amongst the trees. They carry the people they meet "through the air, leaving them 'stupid' for the rest of their lives".

Moldavian Prince Dimitrie Cantemir (1673-1723), a member of the Academy of Berlin, in his book *Descriptio Moldaviae* (1716, in Latin), wrote that Iele are "nymphs of the air, often loving beautiful young people".

The reader who knows the essentials of the UFO phenomenon will recognise, in the above legends, striking similarities between "Iele" and UFOs. The origin of both is mainly nocturnal and aerial; the accompanying noise resembles the bagpipes; both rotate often in a bright circle, affecting the surrounding trees; the grass is burnt, both are attracted to water sources and have fantastic speed of travel and of course they kidnap people. There is also the sexual component which is present in many UFO abductions. It is unlikely that all these details (which can be found in traditions of almost all nations) can be mere coincidences, inventions or fantasies born from fear of the dark.

As an example, I will summarise below two cases, investigated by Gabriel Tudor, in areas of southern Romania and involving, in the minds of the witnesses, encounters with the "Iele".

The first is the account of Basil Pricop, a peasant from Prundu village (35 km south of Bucharest). As the witness recounted: "In 1948 times were very turbulent [as the communist regime changed everything], but us being young did not care too much. On May 1, Labour Day was declared and a large ball was organised in the village of Greaca. I took the horse from the stable without the knowledge of my father and went to the ball. I have did not stop until I reached the ball. It was a great event. Although I had just turned 17, I was one of the most remarkable boys there. In the morning, at five, when there was little daylight, I decided, along with two friends, who had come all on horseback, to go home".

"While crossing a place called Valea Miului, then densely forested, while today it has been transformed into agricultural land, we observed a number of circles "like fire" spinning through the air. We restrained the horses, which had already started to panic. We heard strange noises too. It was like a hissing noise but very pleasant to the ears, almost like hearing a happy tune. In a clearing to our left a fire suddenly started and Marin, one of my friends, said we should take a look as the forest may be on fire. When we tried to ride into the forest all of the horses refused to go near it. So when we finally arrived at the forest I was astonished not to find anything burning or on fire. Instead, in the middle of the clearing, in circle, jumping and holding their hands, were five women. They were tall and thin, with long blond hair and dressed in white. They looked beautiful and I had never seen women so tall; they could have been two meters each! They danced, perhaps to a strange song, as if they were in a *hora* [round dance], twisting and spinning, nimble and so light looking like they were almost floating."

Fascinated, his two friends had dismounted and joined in the dance, being greeted by shouting from the tall women. Our witness resisted, although he confessed "it burned the flesh on me to go and join the dance. But I knew that these women are the Iele and I was very afraid. I called the others to come back, but they did not care. They danced and laughed, chained to the dance and gave no sign that they could even hear me. Suddenly my eyelids felt like lead. I tried to not fall asleep, because I knew that it will not be good, but I could not resist. Dazed, I slipped on to my horse's head and I fell unconscious".

In the morning, Vasile Pricop woke up in a field, without knowing where he was and how he got there. The horse was in the pasture next to him. The young man rose and, still confused, approached the first village, which he discovered in amazement to be Căscioarele, located about 15 kilometres away from the place where he lost consciousness! It was very strange. His horse knew the road well and it would not have been hard for it to go home with his master in the saddle, even unconscious, as had happened on other occasions to other local villagers.

He met a friend and told him the story, but he did not believe him and told him he must have been drunk. Totally confused, the witness returned home, arriving back at around noon. Here heard with amazement that he was wanted by the authorities for allegedly killing the friends that had left the ball with him! They had been found, by a ranger, dead at the place of "hora". What the gendarmes found strange was that the two dead bodies showed no signs of violence. Following further investigations it was established that Pricop was innocent and the case was closed.

Vasile Pricop also said that, at that same location, two years in a row, no grass would grow and even in later years when it did grow it was stunted and discoloured. Most locals have accepted the idea that the "Iele" were guilty of killing the two young men because according to popular tradition, "whoever is dancing the hora with the Iele, can no longer can be a man; or he dies, or becomes disabled".

Gabriel Tudor also found another "realm of the Iele", in the Valea Popii village, Argeş County (120 km north-west of Bucharest). Here, in the forest on the Nucet hill, have been dozens of observations of bright lights moving across the sky at night. The local teacher Cristi Iosif told Gabriel Tudor even that an old neighbour, Filofteia Ciolmei, told him when he was small, that during the Second World War, when she left with her husband to gather firewood in the forest, they had seen flying in the sky "something shaped like a plate turned upside down, inside which there were human-like beings".

One autumn in the early nineties, teacher Cristi Iosif found on the Nucet hill a near-perfect circle with a diameter of 2.5 m, staining the grass where the vegetation was green, unlike the surrounding area, where the grass had yellowed in time with the season. That circle, remembered the teacher, remained there for two years. In the same year, a number of local children had stated that while walking to school one day they observed a bright object in the sky. The object had a very high speed and at times smaller illuminated objects were emitted from it. They flew alongside the main object then merged into it and it disappeared into the distance.

Here as in many places where it is said that "the Iele danced", a distinct species of mushroom grew. People were happy when they found them, convinced that they have magical powers. Among other things, they put these mushrooms in water and the bath the children in it believing that by doing so the children will grow up fit, healthy and strong.

Two tales of the Iele from Transylvania

Everywhere in Romania, the "Iele" are imagined as young women, dressed in white, who appear at night and would hurt or even kill any men they came into contact with. But in various areas of the country, the Iele have different names (şoimane, vântoase, drăgaice, frumoase, mândre, dânse etc.) All these names (polite adjectives or pronouns meaning "beautifuls", "splendids", "falcons", "they" etc.) were used in the past to avoid to upset the Iele or fearing that to use their real name [lost over time] they might appear having been called. Moreover, for the same reason, even "Iele", etymologically means simply "They", that is female people.

Cornel Buta (C.B.), whose interesting experience I will describe in more detail in another chapter, told me, about the Iele, several stories which occurred in his native village, named Bogata Olteană, 40 km northwest of Brașov. In the following, I summarise just two of them.

C.B. knows of the first case from his mother, from an aunt, sister of his mother and even from the witness concerned. In 1920, at 7-800 meters from the village, on a hillside, was a small hamlet inhabited exclusively by gypsies. To the west of the hamlet, nearby was a pine forest. Among the trees, a path was beaten toward a spring which had good clean water. The gypsies made a livelihood by making and selling brooms, baskets, troughs, wooden rakes and forks. Among them there was a 17 year old boy named Ion Florea. One summer evening, he went to the spring to get some water. It is not known whom he met along the way but he was staggered back through the trees as if he was very ill. Another gypsy coming from the village along the same path found him and carried him home. He did not see anyone else but Florea.

By morning, the young gypsy had recovered but could not get up and was talking nonsense. People said that "he was taken by șoimane" (the local name given to Iele). Prayers were performed by a group of priests at his home but even after this he still could not stand up.

Gradually, after about six months, he recovered but was not the same as before. He looked old and was fearful, superstitious and very nervous and evil. He avoided talking about what happened. Before the encounter he could not sing or whistle a tune. But after this experience he frequently sat on the doorstep, humming and whistling some never before heard archaic tunes of rare beauty.

C.B. said that when he was young and Florea was old, "I found him once in a good mood and I asked him what had happened. He told me that going along the path toward the spring, he entered a dense group of 'sparks', like a swarm of bees, which knocked him to the ground and rolled him through the trees. Then he saw himself surrounded by very bright eyes of all colours". A female voice asked him, in an authoritative tone: "What do you want? To paralyse your legs, or give you the gift to play the flute?" The gypsy, though unconscious, said, casually: "Give me the flute and singing". He didn't remember anything after this.

In the same village – Bogata Olteană – is another ancient legend that has passed down from generation to generation. The first gypsy, who settled in the village, was called "Starling" because he was a very good folk fiddler player. Young people often gathered at his house, to have fun and listen to his music. At one point, it was discovered that he knew "the song of șoimane" (of the Iele) and the young people asked him to play it. At first, "Starling" refused, saying that he feared the revenge of

Iele for the disclosure of their secret song. Finally he gave in and agreed to play the song. They locked the door and the gypsy was surrounded by the curious young people. But even before he had touched his fiddle with the bow, that – as C.B. recounts – "an unseen force suddenly opened the door. The young men who were stood by the door were knocked to the floor and Starling was kidnapped and was gone in a flash. As a result of this, all those who had witnesses this event went home absolutely terrified. Starling was found three days later by a villager, only three to four hundred meters from his house. When the villager approached him, Starling was confused, asking "where am I?" He had not suffered physically, but mentally he was never as the same again and become a very reserved and quiet person".

These are just two of the many strange incidents that I have learnt of from only one village. I'm sure there are just as many in each traditional settlement. Of course, these all are all folk tales, which are circulated by word of mouth and were, more and more, supplemented and embellished. Therefore we can not accept them as hard evidence. But there are too many stories like this all of which are very similar to each other. Perhaps there is 'no smoke without fire' after all?

Crop circles

Crop circles are present in Romania, although rare and not of the complexity of those found in other countries. They are mainly found in grass and are considered, in popular beliefs to be enchanted rings of supernatural origin, made, for example, by the Iele.

The best investigated case occurred near the western Romanian city of Arad. On Thursday, June 23rd 1994, engineer Liviu Deznan and his colleagues saw, from the deck of a silo, in a wheat field at the northern limit of Arad, two concentric circles: a central core with a diameter of 8 meters and a slightly elliptical ring, wide 6.5 meters, around him, with the external diameter of about 50 meters. There were also two small signs, also elliptical, with the axes 2.30 respectively 2.75 meters, flattened in the same direction as in the great agroglyphe [Fig. 41]. In both of the circles, the stalks were bent slightly, uniformly, in a counter-clockwise direction and they seemed to have been compacted by the weight of a solid object. There were no tracks or footprints and the wheat was intact. Because the witnesses were busy with farm work, they didn't publicly announce their discovery until Saturday June 25 and the press came only Monday 27.

As of June 28th 1994, the case became public knowledge and was widely covered by the Romanian media. A few investigators visited the scene; they took numerous photographs, including aerial ones, from 1500 to 2000 meters.

Local researchers found that the phenomenon was preceded by many other

Fig.41 Crop Circles in Arad, 1994.

observations in the region: strange bright or black spheres, a large, triangular, grey, "kite unattached to the ground by a rope", a flat, luminous object, which sprouted tentacles like octopus, a trapezoid-shaped object with glowing edges etc. Almost all of these sightings had a great number of witnesses. On June 26, a vortex, seemingly produced by an invisible object, tore tiles from rooftops, without any effect to other buildings just a few meters away. The witnesses said that the whirlwind meandered "intelligently" along the streets of a town near Arad. Three researchers: Raluca Marinache, Ovidiu Someşar, and Sorin Ghilea (the latter now an ASFAN member) published a systematic exposition of the events in a book: *Anotimpul OZN-urilor* (The Season of UFOs, "*Mirador*" publisher, Arad, 1995).

On Monday, June 27th at dawn, Traian Crisan, 49, a former tractor driver, but back then watchman at a sheepfold, not far from the circles in the wheat, came out of his hut, whose roof had been shaken violently by a whirlwind, which ripped several items away, killed three sheep and scattered others. He was knocked to the ground, dragged along and hurt. As he said: "Three sheep were raised in to the air and then crashed to earth and the dog, yelping, went to hide under the hut". The witness then saw, not far away, a bright disc, perfectly round, very big, with a transparent dome, floating three meters above the field of wheat. In the ships door stood two individuals of human appearance with a beard and slanted eyes. Then, after about two minutes, the object shot upward and disappeared. Several people living in the neighbourhoods felt the effects of this incident and believed the testimony of the shepherd.

Peter Leb, journalist and UFO investigator from Târgu Mureş, analysing the soil samples collected at the scene, did not find any radioactivity or magnetic anomalies. He observed that, for the first time in the world, the crop circles could be placed in connection with a close encounter of the third kind. On the morning of June 27, an army team also conducted measurements for radioactivity with negative results. The eerie observations also continued in July, when sightings of bright objects were reported with a relative diameter larger than that of the moon, or a red zigzagging globe, seen several evenings in a row, by different people along with many other unexplained apparitions

On August 30th near the Bârsa village, located 77 km from Arad, between the towns of Ineu and Sebis two locals discovered, in the middle of a maize field, a section of eight lines, over a length of 36 meters, with the stalks bent at a height of one meter. There were no signs of theft; and the cobs, blackened or partially eaten by rodents, suggested that the phenomenon had occurred only a few days earlier. On September 10, not far from this location, similar traces were found in another maize field. At this location a light the size of a rugby ball, with an appendage underneath, moving up and down was reported. There were other bright apparitions too. On August 30, near noon, a grey and white cylinder, 3-4 meters long, with a diameter of 0.4-0.5 meters, was seen hovering about 400 meters from where they discovered the first crop circles in the maize field.

Other crop circle cases were, for instance, in May 1995 near Târgu Mureş, where a weird formation in grass was formed, or on the night of July 14th to 15th 1997, near de village of Cetatea de Baltă, Alba County, where the appearance of crop circles was accompanied by sightings of unexplained lights in the same area. I mention below also several other cases located in various newspaper articles.

On the night of July 7th to 8th, 2008, on the outskirts of the Fântâna village, near Hoghiz, at 03:30, the villagers were awakened by the barking and howling of a number of dogs. A local villager said that she was awoken after three o'clock, and through the bathroom window she saw "a large flame" above the Fântâna village. Other people claim to have seen large, strange lights over some nearby fields. There, in the morning six perfect circles were discovered: a full circle, with ears lying down to the ground, framed by another circle, like a girdle. The concentric circles were surrounded by four smaller circles, arranged symmetrically. Inside them the wheat ears were perfectly superimposed. The owner of the field, George Botoman was the first to photograph the event. It was the only evidence of the crop circles original form, before the curious villagers entered the field. People were convinced that the circles could not be made by humans; the locals, mostly elderly, would not have indulged to do such a thing.

Local teacher Ioan Sorin Apan commented: "The area is flooded with tradition and stories of fairies, *vântoase, frumoase, Iele*. The ethnological hypothesis is the most valid and the most consistent" to explain what happened. He continued noting

Fig.42 Circle in grass at Poiana.

that the phenomenon coincided (using the, old style, Julian calendar) with the feast of "*sânziene*"*, known also as Midsummer, the traditional feast of fairies and of Iele, still celebrated everywhere in Romania. It was superposed, by the Christian Church with the feast of St. John. Moreover – said the teacher – and there was even a full moon. He added: "And at the Bogata Olteana – not far from here, there are often circles in the grass". By 1998 another formation of crop circles was associated with a light phenomenon "that had burned an oak tree leaving it with no leaves at all".

There were, also, relatively recent cases. The village of Poiana, in north-eastern Romania, is situated between wooded hills, 24 kilometres from the county seat, the city of Botosani. Here, in mid-March, 2015, one night, at 02:30, an elder, Valuţă Burlacu, retired Lieutenant Commander in Air Force, saw two lights above the fields. One light departed and the other landed without making a sound. The next day, Dan Pădurariu a younger villager, went to the location and found a circle of grass of a much darker colour, with a diameter of seven meters [Fig. 42]. Since then, the villagers no longer allow cattle to graze there. After this sighting a number of strange characters walked through the village frightening the local villagers.

Locals believe they are ETs in disguise, as, in that remote village, everyone knows everyone and no foreigners were known to have arrived.

On April 27, 2015, villagers from Sigmir (near the city of Bistriţa) said they had found near the village, three crop circles with a diameter of 3-4 meters, consisting of freshly grown grass, a darker green than in the inside and outside. Two circles stuck together and the third was at two meters away [Fig. 43]. A local of 20 years said he had also noticed such circles the previous year, on another hill nearby.

Sânziana is a name of fairies, coming from Latin *Sancta Diana*

Fig.43 Circles in grass at Sigmir.

The Maid of the Woods

In northern Romania, in the historical land of Maramureş, many people still believe in the existence of a "Iele" kind of being, which here is sometimes called "*Fata Pădurii*" ("Maid" or "Maiden of the Woods" or "Girl of the Forest"). That is a female spirit or being, haunting the woods at night and causing much harm, both physically and mentally, especially to men. Sometimes she appears as a woman, with long hair down to the ground, incredibly beautiful and sometimes as a grotesque and ugly woman. Where she walks, from the heart of the forest can be sometimes heard laughter while at other times the sound of crying.

I uncovered a case that combines, strangely and unexpectedly, this popular belief with a "nuts and bolts" UFO abduction. The case is based on the information I been receiving from 2005 until today, by mail and telephone conversations, with Ioan-Dorel Bizeu (D.B.), as well as an on site investigation done in 2014 by Elena Lasconi, who made a documentary about it for a private TV company from Bucharest (*Pro TV*). The case is interesting enough to cover it here with some more details.

D.B. was born in 1968 and raised in Crăciuneşti village, located about nine kilometres east of the city of Sighetul Marmaţiei, near the river Tisa, which here forms the Ukrainian border. As D.B. recounted, when he was little, he often went, for water, to a spring located on the hill above the family property. The path he used passed near the house of a lonely old man, who knew many strange things like stories about a "magic tree" that grew near his fence and was producing small pears, not ripen until a very special day and not every year. Each such special day, "*Fata Pădurii*", with her children came to eat them. But people from around here were saying that she also steals or kills the children that she meets.

In the summer of 1974, the old man died. D.B. was almost six years of age at the time. One day, he wanted to try to see if the miraculous fruits were ripe. While climbing the path, he heard voices singing, but did not see anyone. When he reached the "magic tree", he saw standing around it a girl and six boys, all looking nearly his age. They had bright blue eyes and long blond hair, looking as if all were twins; yet each had well defined features.

When he was at about five meters from them, the girl began to move and take up a hostile stance. But one of the boys came to D.B. and gave him a pear from the 'magic tree'. He also hummed a mixed up tune but D.B. understood that he should eat the pear quickly. The fruit melted in his hand, "became water", so he sipped it from his palm. The taste was more like that of an orange, with lots of mint. As he recounted, immediately after drinking this fluid a tingling sensation went through his body. Then he felt a cold hand on his shoulder. He turned and saw a woman with white blonde hair, more than 2.5 meters tall. She looked at him and D.B. had the impression that her face had a blue tint and her eyes became red with anger. She was the "*Fata Pădurii*".

While the tall woman watched him eating the fruit, her face changed back to normal. Now she had the look of an angel and her eyes became clear and bright green and then she sat down. D.B. even had the impression that she smiled. The benevolent boy conveyed to D.B. something like this: you did well that you eat that fruit, if you had not eaten it, the woman, who is my mother, "would be assimilated you". D.B. speculated that perhaps he might have been kidnapped and taken to their world.

The tall woman had a particularly beautiful face and her body was like that of the fairies. She looked around 40 years of age. She had two large curls in her hair at the back, connected to each other and a golden hair band with pink ribbons. The little girl had the same hairstyle. The boys had just one curl in their hair. They all wore white silk shirts that came to just above their knees. Somehow, they imitated the clothing that had been worn in the area by the locals many, many years ago.

The children sang a strange song about light and the forest, but somehow D.B could make sense of it. They spoke in a 'different but perfect language', which D.B. understood so asked them where they had come from. Their reply was: "our village is above and soon you will forget everything but in your middle age you will remember us". The encounter at the miraculous tree profoundly effected D.B. Even today he is sorry because they did not take him with them. While he was among them, he felt a harmony, a communion and "a fullness of paradisiacal life, where everything is completely different". And they were full of a power that he had never before encountered, anywhere. For a long time he felt that he could not speak to anyone about this encounter. For ten years, D.B. wandered the hills, forests and neighbouring villages, hoping to meet them again, to discover where they lived and to find "their village". His mother said "he is infatuated by the *fata pădurii*". The hardest thing for him was when he realised that actually "they are not of humans".

D.B. said he heard, several times, singing, the *fata pădurii*; He ran through the woods, but never got close to her, though he did see her in the distance. Once she was dressed differently, in a metallic green outfit, "perhaps to hide easier in the landscape". He saw her on another occasion by the river. This time he got very close and ran after her. But the apparition departed at such a speed that no man would have been able to catch her.

The next important encounter took place one day at end of June 1977 and was witnessed also by the mother of D.B. In 2014, when she was interviewed, she was

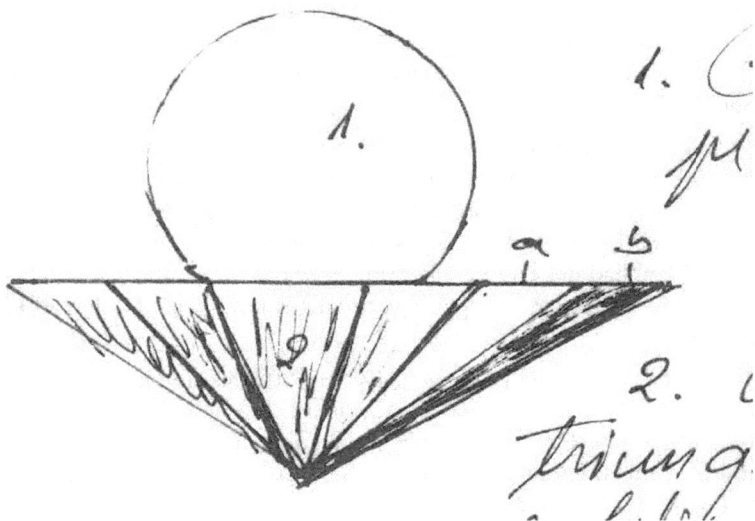

Fig.44 Sketch from a letter of Ioan-Dorel Bizeu representing the UFO he encountered in June 1977, along with his mother and two brothers.

83 years old. She had eight children, of whom four were still alive. Her husband had died long ago. Then, in 1977, D.B. was nine. D.B., his mother, sister M and brother V (three years older), arrived from Camara, a suburb of Sighetu Marmației, located about 3 km from the city centre and walked up a gentle coastal footpath passing near an orchard.

D.B. recounts that suddenly he saw, hovering over the city, a pearly blue coloured disc-shaped object that blended almost perfectly with the colour of the sky. He shouted to attract the attention of others, while thinking how good it would be if the object would come closer. In seconds, the UFO came toward them, stopping about ten meters in front of them and about five meters above the ground. The object was round, about 10 meters wide and 5 meters tall, had the form of an inverted cone and above it was a dome, but when looking more closely, you could see that it was a sphere, that went up and down, from the cone, at a distance of about two meters, at about every 5 seconds [Fig. 44]. The sphere had a greenish-yellow colour, distinct from the pearly blue one of the disc. D.B. said that the sphere was transparent and he has made out an individual on the upper level and two or more at the base. The object emitted heat, as if blowing hot air. In the air was that smell "like when you have a short circuit of electrical power".

D.B. went under the "plate" to see how it looked underneath. He said it was round, but divided into triangles, each with the top in the centre and the base on the circumference, "like slices of pizza". The triangles were illuminated in sequence. When the boy was under the plate, the light went from one triangle to the next, with a click, about every five seconds. But when the object departed, it was just made a fine crackle sound, about ten snaps in a second. D.B. remembered that when the object was near him, "my family members were frozen; they could no longer move; only my mother shouted: don't go, they'll take you with them."

The same scene was described somewhat differently by D.B.'s mother. She said: "I saw something in the sky that came from Sighet and I ran for the children and I got two of them. The boy [D.B.] had stayed there and some women screamed: take care of the children; don't let the saucer take them! And I ran and got two of the children but he stayed behind and looked up. I shouted: come to me, don't go there, they will take you! But he was still looking up at the object". Then she saw a kind of ladder or something, on which walked down a woman all dressed in black. She did not walk but descended smoothly with two lanterns in her hands. She was tall, over two meters, with a white face and she was very beautiful. She called the children to come to her but I didn't let them; I asked her: why do you need my children? Then the woman got back into that flying saucer and was not able to take the children. That object went towards Sighet and soon it was gone disappearing over the forest".

D.B. said he saw something descending from the disc, but he was not looking in that direction. Instead he had the impression that, near that object, time was going slower than in the surrounding area. He added: "I seem to remember I was taken inside. I have a clear picture of one fact: in front of me appeared a number of people dressed in white. There were men and women and children; all of whom stood around me. Several elderly people came out in front of them and each told me something. I do not remember what they told me but I know that everyone told me something. Whenever I try to remember what they told me, I get just an image in my mind and that is what I remember, a semicircle with a light like lightning and around the edge of the circle was some smoke and through the smoke I could see buildings looking like the skyscrapers in New York and other cities and there were smaller settlements all around. This image, that's all I remember. It looks like they sent me a sign about the final destruction of civilisation". Maybe – he said – people need to know only that.

Instead, he believes, he retained in detail almost everything what the children told him. They have told him many things and he also knows something about their songs, but can not reproduce anything in words. Then he said, "they left me; they no longer needed me". He went on to add that for a year after this encounter, he had in his mouth a taste "like mercury". The mother of D.B. described the same episode saying that she had the impression that, at some point, the boy disappeared and reappeared "as in a blink of an eye".

The strange encounter was the talk of the village. The mother of D.B. went on to say that after 2-3 weeks she went with the children out in to the forest to collect wild mushrooms. A man guarding some cattle said to her: "why did you take the kids? The saucer flies around and will take your children". She then went and hid in the bushes with her children so they could not be taken by the saucer.

Was it a coincidence or something else, but both siblings that witnessed the encounter grew up with a serious illness. His sister began to have heart arrhythmias and his brother had asthma. They both died young, the sister aged 35 and the brother aged 45.

The mother of D.B. said that she also saw, quite by chance, about once every year, always in late June, when is the rainy weather, before haymaking, a very tall woman who appeared from nowhere on the same footpath. She never saw her face. She was wearing shiny black clothes and a hood and had two lanterns in her hands and had long golden hair.

Another important encounter took place in 1998. D.B. was then 30 years old, was married and had a child of his own who was now 3 years of age. One morning, he felt as if he was compelled to go to the forest to collect wild mushrooms ("he was carried by the *fata pădurii*" said his mother). Up on the ridge, he saw, coming from Ukraine, a strange cloud. In a miraculously short time, the cloud settled above the forest trough which he would walk and it began to pour with rain.

As D.B. recounted, he was sheltering under an oak tree, when he saw, suddenly, in a clearing located at about 200 meters away, a group of teenagers. All were boys, from 1.80 to 2 meters tall and all looked identical. Accompanying the boys was a woman about 30-35 years old and about 2.5 meters tall. They were all dressed in white robes. Two of them had on their shoulder some golden musical instruments, which D.B. described in the smallest of detail. Their laughter was not like that of humans but it was more of a giggle and they sang exactly as the children he had met back in his childhood. D.B. then realised that they could be indeed the same beautiful children. The woman turned around, saw him, laughed and left.

D.B. said: "Enough! Now I will go with them, come what may". But he was "numb" and did not recover for several minutes. He then ran after them, continuing until he came to a clearing where it felt as warm as a furnace. He ran on, until he was out of the forest but did not see the woman or anyone else.

At home, he found that his hair, eyelashes and moustache were singed, probably

Fig.45 Dorel Bizeu with TV producer Elena Lasconi in a forest, examine strange damages, allegedly produced by a UFO.

in that meadow with the extreme heat. Subsequently D.B. assumed that in that forest an unearthly ship had landed. He believes that, by 2008 or 2009, the same clearing was visited again. D.B. claims that the vegetation and trees in that location had been affected by the UFO.

At the beginning of 2014, when the TV documentary was made, certain signs in the forest suggested that the "ship" may have visited there once again in the not too distant past [Fig. 45]. So D.B. wondered: What do they want? Why do they make so many repeated visits? Why also do they land at the same location?

When investigating this case, several people in the region told me about other strange happenings involving the *„fata pădurii"*. D.B. also had other strange encounters but I will not detail them here.

I would like to mention that these bizarre unearthly contacts with infants and fairies, are far more widespread than is at first believed. As an example, the famous American psychic Edgar Cayce, in a letter in 1933, told that, as a small child, when he was alone, he had as playmates strange creatures, small boys and girls, who could appear or disappear at, will. He once also he saw, out of the window, fairies who called him to come out and play with them. There are many such stories, from everywhere around the world. We now of course label them as folklore or myth and legend but in the 21st century has folklore been replaced and instead we now label such experiences as contact with ET?

THE SPIRITUAL AND RELIGIOUS DIMENSION

The case of Vasile Rudan

LIKE in the USA and Russia, etc., in Romania there were also military projects involving remote viewing and these projects also had some connections with UFOs. A protagonist of these experiments is Vasile Rudan, born in 1934, in a village in Northern Bukovina; in those days it was part of Romania but today it is in Ukraine. His mother was a native clairvoyant. As Rudan recounted, in that region, telepathic communication and extrasensory location of underground water resources is passed from one generation to another and are considered natural attributes.

Since 1965, Rudan had participated, initially as a human subject and later as an instructor, in experimental research made, at the request and under the control of the Ministry of Defence, covering telepathic communications and extrasensory detection of underground targets. Rudan worked as a government specialist in field verification of reports made by archaeologists from surveys conducted at sites around the country, both before and after 1989. He worked also, for several years, with two star general Vasile Dragomir, former chief of Directorate of Military Topography within the Ministry of Defence. There have been localised, by extrasensory means, tens of kilometres of ancient underground ceramic water supply networks (impossible to detect with current technical equipment), ancient walls, various anthropogenic underground cavities etc. After analysing the results, general Dragomir included extrasensory detection among methods for locating the military strategic targets.

Rudan also conducted a number of missions, on the orders of General Ilie Ceausescu, the dictator's brother, as well as of Elena Ceausescu, the dictator's wife and "The No.2" in State, for example for locating possible geopathogenic outbreaks that she feared.

In the 1980s, Vasile Rudan coordinated a group of children, to test their extrasensory abilities. They did not realise that they had any special powers and were told that the tests they were participating in were only games. The children were divided into remote seated groups and told to convey, through the power of thought, from one group to another, different information.

The experiments took place in the commune of Bozioru (in northern part of Buzău County); including Fisici village and Nucu hamlet, up across Gotes Lake. It's a relatively wild area, stretching over ancient hills where geological layers are raised almost vertically. The place is full of human remains from ancient times, including the caves of hermits, some of them dated before Christianity, which is why the place is called by some "The Romanian Athos". In the cave called "*Peştera*" there are strange incisions dated to the Bronze Age. The incisions appeared to some to be vehicles propelled by curved jets, flying through five-pointed stars, toward them being directed spears and daggers. The more popular name of the place is "*Ţara Luanei*" (Country of Luana) either after the name of a mythical king or queen, or even (as some said) of alleged ancient extraterrestrials.

Local legends speak about "gates" opening to an "other realm", which, in some circumstances, "absorb" the unlucky individuals that are around. There are, in a variety of newspapers, unverified stories about people who disappeared and did not reappear and of others who disappeared from one place and appeared at another, after a period of time, without remembering what had happened.

The zone allegedly has some very special properties. Telepathic transmissions made by the children, coordinated by Vasile Rudan, had a greater degree of precision, especially when the temperature in the higher layers of the atmosphere was at its maximum. In an experimental demonstration, two telepath children had succeeded, three times in a row, to transmit and receive complex messages with the seemingly incredible 100% accuracy. On another occasion the participants pinpointed, by extrasensory perception, places where ancient remains were located, a performance which astonished the archaeologists who had been assembled to watch the experiment. In a subsequent test, the children were directed to remote view other areas which were impossible to view by conventional technical methods.

Reports, photos, negatives and films were systematically handed over to the military unit that coordinated these investigations. Rudan was not allowed to keep anything. Subsequently, the training of children was stopped, "by an order from above" (from the Ceausescu family) on the grounds that this would prepare spies "who with the power of thought could sell our geological secrets to some foreign agency", including here archaeological remains hidden below ground level. After the events of December 1989, the extrasensory experimental research group was dissolved. After 2000, Rudan carried on training in techniques of activating paranormal energies as well as those of extrasensory protection and self-defence.

Vasile Rudan had several UFO encounters which he also recounted to me personally. On the night of 22nd to 23rd August 1980, performing his experiments with the children, he was staying in a small hotel in the Fisici village, along with some of the children's parents. The children slept in another building, located at about 30 meters away. At 01:30, a young girl was awoken. Looking out of the window, she saw a lenticular shaped UFO. She immediately woke the other girls and went outside They then saw that in the sky there was also another bigger UFO. They then raised the alarm in the hotel and awoke Rudan by throwing pebbles at his window and shouting "UFOs!" He came out of the hotel, together with about 20 people who were staying there. The big UFO was orange with the shape of a truncated cone with the base facing upwards. Around its upper third gravitated, from right to left, small, red and green, bright lights. On the right, above a hill, at about 2 kilometres distance, was a lenticular orange UFO which appeared to be in some sort of difficulty. It descended toward the hill, oscillating like a leaf falling from a tree. When it was about to crash into the hill, suddenly its orange light became much more intense; the object then rose vertically, remained stationary at a fixed point a few moments and then began to fall again toward the edge of the hill.

After about 40 minutes of observation, the children and some of the others that were present had seen enough and went back to bed. Some people, who remained, said that the phenomenon remained until approximately 04:45. The lenticular UFO recovered, went diagonally to the frustoconical ship, merged with it and the ship accelerated diagonally upward, disappearing in to the immensity of the heavens. Interestingly Rudan, although in the hotel had a professional movie film and photo camera with special high-sensitivity film, had apparently not thought to use them. Rudan commented that: "simply that the idea to use the cameras had disappeared from my mind; the same happened during the three other UFO sightings I have witnessed".

Of the locals, only one elderly villager from Scăieni, a few kilometres away, said to a journalist, a few years later, that he saw the UFOs, but was told, by some officials, that it was a military helicopter operation.

The next day, a team led by Vasile Rudan went to the hill called "La Pini" ("at pines"), over which the UFO was seen that had problems. They were armed with film and photo cameras, without knowing exactly what they are looking for. Rudan said that "I saw, in the grass, a rolling silver sphere, slightly smaller than a tennis ball. When I wanted to film it the object touched my left foot. It sparked a flame and I felt an electric shock in my left hand, which was holding the camera. Simultaneously, a whirlwind sprang to life and that threw us to the ground. My trousers burst at the seams from internal pressure generated by the air. A photo was

Fig.46 Strange effect produced when Vasile Rudan wanted to film an unknown "silver sphere"

taken by my colleague before falling to the ground on all fours. My left arm with which I had held the camera ("x-rayed" as shown on the photo), has not completely healed to this day" [Fig. 46]. What was that silver sphere? An unknown form of ball lightning or an object fallen out of the lenticular UFO?

Towards noon, a "comrade" arrived from Bucharest. He asked Rudan to inform those who had seen the UFOs that it had been a military helicopter, but he refused. The official also demanded to give him any film or photographic images along with all of the negatives.

Rudan told me that he had also "a close encounter with a humanoid crew", an encounter about which he gave no details other than that it was witnessed also by General Vasile Dragomir.

On the night of June 10, 1983, Vasile Rudan was again in the Fisici village, accompanied by a group including a pilot and flight instructor, when someone exclaimed: "Look at that, what a sight". In the clear night sky, at an altitude impossible to establish, a bright "ball" was zigzagging around the sky. Then another "ball", much larger, surrounded by three luminous spheres, travelled in the same, zigzagging "style". "Look at these, they look like some kind of escort for a galactic chief!" quipped Vasile Rudan. The pilot, a sceptic who was convinced that UFOs don't exist, and upon whom all eyes turned, commented: "Well, they are not planes, nor the space shuttle, nor satellites. That's it!"

At the end of August, 1999, Vasile Rudan was in the Orăştie mountains, on the Târsa plateau (altitude 900 meters), where there is an archaeological site, near the remains of Sarmizegetusa Regia (the ancient capital city and main sanctuary of the Dacian kingdom, before the Roman conquest). He slept in an annex building, from which had to descend on a ladder. During the night he was awoken by an inexplicable fear; later he realised it was an emission of infrasound. Sheep in the nearby sheepfold were scared and the dogs were barking with their tails between legs. Rudan came down to a terrace and from here he saw, to the right, a sphere with a diameter of 3-4 meters, hovering at about 10 centimetres from the ground. It was transparent, so that through it he saw the stars. The sphere began to approach and the witness retreated to a shed from where he continued to watch the sphere until around 06.00. His host, who slept in a room in the sheepfold, up the hill, was also a witness to these events and had no explanation for what they had both observed.

Reincarnations?

A case, connected with the mysterious area called "Ţara Luanei", was told to me by Simona Misea (S.M.), a young psychologist from Bucharest. She was interested in transpersonal psychology and in 2012, as a university student, she was subjected to a "past life regression", using the DMP (Deep Memory Process) method, developed by Dr. Roger Woolger. On this occasion she had a vision, which – as she said – has radically changed the way she is looking at life.

She saw herself as an old man. As she recounted to me in writing: "It started with me looking at the ground under my feet. There was a loose soil that had dried in the sun. I had a brown coat on me made of hemp. A cord was tied around my hip. My beard was tangled, as well my hair. I was a monk but I had not been at the monastery for a long time. My house was a hermitage carved into the mountain top, which could be reached only by ladder. I was wondering how to get up there. Then I see myself in my little cell where I also have my little altar. It was an altar without icons, but only with candles and items made from wool. I looked at my weathered hands and I knew that I have a skill useful to many. It was not magic, but something else, but I did not know what. I knew that the villagers were angry with me because they considered that I am working with "the unclean"".

"In the next scene of my vision I was caught by the local villagers and thrown into a pit that had been dug by them. They had hit me in the back with something and I fainted. When I woke up, the earth from the pit was entering my mouth. It was the same warm and loose soil that I felt at the beginning of the vision under my feet. A shudder of horror passed through my body. I was aware of what would happen to me. I was aware that it will be the end as the villagers continued to throw more earth over me. I had a sense of betrayal and not to the villagers, but to those "unclean" forces that could not save me. I was filled with horror, panic and helplessness. While I suffocated I felt a tremendous heat flowing through my body. Death means terror and freedom."

S.M. says that this entire episode lasted about 45 minutes. Impressed, she wrote down her feelings as soon as she got home, but she forgot it shortly thereafter, arguing that it was all related to her imagination and part of her subconscious.

In 2013, in mid-May, she was, for the first time, on a short trip through the Buzău Mountains, in that "Țara Luanei" I mentioned in the former chapter. She reached the cave of the monk Dionisie Torcătorul ("the spinner"), which can be reached only if you climb up a wooden ladder about 4 meters high. As S.M. said: "Inside I had a revelation: It was the hermitage I saw in my vision. It was almost identical. On the left now was a panel describing the life of that monk. The skill with my hands that I could not identify in my vision was to spin wool. People in the village appealed to him because he was a good spinner. Immediately I remembered the wool I had seen on the walls of his cell in my vision. Another significant thing was that Dionisie made exorcisms. I realised that this could be the reason for the murder".

The next day S.M. asked two monks in the area if they knew where the grave of the monk Dionisie was. They replied that we know nothing of his death or his grave and it was unlikely to uncover this after 500 years. They have, however, confirmed that in the area there had been a monastery and it is possible he has retired here.

Subsequently, S.M. added some details of her vision under hypnosis: "In the first instance (before killing the monk) I saw a small green meadow, near which was a rocky wall, not too high and made of limestone. After the death of the monk (when his spirit still dwelt in the area) I could see the whole area. It was a landscape surrounded by mountains, forests, among which was a monastery. It coincides in part with what I saw later in reality. The meadow and the wall are still there, only now trees have grown in the area. It is true that in my vision, the limestone wall was higher and steeper than that which I saw later".

At a first glance, remote viewing and the apparent remembering of past lives do not seem related to the UFO phenomenon. In practice however, there is a subtle connection that we can not ignore. Military remote viewers, as we now know, were nearly all tempted to explore the UFO phenomenon. The case of Rudan, although different, is also an argument of a possible connection. On the other hand, in the published literature, there is a huge volume of evidence concerning the recalling of fragments of past lives which are interpreted as reincarnation. These are often brought to light through hypnotic regression, which is used equally in investigating UFO abductions. Therefore I suspect that behind all these phenomena to which we can add the folkloric and the religious ones, there is a unique texture of processes and it is not wise to consider its components separately.

An illustrating example for this is that of Marius Ghidel (M.G.), an engineer in Bucharest, born in 1957. I had, over the last years, a great number of discussions with him, concerning the memories he has about a great number of strange events in his life (including UFOs), but also about a broader set of situations. I will present his case, in more detail, in a later chapter. Among others, he also has memories of past lives. In two of his recollections, M.G. recounts, in detail, the death of the characters who he feels he is (as with S.M., too!). When you die – said M.G. – "it opens upwards a tunnel and at the end of it is a shining Sun, with rays of love – God ... And I left the body on that delightful tunnel. There is a great happiness in death and a strong sense of relief".

Besides remembering past lives fragments, apparently Marius Ghidel also had a number of premonition type experiences. For example, he made at the beginning of 1992, a trip to Bosnia. After he got off the bus at a gas station near the city of Mostar, he stayed behind, while the others went to eat. Suddenly – said M.G. – he smelt gunpowder, then, for a few minutes, he could see himself in the middle of a war. Soldiers unloaded from trucks crates of ammunition, others loaded howitzers. A year later, the war in Bosnia was in full swing. M.G. viewed on the TV news, the same gas station and the same war scenes he had witnessed before.

Ghidel said he feels as if he had access to "a kind of time capsule, where at the bottom, the events are flowing normally, in their rhythm, but as you rise to the top of the cone, time and space are compressed, therefore you can easily pass through historical periods; and if you go lower, the events are still there". He described, as examples, several moments that he says he had previously lived, as a direct participant in the events. He states he remembers the details of his own beginning, starting from a world of spirits, reaching the womb of his mother, then passing through birth and making contact with the material world which he sees with the eyes of a child. At one point, Ghidel speaks about "a book in which everything was written, what was your soul in previous lives, what he did and what will be in the lives still to come". He knows that the name of this book is "*Arcane*".

Miracles with God the Father

As the reader observed, in many of the cases above, particularly in rural areas of Romania, the witnesses consider the unexplained sightings as "divine miracles", convinced that, in this way, the problem is solved. What else could be a magical light or object descending from heights and returning to the heavens?

As an additional example, Ion Hobana evoked a case that occurred in July 1927 in the Nicolae Bălcescu village (without specifying the area; this name is held in Romania by 12 localities located in 11 different counties). Agronomist George Achimescu said that, on a bright sunny day, with little wind and excellent visibility, a cylindrical object flew over the village at a height of 200 or 300 meters, going from west to east. It was about 15-20 meters long and 3-4 meters in diameter. Its colour was a "smokey" grey; it was not emitting any light and passed without making the slightest noise. A group of children, who were helping with sheep grazing, not far from the village, carefully watched the apparition, being convinced that it was God himself!

Jacques Vallée and many others after him, have pointed out UFO elements in old religious writings as well as a series of parallels between UFO close encounters and apparitions of the Virgin Mary, occurring in predominantly Catholic areas. That descent "as a falling leaf" (present also in the above story of Vasile Rudan) as well as other details (the dance of the sun, sudden lowering of temperature etc.) are reported both in UFO sightings and in theophanies. So, both of them are using, at least, the same type of mechanisms to manifest themselves.

An interesting feature of the theophanies, in the ambiance of predominantly

Christian Orthodox Romania is (unlike in the Catholic West, from which Vallée took examples) that the people always meet God the Father, or Jesus and virtually never the Virgin Mary. The explanation probably lays buried deeply in the collective unconscious. For the same reason, the ones belonging to non-Christian religions meet, in such situations, with their sacred characters. These facts help us understand better the roots of many seemingly illogical and absurd (for example religious) details in UFO encounters recounted by some witnesses, otherwise sincere and eager for truth. These details should not be removed, like embarrassing garbage, which stain the "right" (maybe even "nuts and bolts") mainstream vision of UFOs, but, on the contrary, they should be accepted, just as they were told, without biased embellishments and omissions, while maintaining a positive scepticism. Only when we have gathered enough data, we could try to find out – for example using statistical methods – what actually is behind the countless cultural veils covering those narrated accounts.

Further I would like to reproduce two Romanian cases, that can be (and have been) interpreted both in religious and UFO lore.

On Friday, June 15th, 1935, at around 16:00-17:00, Petrache Lupu (1907-1994), a shepherd aged 28, went with two other shepherds, through a forest located 2 kilometres from the Maglavit village, not far from the banks of the Danube, near the city of Calafat. He suddenly saw, floating in a white cloud, two palms above the earth, a "Moş"* with white beard. Petrache fell to his knees and heard the "Moş" sending him advice to give to the people, to bring them along "the right path of faith", particularly against abortion and abandoning the newborns. If there was any disobedience they would be in big trouble. It is highly interesting that the "Moş" disappeared in a "square cloud". The two other shepherds saw their comrade kneeling and talking to someone but did not see to whom. Moreover, Petrache Lupu was deaf and dumb, which is why he had not attended school and was declared unfit for military service. After this encounter, he began to hear and speak, although still spoke with a slight lisp.

Because of his shyness, Petrache Lupu had not passed on the message he received and a week later at the same location, the "Moş" appeared again, rebuking him harshly. The shepherd apologised saying: "I have not said anything to anybody because I was ashamed that people will laugh at me". Afterwards, the shepherd went to see the village priest and confessed what had happened. The priest did not believe him at first, but then he thought that he would teach the shepherd how to tell the people of what he had encountered. The news spread like wildfire, reaching Bucharest, where Pamfil Şeicaru, the most successful Romanian journalist between

---

*In Romanian „Moş" means primarily „old man" but it is closer to „grandfather", „elder", „greybeard", or „ancestor".

the two world wars, made a huge media campaign about the case.

These two events began a pilgrimage to Maglavit and it is estimated the around one million people visited the site with many claiming miraculous cures of a variety of illnesses.

There were yet even more strange happenings. As reported by the press, one year later, on August 15th, 1936, at 09:00 in the morning, two hundred thousand pilgrims, who came to visit Maglavit, saw the Sun taking on an "accordion shape" and on its surface moving lightning was observed. This phenomenon lasted for about 8-10 minutes, in the presence of the kneeling pilgrims, who followed the scary, strange celestial phenomenon. Was it the same "dance of the Sun" as seen at Fatima (Portugal, 1917)?

Another miraculous event happened on August 29th 1935, in the Parepa-Ruşani village (50 km north of Bucharest). Maria Petre (1923-1996), who was then 12, was running home when she had a strange encounter. As she wrote in her memoirs, she saw in the sky: "like a wave of white cotton, which seemingly was running along with me; and not only that, but it was as if it came down, following me and coming towards me. I stopped running and I looked around: the whole sky was blue and clear, without any other cloud apart from this white one, which seemingly came down for me!" Startled, the girl began to flee, even more quickly, toward her home, but the cloud approached and swept over her. "I fell to my knees, full of fear, trembling and whimpering; I wept greatly". In front of the child, a bright man stood, with blue eyes and a white beard. "He had the face of a gentleness and love. He was dressed completely in the whiteness of that cloud, surrounded by angels and flying doves". Then a gentle voice spoke to the girl: "Fear not, daughter of the Virgin Mary, I am God, the Heavenly Father and I chose you to tell people my word".

On another occasion, she retold the encounter in a different way. It had been "a pillar of silvery white clouds, a tunnel of bright white clouds and I saw thousands of angels from the heights of heaven. There, in the vision, was something bright like the sun, but the sun was elsewhere in the sky. This new sun came down slowly through the tunnel towards me and I saw something approaching me and it had the face of a human of light that spoke to me with a gentle voice. The Heavenly Father told me that a great tribulation will fall over Romania, where our people will not repent: a great war, earthquakes, floods, drought, famine, disease and Russian domination".

Maria Petre was not married and later became a nun. She said that she was commanded to build a church. She has devoted her whole life to this purpose, but the church was not built until 1990. The church was dedicated to the "Beheading of Saint John the Baptist", in memory of 29th August, when the miracle happened.

Encounters with the sacred

In the examples above, we interpreted presumed religious miracles in ufological terms. But there are also cases where, conversely, apparent UFO encounters contain religious elements, just as in the following two cases.

In issue 6 of the magazine RUFOR (1994), Peter Leb reported the case of Mrs S (requested anonymity) from Brasov, a saleswoman, age 27, in 1994. She was not interested in UFOs and was not religious. She had several strange encounters, the first at 12 years of age. In 1983 (then age 16), she woke up one night with the feeling that there was someone in the room. She sat up and saw, through the window, an intense red brightness. As she said: "I was like hypnotised by that light". When she turned her gaze from the window to the room, she saw a short humanoid with a large head, compared to the body and immense, black, unblinking eyes. She saw no mouth or nose. Its body was "malformed" with thin hands. The skin colour was dark grey. She saw nothing below the waist. She wanted to scream but found that could not move. She had a tingling sensation, like by an electric shock, all through her body. The visitor gave her "a sharp look, which penetrated right down to the bottom of my brain"; and she heard the message: "don't be afraid, we won't harm you; you don't know how good it is in our world".

After that, she became completely relaxed. She did not know how long this lasted, but in seconds or minutes in her mind she relived things and feelings from different times in her life. "Then the red light began to fade, arose and disappeared, as well as my visitor". Her cousin, who was sleeping in another room, told her she dreamt that someone had entered the house.

Later, she had a series of short experiences that were really intense. During these episodes, she also had a number of out of body experiences where she saw her body lying on the bed and had "a strong feeling of passing into another reality". She arrived in a round room filled with computer-like devices. There she met people "tall, with long hair, some with beards, dressed in white robes". She identified these people as Christian saints; some of them were presented to her as the apostles Peter, Paul and Simon. She also later met these "strange monks dressed in white".

At one point, she and a little man who accompanied her, stopped at a door at the end of a rectangular corridor. When the door opened – said Mrs S – "I felt that I would collapse. In that room was something that gave me the feeling that "crushes" me. I was enveloped by a powerful white light and fog. My eyes stung and I could barely stand up. I had to hold on to the door edges. I saw a transparent globe crossed by currents of different colours, looking like short circuits. Next to that globe, was standing a tall figure, dressed in a tight black suit". He was about two meters tall, shapely and was wearing a helmet on his head. Mrs S told the little man to ask the entity to remove his helmet so she could see his face. She was told that it was not possible, because, in that case, she will no longer be able to go back and her body will be found dead. As she considered accepting this option, she was told she is not allowed to stay because she "is not yet prepared".

A second case I want to give as an example is one presented, on October 26, 2015, at a private Romanian TV channel (*Antena Stars*). The witness was Maria Ghiorghiu, a graduate of two faculties: Law and Theology, currently secretary in her husband's law firm. She stated that one day in 1997, at midnight, while she was in the kitchen of her apartment, located on the third floor of a building in Bucharest; she saw a hexagonal object "not bigger than the rear tires of a tractor". A hatch opened in it, which absorbed and carried her along a kind of tube, until she reached a rectangular room, about 5 m by 8 m, lined with small triangular mirrors. In the middle of the room was a "stainless steel table" and on it she saw, subsequently, her body lying completely naked.

Around her were five aliens, all dressed in grey overalls. As a feature, they had, from forehead to chin, a stripe in relief. She did not notice any gender differentiation between them. Two of them were the height of normal people; the other three were smaller, about up to shoulders of the other two. They were doing something to her body and when they finished, they forced her to drink a cup a liquid that had the taste as of "a mixture of tree glue and chalk". In an instant she was again back in her kitchen, falling from above in to her chair. It was now two o'clock in the morning. She realised that in this time lapse many things had happened, but she could not remember exactly what. (I mention, in passing, that Jacques Vallée observed that in ancient legends and traditions, if someone is visiting another realm, before returning he must eat or drink a bitter substance that brings forgetfulness. Whitley Strieber also told that after a strange visit he had to bite a terribly bitter fruit, to forget what had happened).

After this incident, Maria often began to see the visitors. Now all she had to do was to close her eyes and to think about them and they appeared, sometimes in the form of "coloured energies". In this way, she communicates with them mentally. She knows that they want good things for mankind. She said she did also extracorporeal journeys in remote areas, even to other planets. She had the vision of some historical and biblical scenes, such as the crucifixion of Jesus, or the beheading of John the Baptist. She said she even saw "the Holy Trinity". She believes that the aliens are creatures of God, as well as the earthlings (an idea expressed in recent years also by prelates of the Vatican).

In the TV show, more people were invited to discuss her case. She attended the debate only by Skype as "the spirits" had advised her not to enter any television building. An Orthodox priest, present at the show, commented that he believed her, but what had happened was a "demonic delusion". When it was pointed out that the Catholic Church has in this regard a different, more nuanced, opinion, the priest said that, from the Great Schism of 1054, the Orthodox Church is the only one holding the right answers regarding the religious Truth.

The case of Cornel Buta

I would like also to present two other cases, in the same category, cases that I have examined personally. I will therefore to provide a lot more details about each case. The first is the case of Cornel Buta (C.B.) from Braşov. From 1996 until today, I have received from him a great number of letters, audiotapes, etc., in which he has reported strange contacts with alleged extraterrestrial beings. I had a long correspondence with him, also phone calls, in which he repeated that he is not interested in publicity and only wants other people to know the facts that he considers important.

Born in 1937, in the Bogata Olteană village, 40 kilometres northwest of Brasov, he was a man of good standing [Fig. 47], is married and has an adult son with

Fig.47 Cornel Buta and his wife, in 2002.

grandchildren. At the age of three, C.B. was adopted by the family of an aunt, his mother's sister, to help and to have an heir, as they had a big household, but no children. From now, until the age of 26, C.B. lived with her in a territory called "Turzun" a peninsula of about 7 square kilometres, almost completely enclosed by a 9 kilometres elbow of the river Olt. This almost virgin area is currently a nature reserve. Back then, his adoptive parents were the only inhabitants of the area, with the household laying at the forest edge. He liked that, benefiting from both the only child status and the wildness and beauty of the place.

The foster parents usually crossed the river in the morning in a boat, to work their land, located on the other side and he remained alone all day, working especially with the animals in the fields. He rarely visited the village, apart from the primary school he attended. The children of his age nicknamed him "the savage". At the age of 26 he moved to Brasov. He went to work in an enterprise with "special production" (military) and, after he completed his studies at evening classes, he became a foreman. He retired in 1997.

C.B. said that, at age of 14 and a half, he had an encounter with unearthly beings. I summarise below the events and his interpretations, as reported to me, by using, where possible, his expressions and trying not to remove details that would seem unlikely. All quotes below are excerpts from his letters.

On Wednesday, March 19th 1952, he was in Turzun. He woke up at 02:00 and went out into the yard for a few minutes. Then he returned to bed and fell asleep. Immediately afterwards he saw himself in another world, with buildings and beings totally different from everything familiar to him on Earth. It was a strange world, monotonous and empty. There was no vegetation. The ground was flat and black like bitumen. Around him, at a range of about one kilometre, everything looked like a gloomy day with thick clouds and black smoke with no breeze.

In this landscape were two buildings. One was somewhat similar to those on Earth but seemed moulded from a plastic, "like black bakelite". The other was light cream, almost the colour of lemon, with a red roof and made of materials that he had not seen on Earth.

In front of him, at about 25-30 meters, stood a "cosmic creature", "an energetic being without shape", whom "the human mind, no matter how hard it tries, can not imagine", of a greatness that the witness was not able to describe in words. The apparition "changed shape and colour at will, from bright white, as strong as sunlight, to red, the colour of blood". It was "a being who was not made of a solid material, but only a living energy field, as a flame, a living form totally different from us" [Fig. 48].

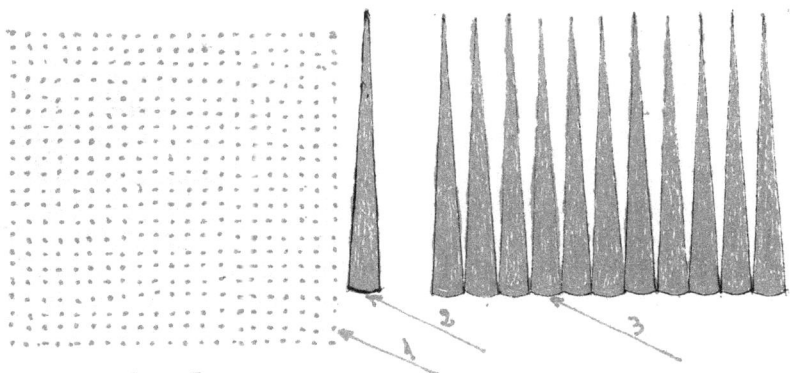

Fig.48 One shape of the "cosmic creature" allegedly encountered by Cornel Buta in 1952, with 50 cm high red "flames", 40-50 on each row, on a 4 square metres area (drew by himself).

To his right, at about 10 meters, was a black athletic looking man, about 1.90 meters tall, with short hair, completely naked. He had a terrible look and made feline movements.

The witness told me that he stayed there for about 20 minutes and had a conversation, in Romanian, with both beings. He asked the glowing creature: "Why have you contacted just me?" The answer was: "You were chosen from N people" (and said a number). As well, when he asked "how do you know all this about me?" the creature said: "We knew you before you were born".

After about 15 minutes of conversation, the bright being proposed him a "plan". C.B. says he asked for time to think. The apparition agreed, provided that he meets three principles of behaviour, that he accepted and respects even today. Then, the being was set a trial period, after which he promised to return. Back then, C.B. did not know that the period will be not of several days or weeks, but for 14 years and a half, during which he will be constantly supervised. He was forbidden to say what else he has learned. He was allowed to say just "ideas and comments from him". At one point, the being of light left him with the black being, wherewith he remained to chat for a short while. His presence seemed to be enjoyed by this man.

While C.B. was there, in that strange world, he had not remembered anything from Earth, as if his memory had been erased. He saw and heard normally, but perhaps because he was deeply focused and attentive on what was around him, he said he did not even see his own body. However, he is inclined to believe that he looked the same as he did on Earth.

After this encounter, he woke up in his bed before sunrise. "It was not a normal awakening but it was as if I was gradually brought back to life by some device". When he opened his eyes, he saw that the door of his room, overlooking the yard, was open. Near his bed, at a distance of about one meter, was standing, facing him, a little man of about 1.0-1.2 meters high. He had the appearance of a Northern European boy of 10-12 years of age. His face was a pinkish white, had blue eyes and blond hair cut short. He wore a kind of tight-fitting bright red jumpsuit, made from a thin, very fine, apparently synthetic and elastic material. On his loins was a belt of 4-5 centimetres wide, which, instead of buckle had a red flat patch, of 2.5-3 cm diameter. From the right shoulder to the left hip a scarf was coming down, with a width of 10-12 cm; but it could have been part of the costume. On the scarf there were embossed flowers. He wore short, tight, elastic, blue-brown rain boots, with thin soles.

He stood motionless, like a statue, with folded arms. When C.B. rose, the little man made a soothing gesture, smiled and said gently, "don't be afraid, I won't harm you". A conversation of about 15 minutes (or more) followed. The little man said that what happened last night was an experiment; he advised him not to listen to everything the black being will ask and not be afraid of him. He said to take care of his body as if it was something holy, to live clean and balanced, to avoid vices, to use his mind as intensely as possible and to evolve continuously through knowledge. C.B. had the feeling that the messenger "seemed independent of the other two and knew all about the events in question".

C.B. asked the little blond man who he was and were was he from? He replied only raising his finger upwards towards the sky. The witness put more questions to this small being and some of them brought no answer but when his questions were answered he was warned not to disclose the answers to anyone.

Then, the little man told him to sleep and C.B. fell asleep. When he woke up, it was daylight. His three dogs were watching him from outside the front door and the little blond man was no where to be seen.

As C.B. said, after that night, for nearly 15 years, day and night, he had become a kind of guinea pig. The bright being left him apparently in the hands of the black "humanoid", which further continuously monitored and subjected him to psychological and physical pressure, contacting him mentally. He even had "elaborate discussions" with him some 10-12 times, but only in certain circumstances: never in a house or under a roof, never in front of anyone, never in noisy places, never when he was sick, tired, nervous, angry, restless, overworked or in any other abnormal state, but only when he was relaxed, "when his thoughts were silent".

The black being demanded that C.B. behave in society the way he wanted. When C.B. opposed him, he attacked him physically. He was paralysed and shaken, as if he had been electrocuted, but without any unpleasant consequences after he managed to escape. Incidentally, in all that time, he had good health. Once, as C.B. says, the black being apparently possessed him, "incarnated himself in my body" for about three hours. But "I drew him out of me. After that, I never had any illness". Following this incident, the black being had not succeeded anymore to overcome him, he did feel his presence from time to time but managed to block him out.

As C.B. explained, he inferred that the black being would not have been allowed to behave this way, but he suffered from loneliness in this hostile place and, by taking him in possession, he would be transposed into the earthly environment, something quite different from his world. When C.B. moved to Brasov, in the crowded ambiance of a larger city and in the noisy environment of his work place, the black being tried to persuade him to return to "Turzun".

The bright entity encountered that night, had not shown itself again throughout this period, until September 1966, when C.B. was "brought in an instantaneous way", for ten minutes, to the same black world. As he recounted: "I appeared before the powerful cosmic interlocutor with the lesson learned". It was the last encounter with this being of light and afterwards he also escaped from the black being forever.

Following these contacts, there remained no physical traces, except that in the 14.5 years C.B. had somehow kept a very youthful appearance. He told me that at the age of 28 he looked more like 17 years of age. Then he began to age normally, but the difference can still be observed even today.

C.B. said that during his contacts, "I asked a lot of questions; some of which went unanswered". "They did not tell me anything about their world and about themselves. Where they come from remains a mystery". "They gave me advice and encouraged me, but they mainly stated: "you're on your own"". "Despite my insistence, both the bright cosmic creature and the young blond man had refused to offer any help". "I was not told to forget, but rather to not forget anything. I was told that I can talk to everybody about anything I want, but had just to be real and objective; but I must not say a word of what they told to me". The first contact has transformed him a great deal. He now sees the world in a completely different way. He became interested in reading more literature on topics such as yoga, UFOs and aliens.

Seeking explanations for what had happened, C.B. reviewed several assumptions that a sceptic could offer for his experiences (including the questions I posed in our correspondence). He could be accused of staging everything, being the only witness of the events. But C.B. contended that between him and a deceiver or hoaxer, there is a fundamental difference. A deceiver always has a purpose such as: advertising, money etc. and supports either something invented or something copied from elsewhere. Such a thing is usually noticed immediately. What has happened to him is, as far as he knows, something new and difficult to invent. In addition, he does not want publicity and he just wants people to know the truth.

He accepts that what he said "cannot be proved in practice" because "I cannot reproduce the event before somebody else", but "you can distinguish immediately the objective cases, because they are exposed with greater accuracy and assurance... They can explain the tiniest details". "It would not have gone through the head of a teenager of 14.5 years, who lived in the wild, to invent such a complex story".

He continued that it was also not a simple dream, as some would think. It was not a sudden awakening but rather like a return to life, assisted by some appliances, like that after clinical death. Something similar was when he came back to life here on Earth. So it was not a dream but something else.

Or were they somehow "hallucinations, visions or other oddities" caused by ingesting some of the hallucinogenic plants in the area? In Brasov there were no such herbs and the contacts continued here for almost four years. In addition, he said, he can distinguish between reality, a dream, hallucination and any other unusual phenomena.

It was also postulated that C.B. may have had epileptic seizures too. But he was at the time and has remained, a perfectly healthy man, according to regular medical examinations, and had no symptoms of seizures, not prior to the first main encounter, or after the second; and in 1966, the encounters ceased completely. Neither was he possessed – believed C.B. The possessed is, among others things, dominated and controlled, which was not the case with him. Although he appreciated that what happened can be considered a "close encounter of the fourth kind", as he had a contact, physically and verbally, with unearthly entities, he stated that "I was not teleported, neither kidnapped by UFOs". Compared to other UFO abductions, he stressed some notable differences: there was no UFO, he did not see any technical tools, he was not physically or medically examined and there were no sexual overtones. But he excuses those who put forward such sceptical explanations: "He, who has lived live such an experience, perfectly understands the inability to comprehend of his fellow earthlings".

C.B. proposes an explanation for its transposition into the bizarre world. He believes that he had two physical bodies, one here and the other there, with their brain interconnected. Only one of these bodies may be conscious at a given moment. As he said: "There are two worlds but I've never been awake (conscious), at the same time, in both worlds, but each time, either here or there". C.B. believes that only through a technique of this kind "can you reach other celestial bodies and communicate with beings from distant worlds". But "it also could be a damned trap", whereas, using the same technique, any human subject could be intercepted and monitored discreetly for a long time, or even contacted like he was.

It could be of interest to reproduce below also his vision, which allegedly he received from his experience. It is a remarkable one, considering his education and occupation, although it is visibly influenced by his readings, rich in UFO topics and related phenomenon.

C.B. considers that the beings he met were representatives of some "brilliant cosmic civilisations", "hundreds of thousands, or millions of years ahead of us". He said: "Imagine what a fantastic difference there is between us and them, from any point of view". "We are, compared to them, worse than a bird on a branch". "As the limited perception of worms, beetles, crickets, grasshoppers, dragonflies, etc. does not allow them to realise our degree of intelligence, so we have no ability to be aware of the size of the development and the activity of the cosmic intelligences".

The entities he met could come, he believes, from a world parallel to ours or which have laws of physics different from what we know and thus, for them, the great cosmic distances appear to be void. He also believes that "among civilisations in space there is no equality. There are privileged castes and classes too, a level of subordination still more authoritative than on Earth".

C.B. remained convinced that aliens have been studying us for "tens of thousands of years". "Earth is for them a kind of biological park". Maybe they are following each of us; that is not too difficult considering that "even we have the technology and computers to achieve such an objective". He stressed that the popular myths, including the Romanian ones, are testimony to this monitoring. But unlike people who lived thousands of years ago, today we are not aware of such monitoring. We are "a generation of amnesiacs". "For thousands of years, each added something and so the truth was lost and has become fiction".

Discussing the assumption that the black being and the blond being could be bio robots, he commented that, however, they were living beings, highly intelligent and civilised, smiling friendly, asking questions and giving intelligent answers, supporting their views, passionately, responsively and lucidly. He furthermore wondered about the striking physical resemblance of the two with earthlings. "Lest we are copies, identical to them, or they are earthlings, abducted and transformed? Lest is our planet an experimental nursery of those super-civilised beings?"

Mankind is – according to C.B. – "a very young pre-civilisation". People still have not emerged from primitivism and savagery, are controlled by animal instincts;

they put first the needs of life and personal interests (wealth, positions, power, sex, health, etc.). People think in a highly rudimentary way and have no passion for knowledge.

If they would like – he said – aliens could kill us all. However, they "love us, they watch us, they follow our developments and consider us even more capable than we think we are. They like to see us close up and they want to see us other than we are, for our good"; but "they are not so favourable to us as some hope". "They have known us for thousands of years but they do not meddle openly in our affairs", as "humans know what to do and they can solve their own affairs" and humans "know what is right and what is wrong". Therefore, the aliens "leave us, to kill each other, to do what we want". "To them time does not matter". "So far they appear to be limited to a number of tests, for experimental purposes". "If we have evolved towards a peaceful advanced civilisation, of a higher level, they will officially contact us and will share their experience and knowledge. And if the earthlings agree, they will integrate us into their community".

C.B. is convinced that the aliens communicated with contactees since ancient times. They "left at the free consent of the subject if he can accomplish or not the mission proposed by them. They do not favour in any way the chosen; on the contrary, they impose stringent conditions". The contactee "will be so impressed after the contacts with the heavenly beings that henceforth there will be a fundamental shift in his thinking and will see the world and earthly life in a completely different way from how he saw it before". However, often he "will witness his incapability of communicating the details of the experience through spoken words". "They will put knowledge first and the necessities of life in the background. The aliens would like that all earthlings become like this". The messages he has received also have an ecological component: "If people knew what I know, they would take care of our planet".

C.B. does not see himself as someone special, compared to other people. The only difference – he said – is the knowledge he has and that others do not know. As he said: "I got a brief audience, at a base, as a guest of a cosmic super-civilised creature and I was under observation for a while".

C.B. is religious without being bigoted. He interpreted, of course, his experience in the key of the Orthodox Christian tradition, in which he was raised. Thereby he said: "From everything that happened to me in the years 1952-1966, I concluded firmly that both God and Devil exist as real physical beings, but they are very far from what we think and how people talk about them". C.B. said he does not believe in an empire of demons and believes that aliens are those "without bodies, masters of power" remembered in biblical texts.

C.B. also believes that the bright being whom he met "was not the Creator, but a creature of the Creator". Maybe it was a representative tasked to pursue life on Earth. But "even if that was not the omnipotent being, the highest in the cosmic pyramid, it really convinced me that there is an omnipotent super-intelligence, unimaginable to the human mind". He added that if the bright being or the blond little man would contact him again, "It would be the most beautiful event of my life".

C.B. also believes that such contacts happened to many people over time. "I think this technique has puzzled and confused people fantastically, as they have become so religious, superstitious and cowardly". He adds that "the Bible, the Book of Enoch and other ancient texts, as well as the myths of popular belief, all attest that the ancients were aware of the existence of beings of cosmic origin. Biblical texts express, that "God sees everything", that "God knows everything" and more. That shows that there were in those times clever people who were contacted and witnessed some events, which otherwise they had no way to know". But, in the meantime, the knowledge thus received "has become myth and religion". At one point, he even concluded: "Religion seems to be just a fossilised remnant of an immense wisdom, sent by aliens, thousands of years ago".

The case of Marius Ghidel

Another case examined by me is that of Marius Ghidel (M.G.), an engineer, born in 1957, with a home, family and a small business in Bucharest. From 2014, I had several meetings with him. On this occasion, he told me and we have recorded the accounts of over 80 unexplained events in his life. Of course, in the following, I will evoke, in summary, only a few of them. Even M.G. acknowledges that "there are paradoxes in these stories everywhere, but they are as real as possible for me". In addition, they "have not happened following accidents, illness, or spiritual practices. All were spontaneous, without knowing anything about such things, even without understanding, then, their significance. I was simply drawn into them. I had not read anything about this subject, I did not know that such unbelievable situations can happen, neither had I heard that other people had experienced something similar".

These stories resemble others detailed in literature, even if they also have unique features. I analysed them, together with Dumitru Constantin-Dulcan PhD, a well known neuro-psychiatrist, university professor and best-seller author from Bucharest, who chatted with M.G. several times, found his case extremely interesting and consistent with other cases he knew of from his practice. None of us has found any reason to doubt neither the sincerity of the witness nor his mental integrity.

Some events reported by M.G. are conventional UFO sightings. At 10 years of age he was at Drobeta Turnu Severin. On a sunny clear day, at lunchtime, he saw a blunt object, like a plate of aluminium, standing still in the sky. It was bigger than the Sun. It changed its colours from: red, yellow, green, orange and blue. It made a soft humming noise. His aunt, who was with him at the time, told him not to look at the sky and that it could be a plane that had caught fire. He had the feeling that other people there were reluctant to look at the UFO. A few years later, he saw a UFO above the sea, from the window of the train he was on travelling toward Mangalia. Again, those around him did not seem to notice anything.

Another interesting encounter happened in 2011. As M.G. recounted, he was walking along the street one evening. The wind raised dust swirls on the street. At one point, he suddenly went into an area where it was quiet, everything seemed calm and still. Over the buildings, but close enough to them, he spotted a formation of UFOs in a V-shaped arrangement. He had the feeling that they had come to see him and that somehow they sent him a message. Right at this moment he saw, coming down the street, a man and a woman. M.G. wanted to tell them to look up, but nothing was there anymore and it was windy again.

In the UFO literature, this condition – reported not only in UFO encounters but also in other related phenomena, like holy apparitions – was called the "Oz Factor", a term introduced in 1983 by UK author Jenny Randles. M.G. said that in January 2014 he went once again into the same type of experience. As he recounted: "I was walking down the street and was just hurrying home. All of a sudden I entered a space where the street noise could not be heard. It was quiet and peaceful. And then in front of me appeared a loved one, it looked at me and approached me and took my hand. We walked a few steps, then it let go of my hand, it looked at me and disappeared, as suddenly as it appeared. Interestingly, the whole experience felt physically real".

A weirder event was that experienced by M.G. when he was 11 years old. He received, as a gift, an oil painting kit and one morning he was on the open balcony of the apartment where he lived with his parents, trying to paint a view. At one point, after an hour or two, he had a moment of "vacuum" after which he saw himself leaving his body, "through the top of the head". He saw his body which remained on the balcony, frozen in time. He saw his residential district, the block houses and all Bucharest. Within 30 seconds, he arrived "in a veil that made a sound like when you stand beside high voltage pylons". It was like a white mist and, as said, he felt a shake and, after that, vagueness lasted 5-7 seconds. He interpreted that the veil is a "layer of thoughts, which separates the two worlds: our world and the one beyond". Then he was immersed "in a space of small golden drops of happiness like shiny confetti of joy".

He had seen himself in this "soup of happiness" on other occasions too, among the multicoloured globes and bright white spheres. Sometimes he was turned into one of these orbs. M.G. commented that this realm was a world where the spirits of people who had lived on Earth were transformed in to balls of light. "It happened sometimes that the surface of a sphere turned in to the shape of a human head and then back to the coloured sphere. Suddenly, appearing in front of me was a bright white globe, bigger than I had seen before, slightly smaller than a beach ball. And this globe did not make any sound but just stood in front of me and looked at me with infinite love. I felt that I must obey. And the love it spread was so great that I could not resist in any way."

Many of these spirits wanted to reincarnate, "because only on Earth you can earn holy love. This is the purpose of our coming alive. Only here is the wealth of feelings and you can live them, you can feel them with your whole being and you can freely express yourself. Only here you have contradictions and you can overcome them. Beyond this there are no temptations, you have nothing to fear and there is an eternal Good".

After these moments of revelation he said that suddenly "I remembered that I was painting on the balcony. In that moment, when this image appeared to me, I turned back". He crossed again "this belt of thoughts that buzzed in my mind" and then he was back in Bucharest. He saw again his home and then his body, which, in the meantime, had remained frozen. Now he noticed that people and cars on the street were frozen too. Once his spirit has entered the body, all went back to around him.

I note that temporal anomalies, in which, during the alleged abduction, the time of material world seems to be stopped, are mentioned in several cases from ufological literature (for example in the book "Witnessed" by Budd Hopkins). But there are other temporal anomalies too. We recall the case of Mangalia, detailed in a previous chapter.

M.G. had several "out of body experiences" (OOBE) and some of them contain elements specific to alleged UFO abductions. One day, when he was 16 years old, while going back home from school, by bus, he had an OOBE. He saw himself going through the roof of the vehicle; then, as he said: "I saw that Bucharest and then Earth, remains small below me. I went into the black cosmic space, the endless void. In front of me I saw away a planet that was illuminated". He then saw, on that planet, a deserted, dusty, reddish landscape, with hills, valleys, then a stone slab, "correctly shaped, with straight edges". He stopped in front of it, then "suddenly I was on it and in my usual form in my high school uniform: blue shirt, with tie, black pants and coat". He pinched himself and pulled the tie to convince him that he was "real" and material. Around him he saw eight beings watching him. "They looked like us, but were thinner, weaker and 1.50 meters tall". They were dressed in green coveralls which extended over their flattened, elongated head, as – he said – like that of the Egyptian Pharaoh Akhenaton, depicted on some statues that he saw later. They had no masks. He could not see more, because a power pressed him to the stone, allowing him to only look up.

The entities kept their hands up, near to their face, "like doctors do before starting an operation" but they had no instruments in their hands. Then "they began to work on something above me at a distance of about 70 centimetres; they worked, removed and I don't know what and gave each other something. I could not see anything and did not feel anything on my body". Finally he felt "as if I was reprogrammed". M.G. mentions that "they had love and therefore you would obey them without resisting".

At one time, those beings "closed their hands then stepped back, stood still for two seconds, after which pushed their hands up. I felt coming from them an immense force that transformed me".

Then, M.G. saw himself on the reverse path. He passed "through the ring surrounding that planet" and after a while he re-entered Earth's atmosphere, seeing Europe, Bucharest and his neighbourhood. Then again he went through the roof of the bus and has found his physical body, which stood inert. He had problems to regain control and to go down to the next station.

Apparently, M.G. was abducted "in spirit", although down on the rectangular stone slab, he was seen "in flesh". The existence of these two possibilities, as well as the difficulty in distinguishing between them, has been known since antiquity. We can quote in this regard, from the Second Epistle to the Corinthians (2 Cor. 12: 2-4) of Paul the Apostle: "I know a man in Christ who was caught up into the third heaven fourteen years ago. I don't know whether it was in the body or out of the body. God knows. I know that this man was taken up into paradise and that he heard unspeakable words that were things no one is allowed to repeat. I don't know whether it was in the body or apart from the body. God knows".

Concerning the words "no one is allowed to repeat" this ban is mentioned in several recent UFO abduction-like cases, among others in that of Cornel Buta detailed before. And because I am reminded of the apostle Paul, we can evoke another parallel. The key word in many reports from abductees or contactees and especially in the case of M.G., is: "an immense love", above anything else. Worth, in this regard, to contemplate the hierarchy of the commands mentioned in the first epistle of Paul to the Corinthians: "Now faith, hope and love remain – these three things – and the greatest of these is love" (Cor. 1, 13, 13). I am convinced that it is not a pure coincidence.

M.G. bears in his mind the memory of several encounters with (obviously male) holy beings of Orthodox Christianity. For instance, one night he woke up with the feeling of a presence nearby. He felt he was beings watched "with amusement, kindness and understanding". The room was poorly lit. He turned and saw only "folds of a bright garment, as Jesus would have. On the feet were Roman sandals. It was a being, made of light, which spread through the house many bright milky white rays". But when M.G. wanted to look closer, the visitor quickly moved into the next room. He ran after him, but it "stood up near the door and went through the ceiling". M.G. added: "I had the strong feeling that it was Jesus".

On another occasion, when he was once more in the other realm, he even met with the "Creator of the Universe, who looked like a marvellous old man, with long white hair, a long white beard and with shiny silvery white garments". He smiled, "and while smiled, he transformed himself into that Sun of Love".

But the most interesting thing is that M.G. claims that he remembers – as if he was present there – the history of the Universe, of Earth, the moments that have marked different human civilisations, including the role of Divinity in this process. I asked him in what moment he became aware of these memories? He could answer only that, as far as he remembers, he always had these things in his mind.

The connection between UFO encounters and the apparition of sacred beings is well documented since at least the works of Jacques Vallée. There are several cases, such as that reported by Betty Andreasson in the books of Raymond Fowler, when the abductions have culminated at a "Great Door" with "beings of light" impossible to describe. We mention that Betty also had seen her spiritual double transformed into globes and then reconverted into a spiritual being who returns to a physical body which had remained inert.

The parallel is all the more striking as M.G. had not read anything about such events, he did not know the Andreasson case, or other stories of this kind; therefore a contamination is unlikely.

M.G. sought explanations for the two sides of his alleged experiences. He asked himself: "Was I on another planet or was I in a parallel reality? I don't know. I am sure it is another type of physics, which we can not even dream of because we have no access to it". He says: "this parallel reality, inhabited by extraterrestrial beings, is everywhere. It is a "second world", but it is not the same world as that of the deceased or of divinity. We are looking for civilisations on other planets, but we don't look inside us, where they are".

CAN WE HAVE AN EXPLANATION?

The limits of mind and of science

WHAT can we conclude from all the cases detailed in this book? An irreducible sceptic will surely label them as a lot of nonsense. Are the sincerity of the witnesses and the honesty of the ufologists who have collected these testimonies a sufficient guarantee to consider these cases as real "facts"?

In the examples contained in this book, I have tried as much as possible, to avoid: tricksters, deception, exaggeration, inventions, misinterpretation of natural phenomena, or of man-made vehicles. It is unlikely, but not impossible for some these cases to have been caused by sleep paralysis, borderline mental pathologies etc. We also remain aware that the stories evoked made that long and tricky travel, from the reality to be perceived, to the stories reported, interposing (unconsciously!) images seen elsewhere, perhaps in a dream, screen memories, all embellished, filtered, rearranged in a logical and socially convenient order, to match beliefs or prejudices, self delusions, wishful thinking, compulsions or even sexual fantasies, all deeply embedded into the subconscious.

However, behind these stories, most if not all of the witnesses went through what was to them very real experiences. How do we approach them? Let us keep only those reports or features which seem credible, according to the investigation methods which are considered correct today? I think it is wiser to keep as much detail as possible from such cases, to see if we can find somehow a clue in this jumble; especially since the cases mentioned resemble each other in many ways and with hundreds or thousands of other cases worldwide and not only in the ufological literature but also in mythology, religion etc.

A famous statement by the geneticist J.B.S. Haldane (attributed sometimes also to the astrophysicist Arthur S. Eddington) says that: "The Universe is not only stranger than we imagine, it is stranger than we can imagine". Our efforts to understand this highly strange Universe are done with our biologically limited senses, with our technically limited tools, as well as using: words, mathematics, logic, or theories, all bearing the limits of our mind and of our culture.

We often speak of "facts", convinced that we perceive reality "as it is". Even if it is hard to believe, we perceive things only filtered by many patterns, acquired starting with our earliest moments of life and continuing with language, family, religion, environment, social pressure, school, science, media etc. These patterns are extremely difficult to be removed later, as the UFO phenomenon clearly shows, because the phenomenon of "imprinting" (known from ethology), which also applies to humans. These filters can change completely what we perceive. There is a "cultural hypnosis" making us "mentally blind" to certain aspects of reality and in the middle of a same culture, everyone suffers from the same type of blindness.

We do not simply see, but, above all, we recognise. And we recognise what we already have in our mind. For example, we classify a potentially infinite number of situations with a finite number of words, as in some Procrustean beds. As a simplified image, it is like in our mind we have some boxes and what we see must fall into one box or into another. This mechanism is particularly disconcerting when we perceive unknown phenomena. If a religious person sees, for instance, something like a light, with a nearly human shape to it, in the air, he will not have for this another "box" other than an "angel" or a "saint". But once the entity perceived fell in to this box, it will automatically receive all of the appropriate attributes. So, for "angel", our man will also see the wings. And once perceived the word "wing" (with the corresponding box) the process repeats and the witness will see feathers, etc. And even if he had in his mind a box for "humanoid", he will know, from school, that the levitation is impossible, so he will reject this hypothesis. Instead, he will have no difficulty accepting an angel in flight, as it was taught by his religion. Such mechanisms, as well as others, more complicated, including subconscious taboos or screen memories, often falsify completely the phenomenon that has been observed. On another meridian, the "filters" of the mind could generate totally different visions. For instance, a Chinese person might say, for the example above, that he saw a flying dragon with glittering scales.

This mechanism also acted, in the previous chapters, in cases with holly apparitions, but also in many others. If G.M. or other witnesses would have been born and raised in a different environment, let's say Buddhist or Hindu, undoubtedly the "cultural filters" of their minds would identify the apparitions with other holy figures. Of course, that does not mean they have not seen anything! Maybe even something holy, but what?

In the process of human understanding of "facts", mathematics adds even more restrictions than those of words. It is enough to mention that $1 + 1 = 2$ is almost never 100% true in reality. A big and healthy apple plus one small and wild do two apples make? Or, there are no two identical apples! And there are also situations in which mathematics is completely unable to describe reality, such as in "The Bald Man paradox" (A man with a full head of hair is obviously not bald. Now the removal of a single hair will not turn a non-bald man into a bald one. And yet it is obvious that a continuation of that process must eventually result in baldness which is inconsistent with mathematical induction).

The benefits that science has brought to mankind are invaluable. However, we must not lose sight of that the scientific method brings new constraints, beyond those of words and Mathematics. Science admits only truths that: persist over time and can be inspected by any interested person, possibly in an experiment. Often science also demands that the observations be quantifiable. But, around us, there are a lot of phenomena which do not meet these conditions. We cannot still duplicate in the laboratory – as science demands – our inner life: our thoughts, our feelings, or our unconscious. Other examples are: intuition, genuine creation, decision based on free will etc. These also make often that, in human activities, a truth valid today that no longer remains valid tomorrow.

There are many other instances that can not be experienced in a laboratory or observed by anyone independently. These include rare phenomena, which do not occur at will, but also fundamental problems: of "ontology" (for instance, whether we live or not in a "virtual reality", or if God exists), or of "gnoseology" (such as infinity of human knowledge process). To split reality in two areas, one of science and another of religion and philosophy is not a solution. The mere fact that the two interact, shows that there is only one reality.

Science often speaks of "laws of nature". The truth is that we do not know any of these laws, but only the laws of Newton, Maxwell, Einstein, etc. They are extremely useful and give predictions with sufficient precision; our wellbeing around is due mainly to these predictions. But any of these human-made-laws may encounter situations in which they are no longer valid, being "falsifiable" as explained epistemologist Karl Popper. So statements like: "it was scientifically proven that X can not exist", or "that Y must exist", have no logical foundation.

Despite the above limitations, we sometimes meet an arrogance of science. Faced with facts that science can not deal with, often science will not say: "I'm sorry, but I'm not competent enough to study that", but instead prefer to give the impression that those facts do not exist. It says, for example, that: UFOs, fairies, OOBE, remote viewing, remembering details from past lives, religious miracles etc. are "scientifically impossible, so they do not exist; therefore please do not bother me with alleged facts".

There is an old comical allegory that depicts that bias: A police officer sees a drunken man searching the ground near a lamppost. The inebriate explains that he is looking for his keys. The officer helps for a few minutes without success then he asks whether the man dropped the keys near the lamppost. "No," is the reply, "I lost the keys somewhere across the street, but the light is much better here".

Science, affected by this "streetlight effect", investigates only the well lit phenomena, which are: observable, experimental and constant over time; although it may be that some "keys", very important for humanity, are to be found somewhere else.

Psychiatrist John Mack (1929-2004), professor at Harvard Medical School and one of the most brilliant ufologists, was a family friend of Thomas Kuhn (1922-1996), one of the most important philosophers of science in the 20th century. As Mack wrote: "What I found most helpful was Kuhn's observation that the Western scientific paradigm had come to assume the rigidity of a theology and that this belief system was held in place by the structures, categories and polarities of language, such as real/unreal, exists/does not exist, objective/subjective, intrapsychic/ external world and happened/did not happen. He suggested that I simply collect raw information, putting aside whether or not what I was learning fits in to any particular worldview."*

Ufology is not under the streetlight of science; it can not bring abductions in to the laboratory, nor can it present a UFO, on demand, to any sceptic. But the fact that ufology is not a science does not diminish its importance and also it would be desirable to not diminish its respectability. When people from different countries, cultures and religions, with different backgrounds and occupations, are reporting the same story, with dozens of details that are consistent – despite the fact that these persons have never known each other and have not read any of the dedicated UFO literature – that means we face no more a fantasy and pure coincidences but a real phenomenon. Applying appropriate statistical studies, ufology can try to strip the primary perception of observations by the many veils placed on it, even if this endeavour will never be perfect.

Hypercivilisations

Could we find a coherent system of truths which explains the strange events collected by ufologists, including those discussed in this book? I ask your permission to present, in the following, only one of these possible explanations. It is rooted in the extraterrestrial hypothesis, but trying to overcome its traditional layout.

Now it is accepted that many of the stars in the Universe have planets around them. The science of spectroscopy assures us that water and the basic components of carbonic life, including amino acids, are to be found everywhere in the Cosmos. More and more specialists admit that the basic cells of life are travelling

---

*John Mack, *Abduction*, Ballantine Books,1995, p.8

throughout space, "infecting" immediately all appropriate planets upon contact. But the favourable conditions for life to thrive should last several (three-four?) billion years, for the random game of mutations and the subsequent changing of the environment to produce the abundance and complexity of life we see on our Earth. In some cases, such a complex life system can give rise to a "technological civilisation". That means intelligent beings capable of building spaceships to travel to other inhabitable planets

How many such "technological civilisations" could be in existence at this very moment (only) in our Galaxy – the *Milky Way*? Astronomer Frank Drake proposed in 1961 a well-known formula to calculate this number. Several researchers made, on this base, their own estimates. The results were varying from millions to a figure near zero. I made again this calculation, respecting more the spirit than the form of Drake equation. The result was that, to date, in the history of our Galaxy could come into being a number of technological civilisations, of which, only a few hundred, survived the childhood diseases (that we face now on Earth) and still exist.

But these civilisations have not arisen simultaneously. In July 2015 it was announced the discovery at 1,400 light years from Earth, of the exoplanet Kepler 452b. It is similar to Earth, orbiting in the habitable zone of a Sun-like star. But that solar system is one billion years older than ours. That means that life and a possible technological civilisation could have appeared here one billion years earlier than on Earth. More generally, the first technological civilisations in the Milky Way could appear a billion years ago, or even earlier. Consequently, we understand that the possible civilisations in the Cosmos are far apart from each other not only in space, but also in time. In our Galaxy, these several hundred surviving civilisations, estimated above, have appeared, most likely, one in a several million years. So, in the Milky Way there is no civilisation close to our level, one that, for example, uses electromagnetic waves for communication.

What will become of our civilisation (if it will survive) over millions (or billions) of years? It is impossible to imagine. We do not forget that we are not able to predict our future, even in a perspective of just several hundred years. How would the inhabitants of a civilisation that has outstripped us with millions of years look like? Maybe they became immortal, maybe time and space do not matter to them, they may have moved into a pervasive virtual reality and so on. But the real answer is probably even much more complex and defies our logic and imagination. We can accept however that they have been transformed into *something else*, beyond our understanding; into something we can name as a "*hypercivilisation*"*.

---

*I exposed this idea also in other books – for example in „*De ce tac civilisațiile extraterestre?*" (Why keep silent the extraterrestrial civilisations?), published in 1983 – using the term „supercivilisations".

If somebody considers that we were too optimistic and the intelligent beings are much scarcer, we should add that our Milky Way is only one of at least 150 billion, more or less similar, galaxies of the Universe accessible to our instruments. And we have strong reasons to believe that there are other Universes too, maybe "parallel" ones, maybe from other states of matter, or parts of a "Multiverse" etc. Therefore it is almost absolutely sure that in the Cosmos there are hypercivilisations.

The preconceptions of the primitive extraterrestrial hypothesis

School and science fiction, but not only, set our minds on patterns ignoring completely the possibility of hypercivilisations. Therefore there are two "extraterrestrial hypotheses": the first is what we might call the "primitive extra-terrestrial hypothesis", the other that of hypercivilisations.

The "Primitive Extraterrestrial Hypothesis" assumes that all cosmic civilisations are more or less at the same level of evolution. Therefore it nurtures some false preconceptions as: very long and difficult cosmic voyages, landing on the lawn of White House, equal rights, conversation, invasion, intervention, aid and so on.

This primitive view is completely implausible. If hypercivilisations exist (and they exist, with a probability of 99.999999%) they exploited, in the smallest detail, our Galaxy, millions of years ago, so they have known, for a long time, about our existence. This reasoning led Enrico Fermi, when he said, in 1950: "they should be here; where are they?" But neither he, nor many others, did consider that representatives of hypercivilisations could be here, among us, but could look so different from our expectations that we cannot recognise them. What prevents us to see them is, also, a set of widespread and deeply rooted prejudices, such as those below.

The *preconception of equal rights*. A difference of millions of years, or even hundreds of millions, is as huge as between us and a lizard or even an ant. If they are here (as it is highly probable), they can examine us, monitor our evolution, even contact us in some form, but they will never put them selves at the same level with us.

The *preconception of conversation*. We interact sometimes with a lizard; but this will never be a conversation, said a researcher. As far back as 1959, Giuseppe Cocconi and Philip Morrison argued that if the difference between two civilisations is of millions of years, the probability that they could exchange ideas is zero.

The *temporal provincialism* (term used by J. Allen Hynek). It states that, in opposition with the previous dark centuries, the last three-four hundred years brought us *finally* to the light of real truth and science. In this light, now we can decide what facts can be accepted and what will never be possible. If one hundred years ago or so we started to use the radio, some believe it will last as the best means of communications forever. If one hundred years ago Einstein postulated that the speed of light is a limit, no other physical law will be discovered until the end of times to avoid this limit and so on. As a peculiar example, we have the *SETI preconception*. According to it, even if the radio signals need thousands of years from one inhabited world to other, the cosmic civilisations will consider that signalling by radio waves will be, forever, the most appropriate means of contact and that we should search for them.

The *preconception of invasion*. For many people (I suspect some of them are linked with the interests of the military-industrial complex) it should be normal if a cosmic civilisation arrives on Earth, it will attempt to conquer us by force (and maybe even to eat us). But the hypercivilisations probably knew, millions of years ago, that we are here; therefore they could invade us at any time and, in a certain sense, probably *we have already invaded* by them, for millions of years. Some OOBE's could be a hint of that.

The *preconception of intervention* and *of aid*. Some hope that the ET will help us (or at least some "chosen") to overcome future catastrophes. But even us, if we discover a valuable piece of land, which has escaped from the human intrusion, we try to declare it a reservation, permitting only a very limited intervention, for scientific reasons. This attitude seems to be strengthening in time. A hypercivilisation observing the Earth and the human technological civilisation should act in a similar manner, avoiding to interfere in our evolution, but taking samples, making some experiments, having very limited contacts (not at all officially or as between equals) with only some individuals, selected upon their and not our criteria.

Therefore no settlement, no destruction, on one hand and no official contact, conversation or substantial help, on the other hand, are to be expected from highly advanced cosmic civilisations, even if they are here now.

A higher intelligence and us

The difference between a hypercivilisation and us could be as high as that between us and ants. Some entomologists who would propose to study the life of an anthill will try to disturb, as little as possible, its life. They could of course make experiments, examining or modifying some ants, or even taking them in remote laboratories, trying to create new "races" and so on. They will certainly try to find out, as much as possible, about the life of the anthill, but will not "present credentials" to the queen of the ants. If the entomologists have the technology, they will create some robot ants, sending them in to the hill and watching from a safe place, for example "on the computer screen", the data transmitted by them. And if a robot ant would be lost in that mission, the incident would add a bit to the costs of research, without being a tragedy.

We can speculate that a hypercivilisation could attempt to realise, using genetic materials from the Earth, new races, with greater brain, with higher intelligence, adapted for some special tasks, etc. Therefore, many "races" described by the alleged abductees (the greys, the tall blonds etc.) can be such artificial human races or even bio-robots derived from the human species. They can be "produced" for example in reservations or bases somewhere outside the Earth. In the same manner we make new varieties of wheat from the traditional ones. Sometimes, the perfect variety of wheat became sterile or exposed to new diseases. At that moment the agronomists will try to find some appropriate genes in the pool represented by the primitive species of wheat, to improve the "perfect" variety. What if humans on Earth are the "wild pool" of genes, suitable to improve some artificial races elsewhere? In this case it will be no problem of compatibility between the visitors and us, as in some of the reported UFO abduction and hybridisation stories, but also, for example, in the biblical note: "In those days, divine beings and human daughters had sexual relations and gave birth to children. These were the ancient heroes" (Genesis, 6, 4). Some people suppose even that there is an ongoing external intervention in the evolution of the human race in order to improve it.

But obviously the comparison above – of mankind with an anthill – is slightly forced, as mankind is, nevertheless, a potential future hypercivilisation. The arising of a technological civilisation could be a very rare event in our Galaxy, occurring probably once in several millions of years. So it is normal for us to be of interest to the higher intelligences. But what could they expect from us?

I mentioned that a hypercivilisation will not give us its technologies; even more, it will forbid that. This is not, only, because of human aggressiveness and xenophobia, making from all new technology new weapons, nor only to avoid a "cultural shock", which could virtually destroy all our social, scientific, religious, economical, political, military and cultural structures. I suppose they have also some other reasons for that. Hypercivilisations could wait (and maybe harvest even now) our original ideas, viewpoints, creations (in art, science, philosophy, ethics etc.), produced as a result of millions of years of our independent evolution. And all that expected crop could be destroyed by a premature contact.

Some old, apparently absurd, stories may be an indication of such an attitude: the punishment for the apple of the forbidden tree of knowledge, the chaining of Prometheus, or the fallen angels (from Book of Enoch), thrown into a pit full of fire, because they were taught earthlings different skills.

Many abductees or contactees (among them M.G. above) spoke about ethereal light balls as "deposits of knowledge and intelligence", recording "everything in the Universe", among others, the life of all (or of the most interesting) individuals. We have some hints for this when we speak about: the "Book of Life", "Akashic Records", "collective unconscious", or even "morphogenetic field" etc. That "super-memory" could be written on a "spiritual" support, or on something around us we are not yet able to imagine. Sometimes, some people, under certain conditions, could gain access to this data warehouse. In that way we can explain: channelling, "xenoglossia", "walk-ins", "reincarnation", ghosts, etc. In such a virtual reality, *time* is different. We can travel in the *past*, live events, without changing the real past, or we can see scenarios of the *future* (sometimes apocalyptical), without accepting fatality.

Obviously, this assumption raises more problems than it solves: What is the "physical" support of this super-memory? Is this support natural or installed by somebody? How are the events recorded? Who writes in it the future scenarios? Under what conditions may someone have access to the records of others and so on.

The Blind Men and the Elephant

It could be that around us there is a hierarchy of hypercivilisations and of intelligence, potentially with no end. Arthur C. Clarke stated: "Any sufficiently advanced technology is indistinguishable from magic". In the same manner, in the limits of rationality, the human mind cannot distinguish between the activity of such hypercivilisations and what we know as sacred, holy, or divine. The realm of hypercivilisations also could be easily be that place named by Jacques Vallée "another reality".

Of course, all the above is not a *proof* that the hypercivilisations are *the* explanation for everything strange and particularly for UFOs. It is only one hypothesis; but one which cannot be easily discarded. We can speculate even further, supposing for example that the spiritual world was before, or that the material world is only a kind of a great virtual reality and so on. Also, the whole Universe (or rather the "Multiverse") could be much older and much more complex than the part we can observe with our instruments. Was there something before the "Big Bang"? What is beyond the limits of our closed Universe (maybe in another dimension or another reality, maybe in a spiritual state of matter)?

Faced with this complexity and trying to understand what lies behind the UFO phenomenon and other connected phenomena, I feel that we are somehow in the situation of the six blind men that – as says a well-known parable from ancient India – touched an elephant, wanting to understand what it is. The blind man who felt a leg said the elephant is like a pillar; the one who felt the tail said the elephant is like a rope; the one who felt the ear said the elephant is like a hand fan; the one who felt the trunk said the elephant is like a tree branch; the one who felt the belly said the elephant is like a wall; and the one who felt the tusk said the elephant is like a spear. Each of them was right and was convinced of his truth, so could not accept the allegations of the others who claimed something so different. The conflict became violent and they fought fiercely.

In the same manner, science, religions, folklore, paranormal studies, ufology etc. touch, each by its own means and in its "light zone", an extremely complex reality; and often one part denies the truths of the others. To overcome this limitation, we must learn, in a pluralistic approach, to respect all truths, as long as we cannot refute them, by *obvious facts*, not only by theories. Therefore we should accept the truths of others, even if they contradict our own truths and we should remain always open to dialogue. It is the only way to ascend to the higher truths we are searching for.

MAIN ROMANIAN SOURCES

Apostol, Dan: *Deocamdată enigme*, Ed. Sport-Turism, București, 1984;

Apostol, Dan: *Urme de pași în Cosmos*, Ed. Științifică și Enciclopedică, București, 1989;

Aramă, Dalila-Lucia: *Să fi fost oare farfurii zburătoare?* in „*Magazin Istoric*" 12/1968;

Davidovici, Doru: *Lumi galactice – Colegii mei din neștiut*, Ed. Științifică și Enciclopedică, București, 1986;

Farcaș, Dan D.: *De ce tac civilizațiile extraterestre*, Ed. Albatros, București, 1983;

Farcaș, Dan D.: *A Close Encounter of the Third Kind in Romania*, in *European Journal of UFO and Abduction Studies* – EJUFOAS, vol. 2(2), September 2001;

Farcaș, Dan D.: *Supercivilisations and the Extraterrestrial Hypothesis*, in *European Journal of UFO and Abduction Studies* – EJUFOAS, vol. 3(2), September 2002;

Gheorghiță, Florin: *OZN – O problemă modernă*, Ed. Junimea, Iași, 1973;

Gheorghiță, Florin: *Enigme în galaxie*, Ed. Junimea, Iași, 1983;

Hobana, Ion and Julien Weverbergh: *UFOs From Behind the Iron Curtain*, Souvenir, London, 1974;

Hobana, Ion: *Janvier 1913 – Des aeronefs fantomes au dessus de la Roumanie*, in "*La Gazette Forteene*", Vol.I, 2002;

Kernbach, Victor: *Enigmele miturilor astrale*, Ed. Albatros, București, 1973;

Kernbach, Victor: *Dicționar de mitologie generală*, Ed. Albatros, București, 1995;

Lazeanu, Ion: *Unusual phenomenon observed with radar device in Romania*, in *European Journal of UFO and Abduction Studies* – EJUFOAS, vol 1(1), March 2000;

Mandics György: *Omul și Universul*, Ed. Dacia, Cluj-Napoca, 1983;

Mandics György: *Explicațiile de lângă noi*, Ed. Albatros, București, 1989;

Marinache, Raluca; Someșan, Ovidiu; Ghilea, Sorin: *Anotimpul OZN-urilor*, Editura Mirador, Arad, 1995;

Mironov, Alexandru: *Enigmatic, Pământul*, Ed. Scrisul Românesc, Craiova, 1977;

Pătruț, Adrian: *Fenomenele de la Pădurea Hoia-Baciu,* Ed. Divya, Cluj-Napoca, 1995;

Pârvu, George: *La voia destinului*, Editura C.N.I. Coresi, București, 2011;

Pârvu, George: *Extratereștrii si Toma Necredinciosul*, Editura Semne – Artemis, București, 2011;

Străinu, Emil: *Fenomenul OZN și serviciile secrete*, Ed. Solaris Print, București, 2008;

Şerban, Mihai E.: *Semeni întru raţiune*, Ed. Dacia, Cluj-Napoca, 1982;

Tudor, Gabriel: *Tărâmul enigmelor*, Grupul de Presă Macri, Bucureşti, 2000;

Turcu, Călin: *Enciclopedia observaţiilor OZN din România*, Ed. Emanuel, Bucureşti, 1994;

Turcu, Călin: *"Extratereştrii în România"*, Ed. Obiectiv, Craiova, vol.I, 2004; vol.II, 2005;

The magazine *"Magazin"*, (1990-2016);

The magazine *"RUFOR"*, No.1-21 (1994-1996);

Personal and ASFAN investigative files.

NOTE: In the above, I included, with few exceptions, only the works about UFOs, written by Romanian authors, published before 1990, and those dedicated to Romanian UFO cases, after that date.